Library of
Davidson College

Colonial Emancipation in the Pacific and the Caribbean

Arnold H. Leibowitz

The Praeger Special Studies program—utilizing the most modern and efficient book production techniques and a selective worldwide distribution network—makes available to the academic, government, and business communities significant, timely research in U.S. and international economic, social, and political development.

Colonial Emancipation in the Pacific and the Caribbean
A Legal and Political Analysis

PRAEGER SPECIAL STUDIES IN INTERNATIONAL POLITICS AND GOVERNMENT

Praeger Publishers New York Washington London

Library of Congress Cataloging in Publication Data

Leibowitz, Arnold H
   Colonial emancipation in the Pacific and the Caribbean.

   (Praeger special studies in international politics and government)
   Includes index.
   1. Colonies—Law. 2. Colonies (International law)
I. Title.
Law   325   75-19801
ISBN 0-275-56000-7

PRAEGER PUBLISHERS
111 Fourth Avenue, New York, N.Y. 10003, U.S.A.

Published in the United States of America in 1976
by Praeger Publishers, Inc.

All rights reserved

© 1976 by Praeger Publishers, Inc.

Printed in the United States of America

To Sandy who makes it worthwhile, with much gratitude
for your forbearance; and

To Mark, Wendy, Susan and Eric who, with less forbearance,
make it even more satisfying

PREFACE

As a result of the decolonization process, a new state is arising among the nation-states: the associated state, the legal and political boundaries of which are yet to be defined. Its powers are being defined in a series of negotiations taking place between the former colonial power (the metropole) and its former colony. These negotiations have tried to strike a balance between the associated state's needs and desire for full sovereignty and the considerations of economic and political security which require a continued relationship with the larger country. There has been to date no careful legal analysis attempting to explore the parameters of these negotiations and thereby the nature of the new entity. This book attempts to fulfill this void.

Every author of either fiction or non-fiction is told that he should write about what he knows. The difficulty with comparative work is that it is very difficult to know all the territory. A number of reviewers have been kind enough to supply that expertise where it has been lacking, and I am pleased to acknowledge it. In many cases their review included discussion and close analysis at considerable length. I am most grateful for their assistance. The final decision on omissions and inclusions in the text was, of course, my own; but their assistance prevented a number of blunders and provided useful nuances.

The Philippines chapter was discussed with Dr. William Tansill, specialist, American National Government, Library of Congress, who, as usual, brought to bear an unusual degree of knowledge and careful deliberation in the United States territorial field.

During the preparation of the chapters on Puerto Rico and Guam, I had the privilege and pleasure of discussing the issues with the officials of the Commonwealth Office of Puerto Rico in Washington and the staff of the Guam Delegate to the Congress. All were uniformly helpful, providing a number of useful insights in addition to correcting specific statements. I want to thank them for the free interchange that they provided.

The Cook Islands chapter was discussed with Mr. M. J. Powles, political counsellor of the New Zealand Embassy in Washington, and was reviewed by Professor Quinton Baxter of the New Zealand Mission to the United Nations and Professor C. C. Aikman of the Victoria University in Wellington, New Zealand. Mr. Powles and Professor Baxter were kind enough to take the time to explain the operative facts in an area quite foreign to me.

The Papua New Guinea chapter was reviewed and discussed with Mr. Peter Paypool of the Papua New Guinea Foreign Service and Messrs. Timothy Blaine and Warren Lang, formerly with the Australian Embassy in Washington, D.C. The personnel at the Australian Embassy was uniformly kind to me, making available essential documents and books that were unavailable elsewhere.

The West Indies Associated States chapter was reviewed by Mr. David Walker, first secretary of the British Embassy, who gave me the benefit of his experience in the area.

The United Nations chapter was explored with Mr. Francis Vendrell, political affairs officer, Department of Political Affairs and Decolonization of the United Nations, who gave me the benefit of his vantage point from within that institution.

My special thanks go to Ms. Ruth Van Cleve, former director of the Office of Territories in the Department of the Interior, a lawyer and an author in this area herself, who was kind enough to review the entire manuscript and comment upon it. Her review was most painstaking, raising numerous questions of both fact and approach. I am most grateful to acknowledge her generous assistance.

Much of the author's experience and interest in this area and initial writing resulted from two positions: as general counsel to the United States-Puerto Rico Commission on the Status of Puerto Rico; and, more recently, as retained counsel to the Commission on the Status of Guam established by the Twelfth Guam Legislature. Many of the chapters in their early form were presented and discussed with the latter commission and I am grateful to Senator Frank Lujan and Senator Paul Bordallo, former chairman and vice-chairman of that commission, for their insights into the status problems of Guam and its counterparts.

I should also acknowledge the assistance of Mr. Barry Kriebel, who assisted in the research and initial drafting of the Micronesia and Papua New Guinea chapters; Ms. Hasia Diner, who performed a similar function with respect to the Cook Islands chapter; and Mr. Richard Caples, who assisted in the research on the West Indies Associated States chapter.

I was also fortunate enough to have my daughter, Wendy, assist in the proofreading and in the preparation of the index, a fact which provided me not only with efficient service but great pleasure.

Finally, I should express my deep appreciation to Ms. Hilda Vanover, who typed the manuscript, keeping up with the seemingly endless revisions with her usual efficiency and maintaining through it all an appropriate degree of tolerance and good humor.

CONTENTS

	Page
PREFACE	vi
LIST OF TABLES	xi
LIST OF MAPS	xi

Chapter

1	INTRODUCTION	1
	Military Security and External Affairs Representation	6
	Tariffs and Trade	9
	Immigration	10
	Taxation and Duties	11
	Applicability of Federal Law	11
	Political Representation	11
	Agreement Modification and Dispute Settlement	12
	Termination	12
	Notes	12
2	THE PHILIPPINE ISLANDS	14
	Historical Background	15
	The Philippine Commonwealth	21
	Changes Made During the Commonwealth Period	24
	Independence	26
	Notes	32
3	PUERTO RICO	35
	Economic Structure	37
	Historical Background	38
	The Development and Goals of the Commonwealth	54
	Notes	63
4	TRUST TERRITORY OF THE PACIFIC ISLANDS	67
	Historical Background	69
	United States Administration	71

Chapter	Page
Trust Territory Negotiations	77
Micronesian Negotiations	80
Marianas Negotiations	90
Notes	101

5 GUAM — 105

Economic Structure	107
Historical Background	107
The Development and Goals of the Territory	117
Notes	129

6 THE COOK ISLANDS — 132

Historical Background	133
The Cook Islands Constitution	137
Political Relations	138
Transition to Internal Self-Government	143
Economic Relations	144
Notes	145

7 PAPUA NEW GUINEA — 147

Historical Background	149
Shift in Australian Position	152
Development of the Ministerial System	155
Movement Toward Internal Self-Government	157
Internal Self-Government	159
Political Relations and Structure	161
Economic Relations	169
Notes	170

8 WEST INDIES ASSOCIATED STATES — 174

Leeward Islands	174
Windward Islands	177
Historical Background: 1624-1945	180
The Postwar Period: 1945-1967	181
The Situation Since 1967	183
Economic Aspects of the Relationship	190
Termination	191
Notes	192

9 THE UNITED NATIONS AND DECOLONIZATION — 194

Article 73: Non-Self-Governing Territories	194
The Events of 1953	195

Chapter	Page
The Special Committee of 24	201
Notes	211
10 CONCLUSION	213
INDEX	216
ABOUT THE AUTHOR	223

LIST OF TABLES

Table		Page
1	Proposed U.S. Financial Support of Micronesia, 1976-80	87
2	Ownership of Papua New Guinea's Resources	168

LIST OF MAPS

Map		
1	Islands of the Caribbean	frontispiece
2	Philippines	16
3	Puerto Rico	36
4	Trust Territory of the Pacific Islands	68
5	Guam, Showing Communities and Military Installations	106
6	The Cook Islands	134
7	Papua New Guinea	148
8	Leeward Islands	176
9	Windward Islands	178
10	Oceania	214

Colonial Emancipation in the Pacific and the Caribbean

MAP 1

Islands of the Caribbean

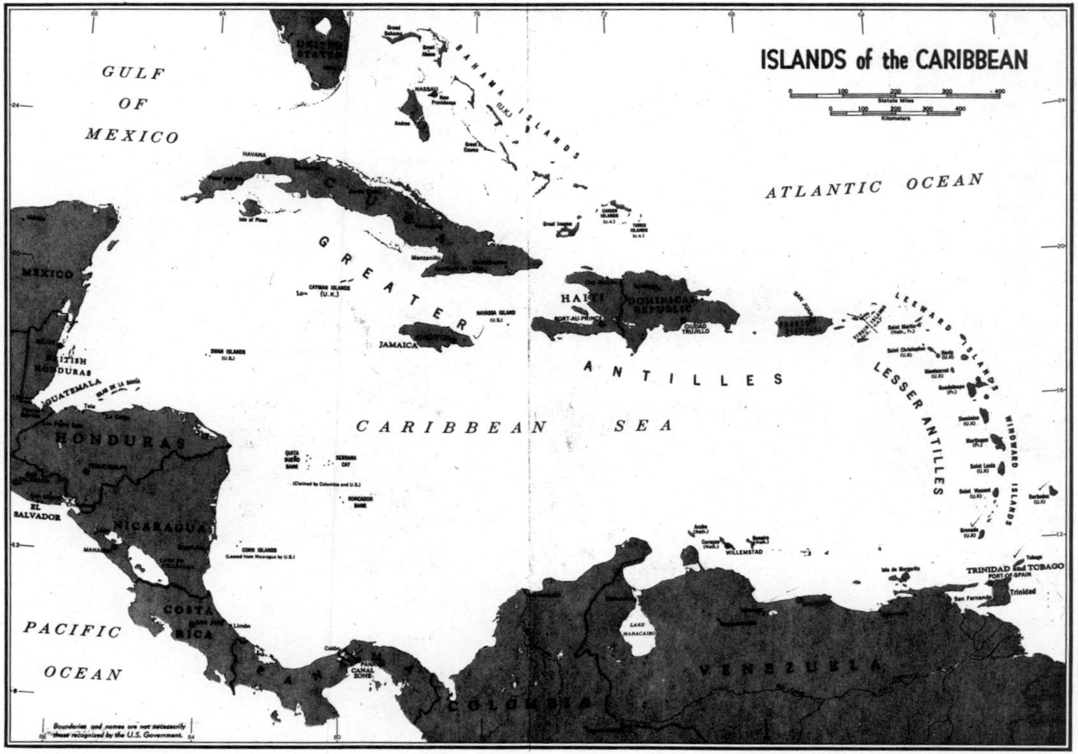

Source: U.S. Department of State

CHAPTER 1

INTRODUCTION

The major phenomenon in international affairs since World War II has been the breakdown of colonial empires of the eighteenth and nineteenth centuries. Since World War II almost a hundred new entities have appeared on the world scene. The result has been a series of states—some of them quite small—with economic and political needs quite different from those of the larger sovereignties. Many of these, although self-governing, have retained a continuing legal association with their former metropoles.

These legal/political analyses of selected insular territories are designed to facilitate comparison of the varying federal relationships of the associated state to the former metropole. While the emphasis is on those relationships within the U.S. federal system, the inquiry will also go beyond this to explore the relationship of associated states within the various British Commonwealth polities. Such comparisons are always dangerous since each area has a somewhat unique historical relationship to the larger power. Add to this the multitude of imponderables which go into any political decision at the national level, and the need for caution increases rapidly.

The relationships to date have been very much the product of each major power's own limited experience. As the association concept takes hold, the examination of the experience of other federal associations will be necessary to determine realistic and legally possible alternatives.

In recent years the United States has tried to change its relationship with the island territories to permit them to be more self-governing and reach a relationship other than integration (statehood) within the United States. The model for this was the Philippine Commonwealth experience of the 1930s, although Puerto Rico was the first area to suggest this association status may be a permanent one. In 1952 Puerto Rico became a commonwealth; in part as a conscious choice of the United States leadership, but in greater part because of the political skill and legerdemain of Puerto Rico's leaders. The commonwealth role was initially regarded at the federal level as unique and not as the pattern for the other U.S. territories such as the Virgin Islands, Guam, or American Samoa.

But the Trust Territory of the Pacific Islands (TTPI) changed that. As of 1975 the United States is actively engaged in negotiations with the Trust Territory which, it appears, will separate into two different entities. Negotiations with the northern Marianas—the Mariana Islands District of TTPI—have followed closely the pattern of Puerto Rico's establishment as a commonwealth; but TTPI as a whole and the remaining five districts of TTPI (which will be referred to as Micronesia) have suggested new ideas seeking a looser relationship. Guam, formerly directed only toward statehood, has been influenced by these events and it, too, is now thinking seriously about a commonwealth relationship.

The Cook Islands' association with New Zealand has been influential throughout the Pacific and within the United Nations organization. Papua New Guinea, much larger and more diverse, has wrestled with the association problem as it has moved toward independence. Its relationship with Australia is significant for the associated state that must accommodate to a closer association to its former governing power, but wishes prior to independence some of the powers of a larger, more independent country.

The major issue—sometimes stated but frequently unstated—in the relationship is the reserve power in the colonizing country. The extent of this is rarely tested. In only one modern-day case has this reserve power been exercised: England took the major step of actually invading one of the islands comprising the West Indies Associated States, attempting to both arbitrate and superimpose a new structure over that previously established. We will examine the West Indies Associated States experience at considerable length in order to understand the significance of this event.

For this reason, this book will, after examining relationships with the Philippine Islands, Puerto Rico, the Marianas, Micronesia, and Guam, look carefully at the Cook Islands, Papua New Guinea, and the West Indies Associated States. Our analysis will discuss each association within its own historical and national context but then will discuss the United Nations (UN) standards for decolonization and the treatment of these associations before the UN Decolonization Committee and the General Assembly. Finally, we shall suggest in the conclusions the possibilities and dangers in the relationship.

All of the states to be discussed have certain things in common. They are, for example, all islands; but they vary considerably in size (from more than 40 million people in the Philippines to less than 20,000 in the Cook Islands and the Marianas) and vary substantially, also, in density and cultural unity (from the highly dense and culturally unified population in Puerto Rico to the more widely dispersed, disparate population of Papua New Guinea).

INTRODUCTION

These factors, however, should not be viewed only in absolute terms. They need to be related to the other partner in the association. For example, Puerto Rico's rather homogeneous cultural background would be a great asset were it not for the fact that the culture is so different from that of the United States. The Cook Islands are geographically isolated, it is true, but are far less isolated in relation to New Zealand than TTPI is with respect to the United States. Issues, then, of relative size, relative distance, and cultural interaction are critical.

Full political integration, such as statehood, bestows a standard set of rights, powers, and responsibilities upon the territory and its inhabitants following the pattern of other entities already integrated into the system. A status short of full integration does not guarantee or require any particular division of power or uniformity of political institutions. This can be of great benefit to the smaller associated state. The relationship need not start with any particularized form but can evolve over time to meet the common aspirations and goals of the former territorial populace and the larger community. But there is a corresponding danger. Since the bargaining power is, and will remain, unequal and the negotiation is without defined ground rules, the smaller community is likely to find itself in a continuously deteriorating position.

The benefits and dangers need to be emphasized since the legal/political relationship between the associated state and the larger power is an unstable one. No matter how firm the original structure, the association agreement is likely, in a very short time, to be amended both in fact and in law as the needs and the desires of the parties rapidly change. By its very nature, the associated state relationship is a continuing struggle to obtain unsatisfied goals. Rather petty, or at least nonmajor, issues can take on great significance so that the broader areas of agreement are forgotten or at least fade in the background as the struggle continues over a particular issue.

All of this has to be set against the fact that the historical circumstances which brought the parties together have embedded within them bitter memories. Conquest may, in fact, be the tie that binds, but every colony must wish that it were not so. Further, the economic and political power of the former colony is relatively small, almost nonexistent when measured against that of its colonizer. Whatever agreements are struck must appear inequitable given the relative bargaining positions of the parties, and will be a continuing source of political concern to the lesser sovereign and an irritant to the larger power.

The focus here is upon alternate legal and political relationships. The geographical and economic situation in which each associated state finds itself is mentioned briefly to permit the reader to gain his bearings. Each study explores certain common key areas which are of continuing concern and go to the heart of any federal relationship being established:

1. the applicability of national legislation
2. the rights of movement (immigration) and to investment (land ownership) of the citizens of the associated state and the metropole
3. the continuing financial role of the former colonial power
4. the continuing military role of the former colonial power
5. the degree of local autonomy accorded the associated state
6. the degree of autonomy in the international sphere accorded the associated state.

We can, perhaps, make a number of generalizations on the United States experience which may assist the reader as he proceeds. Although relative size has been an important issue in other federal systems, this has not been true in the United States. The United States has always been overwhelmingly dominant in comparison to its offshore territories. This dominance, coupled with America's limited colonial experience, has resulted in a tendency to treat all colonies similarly despite their major differences and has resulted in a very cautious treatment of the federal relationship.

The United States tends to follow a legalistic, conservative, and fairly rigid course in its territorial relations. (This generalization is, I believe, correct although it should be noted that the United States did develop varying political relationships and institutions with its outlying areas so as to have been able simultaneously to govern Alaska as a new state, Hawaii as an incorporated territory, Puerto Rico as a Commonwealth, Guam as an unincorporated territory under an organic act, American Samoa without an organic act, and the Pacific Islands as a Trust Territory.) However, the United States has assumed, with very minor exceptions, the equal applicability of federal law and interpretation of the U.S. Constitution. This has meant, as federal power has expanded, the extension of federal power to the territories, potential and actual exercise of military powers of eminent domain, and the restriction of any international presence for the associated state. On the other hand, this approach means that the United States takes the grant of citizenship very seriously. There is no restriction on immigration to the mainland for citizens of the territories because of the perceived constitutional consequences of American citizenship. Similarly, the United States has assumed that the traditional state pattern of separation between the executive and legislative branches would be followed in the territories. In 1966 the Virgin Islands suggested a parliamentary system of government and this was immediately scotched by the chairman of the congressional committee.[1]

The British Commonwealth colonial powers have been, on the other hand, much more flexible; more ready to restrict their own federal power in all areas, more ready to permit an independent, international presence for their associated states. But the ground rules are less clear;

the boundaries for the relationship are almost totally unlimited and subject to improvisation, so that the act of restricting immigration by Commonwealth citizens to the British Isles was legally less shocking than a similar act by the United States would have been.

Within the United States experience, the military issue appears much more dominant. All of the United States areas, during their colonial experience and even afterward, have been subject to a large military establishment maintained directly by the federal government, generally unchecked by local authority. This role for the military in colonies or associated states is not, of course, unique to the United States but its omnipresence is unusual. The result is that, both in the U.S. Congress and the executive branch, defense and military implications are involved or color attitudes on minor points more frequently than in other federal polities.

The United States has also been very slow to permit political involvement of its offshore areas at the national level. No offshore area has ever been able to vote on legislation relating to it and, with the single exception of Richard Taitano from Guam, who was director of the Office of Territories in the Department of the Interior from 1961 to 1964, no offshore representative has ever played a continuing, major role in the executive branch in areas of importance to his homeland's welfare. The flexibility of the Constitution has not been put into play to permit broad-scale political representation at the national level for colonial areas.

On the other hand, in the economic and social area, the large size of the United States has served the colonies well. The United States' humanitarian, liberal attitudes encourage from the outset a social concern (this is most clearly seen in connection with health and education efforts) and have generally meant an economic standard of living higher in the United States offshore areas than elsewhere. As federal economic programs have expanded in the United States, this has resulted in greater financial assistance as well—although not necessarily proportionately—to the offshore areas, a relationship not found in other federal polities.

But generalities in this area are almost impossible. There are too many exceptions and accommodations. The question, of course, is one of power and in broad terms relates those powers retained by the larger polity to those given to the associated states (and, most importantly, to those left rather unclear or required to be exercised jointly). In the next few pages some aspects of the problems and issues are noted, but the full answer rests in the detailed analysis to be found in the individual case studies.

MILITARY SECURITY AND EXTERNAL AFFAIRS REPRESENTATION

National Security

It has been common, almost pro forma, for the larger power to insist on the control of national security affairs and foreign affairs of the associated state. For example, in Guam, the Marianas, Puerto Rico, the Philippines under commonwealth, and Micronesia, the United States obtained this right.

British Commonwealth practice appears somewhat different, at least in theory. Technically, Australia retains similar rights with respect to Papua New Guinea, New Zealand has similar control in the Cook Islands, and Great Britain certainly has such control of the West Indian associated states. But the extent of this power when implemented is harder to judge. Australia has announced that during the interim period—prior to independence—Papua New Guinea would be treated as if it were already independent, so that in fact the military power may not be there; or, if there, is in a form similar to a defense treaty arrangement. But at present Australian and Papua New Guinea military armed forces are comingled in Papua New Guinea, so matters are far from clear.[2] The New Zealand-Cook Islands agreement requires consultation before action in the area of national security. But the same constitutional provision was present in the case of the West Indies Associated States in the Caribbean. In light of Great Britain's action in the Anguilla situation, the reserve power may permit stronger unilateral action by the larger power than had been thought previously.

There are corollary questions, such as that of compulsory military service. In the case of Guam, Puerto Rico, and the Marianas under the proposed covenant the United States imposed the requirement of compulsory military service similar to that which prevails in a state of the Union. In the case of Micronesia, although the military has the power to use Micronesia for military purposes, the United States does not retain the power to require compulsory induction of the population into the armed forces. In Papua New Guinea and the Cook Islands, no such requirement of service in the armed forces is imposed.

Foreign Affairs and the International Presence of Associated States

With respect to external affairs, it is also unclear what is being retained by the larger power. There are at least three aspects of the issue: treaty-making powers with foreign governments, international representation, and control over foreign trade.

The United States has, perhaps, been the most rigid of all colonial powers on all of these issues. Although there are many international

INTRODUCTION

organizations in which full sovereignty is not required, the United States has resisted membership in these institutions by Guam, the Marianas, Micronesia, and Puerto Rico. Puerto Rico has commercial attaches in U.S. embassies and has had representation in international conferences as part of the U.S. delegation. But, in general, Puerto Rico has been viewed in these areas as similar to a state of the Union. The major breakthrough is Puerto Rican membership in the Caribbean Development Bank. As of 1975 Congress was in the process of passing special legislation to permit this, although there appears to be little necessity for such an act. In the case of Guam the United States government has resisted Guamanian membership in the Asian Development Bank, the United Nations' Economic Social Council on Asia and the Pacific (ESCAP), and the various South Pacific international forums such as the South Pacific Commission.

It is hard to know the reason for the U.S. rigidity. There are two questions with respect to an associated territory of the United States joining an international organization: one constitutional, the other international. The constitutional question revolves around Article I, Section 10 of the U.S. Constitution, which provides as follows:

> No State shall enter into any Treaty, Alliance, or Confederation. . . .
> No State shall, without the Consent of Congress lay any Duty of Tonnage, keep Troops, or Ships of War in time of peace, enter into any Agreement or Compact with another State, or with a foreign Power. . . .

Thus, there is an absolute prohibition of any state's entering into a "treaty, alliance, or confederation" with a foreign power, and a partial limitation with respect to a foreign "agreement or compact" since the latter requires congressional consent. However, in a series of cases, the Supreme Court has held that a state may, without the consent of Congress, enter into a compact where it did not "tend to increase and build up the political influence of the contracting States so as to encroach upon or impair the supremacy of the United States or interfere with their rightful management of particular subjects placed under their entire control."[3] By its terms, in any event, the constitutional provision applied only to states; and in the case of Puerto Rico, it has not prevented that territory from entering into a variety of bilateral and multilateral relationships such as the Caribbean Organization, and various relationships with the Dominican Republic.

There would not appear to be, then, a bar in U.S. domestic law. The issue would thus be one of international law, which in general means an examination of the practice and legal requirements of the international organization involved. If the area is considered a nation-state, then it may join all organizations, including the United Nations. The traditional attributes of statehood are population, area, stable government, and, according to traditional textbook writers, independence, especially with respect to external affairs. The question of statehood in an international sense has arisen with respect to several smaller countries which have become members of the United Nations, since many of them delegate some of their responsibilities for defense and foreign affairs.

The statehood requirement for membership in the United Nations has been met by states with very small population, such as the Maldive Islands (93,000) and Iceland (185,000) and by others with very small land areas, such as the Maldive Islands (298 square kilometers) and Malta (316 square kilometers). Some accommodations were also made initially for countries which were formally tied to a metropole but were soon likely to become independent (the Philippines, India, Syria, and Lebanon) in addition to the Soviet provinces of Byelorussia and the Ukraine. But in the 1950s the issue rarely arose, so that one writer could say that in general "where the claim has been for comprehensive participation, the U.N. has required a high degree of sovereignty in the conduct of its foreign relations."[4] Seventeen states were, however, admitted en bloc in 1960; many, such as Cyprus, with extensive military and external ties with larger states. This continued throughout the 1960s (the most notable instances, perhaps, being Mongolia, Mauritania, and the 1971 admission of Bhutan). In short, whatever the traditional views of the nation-state, they are obviously being modified in UN practice to permit a good deal of flexibility in interpretation.

But even if an area cannot meet the requirements of a nation-state for the purposes of UN membership or for other reasons, a territorial community is not thereby excluded from other types of international participation. Many of the United Nations-related organizations provide for associate status as well as consultative status.* The World Health Organization (WHO), the Food and Agriculture Organization (FAO), the United Nations Educational, Scientific and Cultural Organization (UNESCO), and the International Telecommunications Union (ITU), for example, envision associate memberships for "territories or groups of territories which are not responsible for the conduct of their international relations." ITU goes further in providing associate membership, on majority approval, for "any country not a [full] member."

---

*The UN Department of Legal Affairs advised that full membership for non-self-governing territories would be contrary to the charter and that only in very exceptional circumstances should it be granted by a subordinate UN organ to a state that is not a member of the United Nations. (See David Wightman, Toward Regional Cooperation in Asia [New Haven: Yale University Press, for the Carnegie Endowment for International Peace, 1963], p. 22.) The opinion seems to have been more honored in the breach than strictly observed. An extended argument in favor of Puerto Rico's assuming an international role may be found in Reisman, Puerto Rico and the International Process, American Sec. of International Law (1975).

INTRODUCTION

Other organizations have adopted other phrasing. The Pan American Health Organization's constitution provides, for example, that non-self-governing territories have the "right to be represented and participate in the organization;" although the meaning of this phrase has been the subject of considerable debate over the years. Associate members are generally not entitled to vote or to hold office in plenary bodies or in key committees, but this practice is by no means uniform and is rapidly changing. Thus, international law could also permit an international presence for U.S. territories. Great Britain, New Zealand, and even France have been much more forthcoming and willing to permit their smaller island associated states to be represented in the institutions noted above.

Treaty making is a more complex question and seems to raise international law questions rather than political ones, although recent practice involving Quebec would suggest that the legal situation is more permissive of this than some would have it.[5] The United States has resisted this possibility for its commonwealths and territories; for example, by resisting Puerto Rican efforts to sign, on behalf of itself, an international treaty obligation, even when the Puerto Rican government provides the funding. There has, however, been some give in the United States position recently. With mutual consent, the Marianas may enter into treaty obligations; and Micronesia was negotiating a treaty-making power, except for agreements involving national security. Again, the British Commonwealth associations are more permissive, with almost no restriction in this area for the Cook Islands, Papua New Guinea, and the West Indies Associated States.

TARIFFS AND TRADE

It is interesting that in the area of trade, which gave rise in the United States to the constitutional distinction between unincorporated and incorporated territories, the United States has been very flexible. Thus, Guam, like the Virgin Islands, is considered a free port outside the customs territory of the United States and is permitted transshipment of foreign goods freely into the United States, provided 51 percent of the value of completed goods derives from territorial operations. Special restrictions, however, have been placed on watch manufacturing because of injury or potential injury to the United States industry. In the case of Puerto Rico there is a sugar quota; but outside of that, transshipment to the United States is completely free. In addition, Puerto Rico is given the power to place duties on foreign importation of coffee (which affects Puerto Rico uniquely), although the United States itself has no such tariff on the product. In the case of the Marianas and Micronesia, local control is complete and these territories can restrict fully, by tariff or quota, importation of foreign—that is, non-U.S.—goods into their islands.

The above flexibility is, however, limited by the possibility of the metropole's changing the situation unilaterally. All the metropoles retain this kind of power; and although they use it infrequently (sugar quotas, for example, in the United States, or citrus and banana quotas in Great Britain), it is there.

The corresponding power seems also to be present in the territory, usually restricted by political realities rather than legal necessity. In the case of the United States territories, it appears that Guam or Puerto Rico could impose export duties on transshipment (although they have not done so). The Marianas could go even further to control exports. Micronesia could go the furthest of all and impose any type of control it wished, provided most-favored-nation treatment was accorded.

IMMIGRATION

Finally, there is control over the movement of persons. The United States has been rather forbidding on this point, denying requests by both Guam and Puerto Rico for control by them of migration into the islands (or at least for individual variations from the centrally set immigration policy). The Virgin Islands have made a similar request, since the United States' liberal immigration policy has resulted in serious racial and political difficulties. Some accommodation has been made for American Samoa, which is considerably smaller in population than any other U.S. territory. (The constitutionality of this, it should be noted, has never been tested.) American Samoa can restrict immigration of foreigners and of U.S. citizens, a power accorded no other territory. In the Marianas, the question is still being negotiated as of the mid-1970s; but in the case of Micronesia, the U.S. negotiators had agreed to complete local control by the Micronesian government.

With respect to immigration from the associated states to the mainland, the United States has been similarly consistent. In all U.S. territories, free immigration is permitted from the territory to the United States. In the case of Micronesia, while immigration to the States is permitted, Micronesian immigration to Guam and American Samoa is not.

Outside the United States, in the British Commonwealth associations, the associated state is given much more control over the movement of foreigners or the larger power's citizens. The smaller associated states completely control the ability of all nonislanders to move to their island. On the other hand, the free movement of the associated states' citizens that is available in the United States is not available in Great Britain.

A key issue has been control over land ownership. In the Commonwealth associations, nonresident citizens may not invest or own land on their island. In American Samoa and the Marianas a similar provision is found, but attempts by Guam to restrict nonresident United States citizens from owning land on that island have been ineffectual.

TAXATION AND DUTIES

The United States has treated the matter of duties quite casually, viewing this as a means whereby the territorial expenses can be defrayed without drains on the federal treasury. Thus, in general, duties collected on shipments to the territory are turned over to the territory.

Taxation is less consistent. Puerto Rico, because of a provision inserted in 1900, is free of federally imposed taxes, while the Virgin Islands, Guam, and American Samoa pay taxes to their own treasuries to satisfy the federal obligation. But it is federal legislation which can change, and has changed, the local tax structure. The commonwealth associated states are more autonomous in this regard; their tax legislation is controlled by themselves.

APPLICABILITY OF FEDERAL LAW

The issue of applicability of federal law to the territories is part of a broader one, the applicability of national legislation. In the case of the Cook Islands, the Caribbean, and Papua New Guinea, the larger sovereign's laws do not apply without the smaller territory's consent. Puerto Rico has argued for something similar without success. There is a provision indicating that federal law does not apply where local conditions do not permit,[6] but this to date has never checked federal legislative or executive action. Guam and the Virgin Islands do not even have this saving clause,[7] and federal law applies unless Congress states to the contrary.

POLITICAL REPRESENTATION

The issue of political representation touches upon the method of participation in the federal decision-making process. One would expect this situation to be the obverse of the issue already mentioned, that of applicability of federal law. That is, if the federal law applied generally, the federal body would have a territorial participant; while if it generally did not, then no such participation would be required.

That has not been true in the United States. Although, as indicated above, federal law generally does apply to the outlying areas, the United States has accorded its associated areas at best (Puerto Rico and, more recently, Guam) a nonvoting resident commissioner who is expected to handle the area's legislative and executive interest. The Marianas are not given any official legislative role at the federal level.

Papua New Guinea, the Cook Islands, and the West Indies Associated States do not have any parliamentary representation. There is an official representative of the larger power in their area, a vestige of the governor-general or a forerunner of the ambassador, depending upon one's point of view. In any event, federal action affecting them is much less frequent than in the United States context.

AGREEMENT MODIFICATION AND DISPUTE SETTLEMENT

One of the issues that is less frequently discussed is the question of how to settle disputes between the associated state and the larger power. In United States practice it has always been assumed that the U.S. federal courts would decide. This is set forth explicitly in the Marianas agreement; but in the case of Micronesia there is a requirement of "good faith negotiation" although what that entails is rather unclear. It does seem to limit the U.S. court jurisdiction somewhat.

If the issue was contemplated in the commonwealth associations, a decision was apparently made to keep a discreet silence.

TERMINATION

The issue of how relationships between territory and metropole are to be terminated has been critical in recent negotiations. The Cook Islands pioneered the idea of unilateral termination, balancing the unequal bargaining position with an "option out" on the part of the associated state if the negotiation, over time, became too one-sided. Micronesia, in its negotiations with the United States, envisioned something similar, but the United States refused to discuss the issue and the negotiations foundered as a result. Puerto Rico has argued that the "compact" may be modified only by mutual consent, although this has hardly been the rule to date. Termination of any associated state relationship with the United States is never clearly set forth or envisioned.

NOTES

1. Discussed in S. A. DeSmith, <u>Microstates and Micronesia</u> (New York: Center for International Studies, New York University, 1970), p. 97.
2. The role of Papua New Guinea in international relations and the national security tie with Australia are discussed in Miller, <u>Papua New Guinea in World Politics</u>, 27 <u>Australian Outlook</u> 191 (1973).

3. <u>Virginia</u> v. <u>Tennessee</u>, 148 U.S.503, 518 (1893); see <u>McHenry County</u> v. <u>Brady</u>, 37 N.D. 59, 163 N.W. 540 (1917). Frankfurter and Landis, <u>The Compact Clause of the Constitution—A Study in Interstate Adjustments</u>, 34 <u>Yale L. J.</u> 685, 749 (1925) lists eleven interstate agreements made without congressional consent, some expressly approved by the Supreme Court. The subject is thoroughly reviewed in Zimmerman and Wendell, <u>The Interstate Compact Since 1925</u> (1951). Some contemporary examples of state compacts providing for foreign participation are the Northeastern Interstate Forest Fire Protection Compact, 63 Stat. 271 (1949) (art. II permits any province of Canada to join with the consent of Congress which was given in 1952, 66 Stat. 71), and the Great Lakes Basin Compact (art. II [B] permits the Provinces of Ontario and Quebec to become parties). Congressional consent authorized a New York compact with Canada relating to the bridge across the Niagara River between Buffalo and Fort Erie, 70 Stat. 701 (1956), as modified, 71 Stat. 367 (1957), and allowed the State of Minnesota to enter into compact with Manitoba for the development of an access highway, 70 Stat. 701.

4. Cohen, <u>The Concept of Statehood in United Nations Practice</u>, 95 <u>U. of Pa. L. Rev.</u> 1149 (1961).

5. Fitzgerald, <u>Education and Cultural Agreements and Ententes: France, Canada and Quebec—Birth of a New Treaty Making Technique for Federal States</u>, 60 <u>Am. J. Int'l.</u> 529 (1966).

6. Leibowitz, <u>Applicability of Federal Law to the Commonwealth of Puerto Rico</u>, 56 <u>Geo. L. J.</u> 219 (1968).

7. The issue is examined in the Legal Appendix (prepared by the author) to the Report on the Status of Guam of the Twelfth Guam Legislature (September 1974).

CHAPTER

2

THE PHILIPPINE ISLANDS

Although the Philippine Islands came under United States suzerainty at the same time as Puerto Rico and Guam, and only a year after the acquisition of Hawaii, they became the bellwether for subsequent associated-state thinking in the United States. This was the largest of the offshore territories, with the strongest sense of nationality and a culture distinct from that of the United States. Although its territorial relationship has, perhaps, long faded from the public mind, the recent proposals with respect to Puerto Rico, and to a lesser degree with respect to the Marianas and Micronesia, take many of their ideas and specific provisions from this earlier relationship. This fact warrants a discussion of the United States' relations with the Philippines before turning to those other areas.

The Philippines consist of approximately 7,000 islands of varying size, stretching over 1,100 miles from north to south with a total area of almost 115,000 square miles. They are strategically located between the East Indies and Japan, not far from the coast of China. The country consists of three main island groups: the Luzon group in the northern Philippines (containing the largest and most important island of Luzon, with an area of 41,000 square miles), a middle group (the Visayas), and the most southern group, which contains Mindanao, the second largest island in the chain.

The Philippines have a warm, humid climate with little variation in temperature, although the islands are subject to strong typhoons between August and October and earthquakes are not unusual.

The islands are heavily populated, with more than 40 million people, a sharp increase over the 7,635,426 counted at the time of the first United States census in 1903. They earn their living primarily in agriculture, with sugar, rice, and coconut copra products predominating. There are large, undeveloped mineral deposits with considerable economic potential on the island of Mindanao.

The islands are overwhelmingly Christian; this is, in fact, the only Christian country in Asia. No single language predominates. About nine different languages and about 100 different dialects are actively spoken. Under Spain, Spanish was the official language of the islands; but after acquisition by the United States, English was added as another official language. After the achievement of independence, a variation of Tagalog, Philippine, was adopted as the national language.

HISTORICAL BACKGROUND

Relationship with Spain: 1521-1898

The native Philippine civilization prior to Western contact had developed considerable sophistication in some areas. It was a culture of developed skills in various artistic fields, widespread literacy, and some settlements of unusual size that carried on extensive trade both within the archipelago and with China, Indochina, and possibly Japan.

The islands were opened to the West as a result of their discovery by Magellan in 1521 in the course of his around-the-world voyage; but it was not until almost 50 years later that the Spanish established permanent settlements on the islands. The islands were conquered with relatively little bloodshed; and the basic tax, the tribute, was not in itself overburdening. In addition to the tribute, however, the government exacted forced drafts of labor to obtain increased food and timber production, with consequent great pain and suffering.

The Philippines were ruled by a governor-general endowed with enormous powers, including the ability to determine the applicability of royal decrees in the islands. In addition, there was an <u>Audiencia</u> which acted as both a supreme court and an advisory body. But this centralization of control was more in theory than in fact. The Spanish government relied heavily upon a form of indirect rule, using traditional elites in the isolated, tribally oriented countryside and using local leaders to fill offices below the rank of "mayor." This administrative method, adopted perforce both because of the great distance from Spain and the nature of Philippine Island society, also reinforced the role of the Catholic Church, since at the local level the only Spanish official was likely to be a friar.

The position of the friars, the profitability of the galleon trade, and the rugged topography and decentralized population pattern of the archipelago separated the Spaniards' society and economy from those of the natives for most of the first two centuries of Spanish rule, reducing friction between the conquerors and the conquered. In the nineteenth century, a series of events changed matters considerably: The demise of the galleon trade between Mexico and the Philippines, due to the increased popularity of European cottons instead of Chinese silk, required the Spanish, in 1839, to open the Philippines to foreign trade. Racial friction grew. The Filipinos resented the ethnic tax categories

MAP 2

Philippines

Source: T. F. Kennedy, A Descriptive Atlas of the Pacific Islands (New York: Praeger, 1969).

established by the Spanish and the difficulty of obtaining better church appointments which they saw as a racial bias.[1] The ownership by the church of large tracts of agricultural land exacerbated the situation. And, of course, nationalism was in the European air. The 1880s brought the first railroad, telegraph, and telephone to the Philippines; and with them the liberal currents of the continent.

On the night of 20 January 1872, Filipino soldiers in Cavite mutinied. The Spaniards suppressed the mutiny easily—in less than a day—and the mutiny in Cavite was not duplicated elsewhere. But the Spanish magnified its importance, viewing it as part of a widespread conspiracy seeking separation from Spain. They focused on the discontent of the Filipino priests and issued a series of investigations and repressive measures against them, culminating in the execution of three priests who had been leaders in the movement to secularize the parishes. As a result, the Cavite mutiny became the turning point in Philippine-Spanish relations.

The next two decades saw growing political and social consciousness and discontent among the Filipinos. The Spanish attempted reforms, such as the celebrated Marua Law of 1893 which increased local autonomy, broadened the electorate, and reduced the role of the priest. But the reform was too late.

In August 1896 a major revolt was begun, headed by Andre Bonifacio and the secret society he had founded, the Katipunan. This revolt was continuing with considerable success when, as a result of the Spanish-American War, the Philippines came under United States control. The United States then fell heir to the racial and national assertiveness of the Philippines which had directed itself at the Spanish.

Relationship with the United States: 1898-1934

The Philippine insurgents had hoped the United States would treat them as allies fighting for independence; but instead, the United States viewed them as a combatant against a common enemy. In 1899 after the Treaty of Paris, when the United States obtained the Philippines and occupied them, Philippine nationalism reasserted itself. There was intermittent shooting, fighting, and guerrilla warfare which continued until 1904.

It was in this context that judgments covering the United States policy in the Philippines were to be made. The question of the propriety of annexation was a partisan issue (with the Democrats holding to the antiimperialist position while the Republicans were less certain), even so, from the time the United States obtained the Philippines together with Puerto Rico and Guam (by the Treaty of Paris), official American policy—although it was to waver and frequently promise more than it delivered—usually assumed that one day the Philippines would be independent. Thus, the Philippines never were incorporated into the United States tax system and always had a separate coinage and monetary system. Nevertheless, the credit of the United States stood behind the bonds issued by the Philippine government up to the passage of the 1934 Act. The Philippine government was also given power to regulate tariffs, except where Philippine-U.S. trade was involved, but the Philippine legislation was to set the pattern in key areas for the governance by the United States of its territories.[2]

In 1902, the first organic act for the islands was passed; its substance was similar to the Foraker Act of 1900 for Puerto Rico. There was a bill of rights patterned on the first ten amendments to the U.S. Constitution, except for the omission of the right to jury trial and the right to bear arms. (Since the Philippines were held by the Supreme Court to be an unincorporated territory, only the fundamental provisions of the U.S. Constitution applied to the island's inhabitants.)

Executive power was vested in the civil governor appointed by the President of the United States. A single-chamber Philippine Assembly was established, composed of Filipinos elected by Filipino voters for a term of two years. A Philippine commission represented the upper house with the governor acting as chairman. The U.S. Supreme Court exercised jurisdiction over the Philippine Supreme Court. The bill also provided for two Filipino resident commissioners, one more than in the case of Puerto Rico, to represent, without voting powers, the Philippines in the U.S. House of Representatives.

In August 1916 the United States Congress passed the Jones Law to "declare the purposes of the people of the United States as to the future of the political status of the people of the Philippine Islands, and to provide a more autonomous government for the Islands." In its preamble, the Jones Law declared that "it was never the intention of the people of the United States in the incipiency of the war with Spain to make it a war of conquest or for the territorial aggrandizement," and that "the purpose of the people of the United States is to withdraw their sovereignty over the Philippine Islands and to recognize their independence as soon as a stable government can be established therein." (Between 1919 and 1934, the Philippines sent twelve independence missions to inform the U.S. Congress that a stable government existed there and that the time had come to grant independence.)

The act also provided for some expansion of Philippine control of the various branches of the islands' government which was established along U.S. lines. The legislative power was to be vested in a bicameral Philippine Legislature, composed of the Senate (upper house) and the House of Representatives (lower house). The Senate was to replace the old Philippine commission. It was to be composed of 24 senators, 22 of whom were to be elected by the Filipino voters and 2 to be appointed by the American governor-general. The House of Representatives was to consist of 90 representatives. Executive power was to be exercised by an American governor-general appointed by the president of the United States.

PHILIPPINE ISLANDS

Judicial power was to be vested in a Philippine Supreme Court which, together with the lower island courts, exercised considerable autonomy since the United States courts never functioned directly in the islands but only indirectly by means of review by the U.S. Supreme Court. There was no U.S. federal district court for the islands; instead, the lower courts were enabled by law to enforce certain federal statutes. Almost until commonwealth was established in 1934 the Supreme Court of the Philippines was composed of nine judges appointed by the president of the United States—five from the States and four from the islands. By law, the court's decisions were to be reported in English.[3] The effect of the Jones Act was that although final political authority rested with the United States officials, for many years prior to 1934 the day-to-day affairs of government (except for foreign affairs and defense) were handled by the islanders themselves.

Restrictions on Filipino self-government, however, included the following:

1. The American governor-general and the president of the United States could veto any law passed by the Philippine Legislature.
2. All laws promulgated by the Philippine Legislature affecting coinage and currency would require the approval of the president of the United States.
3. All accounts pertaining to the revenues and expenditures of the Philippine government were to be subject to audit, approval, or disapproval by the insular auditor appointed by the president of the United States.
4. Trade between the Philippines and the United States was to be subject to regulation by the U.S. Congress.
5. Important cases decided by the Philippine Supreme Court could be appealed to the U.S. Supreme Court.
6. The public schools were required to be conducted in English.

Limitations on Philippine residents becoming U.S. citizens and lack of full reciprocity with respect to the rights enjoyed by the citizens of one country in the other, have been sore points to this day. After the American occupation and up to independence, inhabitants of the Philippines were citizens of the Philippines who owed allegiance to the United States. They were never given collective citizenship and although they were allowed to enter the United States freely until 1934, they could not become naturalized citizens since they were not of the white race or of African descent.[4] However, exception was made for those who served in the U.S. Navy, Coast Guard, or Naval Auxiliary Service after 1918.[5]

We may view this racial slight as the product of a bygone time, but insults such as these cut deeply and last longer than we wish. Fortunately, it no longer affects our territorial relationship. Further, U.S. citizens and corporations in the Philippines enjoyed the civil rights of the native citizens and corporations although the reverse was not true. This economic advantage was part and parcel of the benefits of "empire" but its attempted continuation after Philippine independence has given rise to considerable tension.

Trade and its terms have been a continuing area of tension, both at the time of commonwealth negotiations and when the Philippines received their independence. Trade between the Philippine Islands and the United States prior to 1934 was governed primarily by two acts passed in 1909: the Tariff Act of 1909 and the Philippine Tariff Act of 1909.[6] These acts established, in effect, free trade between the United States and the Philippines, although under their terms the Philippines, together with Guam, was—unlike Puerto Rico—placed outside the United States domestic tariff area. The key provisions stated that goods entering the United States from the Philippines would be subject to the same tariff as foreign goods, except for U.S. or Philippine articles which could enter duty free.[7]

The laws, however, were not quite reciprocal. There was a 20 percent limitation on the value of foreign materials in the case of Philippine goods entering the United States, but no limitation in the reverse situation. An illustration shows what the difference might mean in practice. The Philippines might import silk cloth from Japan, embroider it, and make it into blouses. But if the value of the Japanese cloth exceeded 20 percent of the blouse, the blouse could not enter the United States free of duty. The United States could import coffee beans from Brazil, grind them, and can the ground coffee. No matter what percentage of the value was represented by the original coffee beans, the whole product could enter the Philippines free of duty.

In addition, there were tariff quotas on certain Philippine articles (sugar and tobacco), and rice imported from the Philippines was subject to the full tariff. ("Absolute quotas," which are usually duty-free, represent the quantitative amount of a product that may be entered from another country. Once the limit is reached, no more of that product may be imported. "Tariff quotas" are used to refer to an amount of a foreign product that may enter a country paying a reduced tariff. Once the limit is reached, any further amount of that product which may be imported incurs the full tariff.)

Sale of Philippine goods was limited more closely to the United States by a provision imposing export duties on the principal Philippine exports—cordage, sugar, copra, and tobacco products—except when they entered the United States or its possessions.[8] However, at this time the practice began of restricting imports into the United States to goods entering in vessels of the United States or of the country of origin. It was also provided that tariff duties and the taxes (such as processing taxes) paid in the United States on Philippine products would be set aside and returned to the Philippine treasury. This practice continued until independence and has been followed by the United States in all its offshore areas prior to statehood. Since the Tariff Acts of 1913,[9] 1922,[10] and 1930[11] made no substantial changes, this was essentially the American-Philippine trade situation when the Independence Act of 1934 was passed. The effect of the tariff limitations was to provide a market for Philippine raw materials in the United States resulting in an almost unbroken favorable balance of trade with the United States[12] and an increasing unfavorable trade balance with other countries, notably Japan. In addition, the American investment in the islands during the period prior to commonwealth had grown substantially,* as had the number of islanders and Americans in one another's countries.†

THE PHILIPPINE COMMONWEALTH

During the depression a number of bills were introduced which provided for the exclusion of the islanders and their products from the United States and for immediate severance of the territorial relationship, proposals which found support not only on economic but on racial grounds. Feeling aggrieved, the Philippines vigorously renewed their demands for independence which had waned in the late twenties.[13]

The Philippine Independence Act of 1933,[14] providing for independence within ten years and a "commonwealth" government in the interim, was vetoed by President Herbert Hoover. The president felt that there was no consensus in the Philippines in favor of independence and that the situation in the Orient was extremely unstable. If independence were to be granted, he favored increased United States control in the interim and a more gradual staging of independence.[15] The act was passed by Congress over President Hoover's veto, but never went into effect because the Philippine Legislature rejected it unanimously. They felt that (1) the economic provisions were inconsistent with independence; (2) the immigration clause was objectionable and offensive; (3) the powers of the high commissioner were too vague; and (4) the

---

*An estimate in 1930 by the Trade Commissioner of the United States Department of Commerce placed American investments in the Philippines, other than those of the United States Government, at about $200 million. <u>Hearings Before the Committee on Insular Affairs on H.R. 7233</u>—a bill to provide for the independence of the Philippine Islands, House of Representatives, 72nd Cong., 1st Sess.), p. 68.

†According to the American census of 1930, there were 45,208 Filipinos in the United States, around 35,000 in the Pacific Coast States, the rest scattered throughout the United States. (Ibid., p. 71.)

U.S. retention of military bases was inconsistent with true independence or national dignity.[16] A delegation from the Philippines came to Washington to negotiate, unsuccessfully, more favorable terms. The following year a similar law was enacted,[17] and this time it was reluctantly accepted by the Philippines.

The 1934 act, in addition to the promise of independence, gave the Philippines the right to draft their own constitution. The constitution was to be voted upon but the question of independence itself was not submitted to a plebiscite. Philippine authorities had opposed such a plebiscite and, therefore, the Independence Act of 1934 provided for it only indirectly by saying that a vote in favor of the constitution would be "deemed an expression of the will of the people of the Philippine Islands in favor of independence." The United States subsequently has required direct referenda on status changes in its offshore areas although the practice has been endorsed by the United Nations.

Powers Retained by the United States

The commonwealth constitution was limited in the areas and powers it could cover. Foreign affairs remained "under the direct supervision and control of the United States." Commonwealth public debt would be subject to limits set by the U.S. Congress and all foreign loans needed the express approval of the president of the United States. Property owned by United States, or by religious, educational, and charitable institutions, was to be tax-exempt; United States citizens and corporations retained the same rights as residents of the Philippines, and public school instruction was still to be "primarily conducted in English." Review by the United States Supreme Court of the decisions of the highest commonwealth court was also continued.

During commonwealth the United States also retained many other important powers. Most importantly, the president of the United States could

> suspend . . . the operation of any [commonwealth] law, contract or executive order . . . which in his judgment will result in a failure of the government . . . to fulfill its contracts . . . meet its bonded indebtedness . . . [impair its currency] reserves . . . or will violate international obligations of the United States.

Also, the United States executive continued to have the right to expropriate property for public use, to maintain military bases and men in the Philippines, and to call into United States military service commonwealth servicemen. In addition, the president of the United States had the right to intervene "for the preservation of the government of the

Commonwealth of the Philippine Islands . . . for the protection of life, property and individual liberty and for the discharge of government obligations under and in accordance with the provisions of the constitution." Further, the president retained the right to approve all amendments to the Philippine Constitution. The act provided for the appointment by the United States of a high commissioner who had access to all official records and was to keep Congress and the president informed

Trade and Tariff Provisions

Tariff quotas during commonwealth were to be imposed on major Philippine exports (sugar, coconut oil, and cordage). Beginning with the sixth year, Philippine export taxes were to be imposed in gradually increasing percentages of United States import duties so that, when independence day arrived, export taxes on most Philippine goods would be payable to the Philippine government at a rate equal to 25 percent of the United States tariffs. Funds thus collected were to go into a sinking fund and be used to pay the principal and interest on Philippine bonded indebtedness which until this time, as mentioned above, had been guaranteed by the credit of the United States. The law stated that after independence all Philippine articles were to be subject to the full United States duty. However, one year prior to the date fixed for independence a conference would be held between representatives of both governments "for the purpose of formulating recommendations as to future trade relations."[18]

These tariff quotas and duties were less favorable to the Philippines than the islanders has hoped. They had agreed to tariff quotas on their prime products but had desired the duty-free quotas to be higher than actually imposed, and they had opposed any tariffs on other goods during the interim.[19]

Military Bases

The Philippines had wanted the transfer of sovereignty to include all military and other reservations of the government of the United States, with a provision whereby the Philippine government would agree to sell or lease to the United States lands necessary for coaling and naval stations.[20] In this matter, too, the Philippines were disappointed. Section 10 of the 1934 act provided that the transfer of sovereignty would take place except "such naval reservations and fueling stations as are reserved under Section 5."* It authorized the president of the

---

*This section refers to the designation by the president of land and property for military and other reservations of the government of the United States.

United States to negotiate with the government of the Philippines not later than two years after his proclamation "for the adjustment and settlement of all questions relating to naval reservations and fueling stations . . . and pending such adjustments . . . the matter . . . shall remain in its present status."

Immigration

The Philippines had objected strenuously during the hearings on the 1933 act to the proposed exclusion of Philippine residents from the United States. They had indicated that they would accept restrictions on travel and residence in the United States only if it were on economic grounds—rather than on racial ones—and then only if included as a measure preparatory to independence.[21] Section 8 of their proposed bill provided that during the commonwealth period the Filipinos would be classified as nonquota immigrants but the number of immigrants would not exceed 100 a year. In the Independence Act of 1934 Congress treated citizens of the Philippines for the purposes of the immigration laws "as if they were aliens" and set the quota on entry at 50.[22] After independence the Filipinos would be treated like any other foreign country, which meant total exclusion.

CHANGES MADE DURING THE COMMONWEALTH PERIOD

Congress, to respond to expressed Philippine concerns before the new commonwealth government was established, enacted three new pieces of legislation in the trade area which modified the Independence Act:

1. The Jones-Costigan Act,[23] which authorized the Secretary of Agriculture to impose absolute quotas on sugar importations, including those of the Philippines.*
2. The imposition of a tax of two cents per pound in the Revenue Act of 1934 on the domestic processing of coconut except when its copra was an import of the Philippines (an obvious benefit to the Phil-

---

*The Sugar Act of 1937 gave the Philippines 34.7 percent of the total sugar importation from foreign markets, but it was provided that in no case would it be less than the duty-free quota established by the provisions of the 1934 Independence Act. (Sec. 202 (b), P.L. 414, (1 September 1937); 50 Stat. 903.)

ippine industry) and an additional three cents per pound tax on certain domestic processing of this and other oil sources.[24]

3. The imposition of an absolute duty-free quota on Philippine cordage in place of the tariff quota previously in force.[25]

Although the Independence Act had provided that the provisions of the act would not take effect "until accepted by concurrent resolution of the Philippine Legislature or by a convention called for the purpose of passing upon that question," which suggested a bilateral agreement, these changes were made unilaterally.

In 1936-37, after it had been suggested by Philippine President Quezon that the independence date be advanced to December 1938 or 4 July 1939, a Joint Preparatory Committee on Philippines Affairs was established with representatives from both countries and, after extensive hearings, made a report. The report, like the Congressional actions, was to be sympathetic to the Philippine economic concerns, but to resist greater exercise of Philippine sovereignty. The committee recommended that the date of independence not be advanced since the revenues being gained by the Philippines from export taxes (used to retire bonds) and from the return of excise taxes paid on Philippine products in the United States would cease at the same time that the commonwealth government would have to make provisions for its defense program. The committee also recommended "with a view to affording both American and Philippine interests a reasonable opportunity to adjust to the changed relationship" that trade preferences should not be ended in 1946 but should continue until the end of 1960.[26]

The report pointed out further that an undesirable situation had arisen in each country regarding the rights and interests of the citizens of one country in the territory of the other. Noting that the Independence Act had not provided for the rights of the residents of the Philippines in the United States during the interim period, although citizens of the United States were required to have the rights of Philippine citizens when they were in the Philippines, the committee indicated: "Because of this and possibly for other reasons, there has developed in the United States a feeling and, in some instances, a legislative tendency, to consider citizens of the Philippines as if they were aliens." The committee recommended that during the commonwealth period "the authorities of the two countries, in both legislative and administrative action, should adhere to the policy of not curtailing the rights and privileges which [the citizens of the other country enjoyed] prior to the inauguration of the Commonwealth government."[27]

The committee also recommended that "in view of the extensive properties which will be turned over to the independent government, as a matter of equality" some arrangement be made to retransfer title to the United States of such properties as would be needed for the official establishments similar to those which the United States maintained in other foreign countries.[28]

In 1939 the Act Amending the Philippine Independence Act was enacted[29] incorporating some of these recommendations. Thus, Section 8 of the Independence Act was given a new subsection to grant citizens of the Philippines during commonwealth the same rights within the several states that they had prior to commonwealth. This still fell short of full reciprocity with the rights of United States citizens in the Philippines. Section 10 of the Independence Act was amended to give the president of the United States the right to transfer to the Philippine government or private persons property owned by the United States in exchange for property which would be suitable for diplomatic or consular establishments, or to designate by presidential proclamation property owned by the United States which would be suitable for this purpose. Property thus designated or acquired would remain the property of the United States following independence. The amendment also provided that the official residence of the United States high commissioner in Manila and Baguio would continue to be the property of the United States after independence.

Adjustments favorable to the commonwealth were made in the trade arrangements between the commonwealth and the United States. The restriction of foreign material to 20 percent or less was now applied also to American articles entering the Philippines. The total sugar quota remained the same (in accordance with the joint committee's recommendation) but could now be filled more flexibly. The committee's suggestions to increase the cordage quotas to 6 million pounds and to impose a duty-free tariff quota on coconut oil, tobacco, and pearl buttons were carried out in the act. In addition, Congress added cigars to the duty-free tariff quota list. These duty-free quotas, with the exception of that for sugar, were to diminish each year by 5 percent.

The Japanese invasion and occupation of the Philippines caused the operation of these laws to be suspended. The destruction caused by war was greater in the Philippines than in any other country in the East. The physical damage, estimated by the War Damage Corporation, was over $800 million, as follows:[30]

Property Losses	Millions of Dollars
Public property	196
Private property	464
Religious property	139
TOTAL	800

INDEPENDENCE

At the beginning of 1946, only months before the Philippines were to receive independence, little had been done to establish the terms of independence or assist in relieving the war damage. Congress was put under intense pressure to enact legislation before independence day by President Truman and United States High Commissioner McNutt. During this period there was increasing unrest in the islands due to four factors:

1. The noncompliance with the proclamation prepared in American (General MacArthur's) headquarters and signed by Philippine President Osmena indicating that all Philippine soldiers who served in the American armed forces would receive the pay of American soldiers.

2. The repudiation of guerrilla currency issued under written instructions after the decision to use it was made by General MacArthur and President Quezon before leaving Corregidor.

3. The nonpayment (up to that time) of GI benefits to Philippine soldiers, even though the Administrator of Veterans' Affairs had announced the benefits were to be available.*

4. Nonaction by Congress more than a year after Senator Tydings had made a hurried trip to the islands and informed Congress regarding the situation and Commissioner McNutt had obtained from the president and his advisors agreement on American-Philippine policy, including legislation for payment of war damages and extension of the trade privileges for a period of years after independence.[31]

On 30 April 1946, Congress passed the Philippine Rehabilitation[32] and the Philippine Trade Acts.[33] The Rehabilitation Act authorized $400 million as compensation for war damage suffered by private and religious property.[34] In addition, it authorized the transfer of $100 million worth of United States surplus property to the Philippine government[35] and an additional $120 million for the restoration of public property and essential public services.[36] Section 601 of the Rehabilitation Act provided that no compensatory payments exceeding $500 were to be made by the War Damage Commission until an executive agreement had been entered into by the president of the United States and the president of the Philippine Islands and had become effective. This latter provision was opposed by the State Department.†

The Trade Act directed the terms of the agreement between the two countries, and stated that the agreement was to continue unchanged for 28 years. The explanation given for the long duration and prohibition

---

*Congress had subsequently attached a rider to an appropriations bill excluding commonwealth army veterans from any United States veterans' payments except in the case of death and disability payments.

† The Philippines had sought $1 billion for rehabilitation, $800 million estimated by the War Damage Commission plus a sum to take into consideration the price increase involved in replacement. <u>Hearings Before the Senate Committee on Territories and Insular Affairs on S. 1488</u>, 79th Cong., 1st Sess., p. 151.

against change was that American capital was needed to rehabilitate the islands and would not go there unless long-term assurances were provided. It should be noted that the State Department objected strongly to this provision.

Trade and Tariff Provisions

The terms of trade were favorable to the islands. Philippine articles, including Philippine sugar, were to enter the United States free of duty for eight years, up to 3 July 1954. After that they were to have increasingly applied percentages of the lowest United States custom duty at the following rates:

Period	Percentages of U.S. Duty
4 July to 31 December 1954	5
Calendar year 1955	10
Calendar years 1956-72, yearly increase	5
1 January 1973 to 3 July 1974	100

They were thus given the most-favored-nation treatment, placing them on a par with Cuba.

Philippine products which were not Philippine articles—the 1939 act's reciprocal definition of Philippine and United States articles (less than 20 percent of foreign material) was continued, with the addition, however, that in calculating foreign material the whole chain of production would be considered—and the difference between the declining duty-free quota of cigars, scrap tobacco, coconut oil, and buttons and its absolute quota would be subject to the next lowest United States duty (most-favored-nation treatment, excluding Cuba) during the 28 years.

At first Congressman Bell and others, Commissioner McNutt among them, had tried to get a period of 20 years of free trade. In the Senate, which had before it the Tydings Bill, a bill far less favorable to the Philippines,[37] a compromise was reached. Senator Tydings argued that free trade between the United States and the Philippines was not beneficial to the islands since the Philippines would never be truly free as long as they were economically dependent on the United States.[38] The State Department had opposed the 20 years of free trade—a quite prolonged trade preference for the Philippines—since it was trying to get reduction of trade barriers throughout the world and this would hamper its effort to persuade the British to abandon trade preference agreements with their former colonies.

United States articles were to be subject to customs duties in the Philippines in the following progression:[39]

PHILIPPINE ISLANDS   29

Period	Percentage of Philippine Duties
4 July to 31 December 1954	5
Calendar year 1955	10
Calendar years 1956-72, yearly increase	5
1 January 1973 to 3 July 1974	100

Philippine export duties could not be imposed on articles exported to the United States.[40]

The absolute duty-free quotas on cigars, scrap tobacco, coconut oil, and buttons remained exactly the same as set by the 1939 act, except that the scrap tobacco quota was increased by 2 million pounds.* Despite objection by the Departments of State and Commerce and the Philippine government, it was provided that these quotas had to be distributed by the Philippine government to the producers on the basis of what each had exported to the United States in the year 1940.[41] Only when producers failed to meet their quotas was reallocation by the Philippine government permitted. In effect, then, the act granted a virtual monopoly for 28 years to those producers—many of whom were Americans—who had dominated the principal Philippine industries in the years before the war.[42] The duty-free imports were to diminish at a rate of 5 percent per year, until in 1974 they would be down to zero.

The sugar quota (which was absolute and fixed, not diminishing) was again set at 850,000 long tons and was to last until 1974.† It was to be allocated to the manufacturers of refined sugar in the Philippines of 1940 on the basis of what they had exported to the United States during that year.[43]

A major objection of the State Department, but not of the Philippines, was the tying of the Philippine currency to the American dollar:

> The value of Philippine currency in relation to the United States dollar shall not be changed, the convertibility of pesos into dollars shall not be suspended, and no restrictions shall be imposed on the transfer of funds from the Philippines to the United States, except by agreement with the President of the United States.[44]

---

*Cordage (including binding twine) was given a fixed, absolute, not duty-free quota of 6 million pounds—lasting until 3 July 1974—to be allocated to producers of 1940 on the basis of what they had exported to the United States during the 12 months preceeding the inauguration of the commonwealth government (Sec. 212). No excise taxes would be imposed on the processing of undressed cordage. Rice was given a fixed, absolute, not duty-free quota of 1,040,000 pounds to last till 3 July 1974. There were no provisions for its allocation (Sec. 213).

† After Cuba and the United States broke off relations, the sugar quota for the Philippines was increased to 1,050,000 short tons raw value, approximately 937,500 long tons.

The Department of State pointed out that this was a restriction far more stringent than imposed upon Bretton Woods signatories. The effect of this limitation was to make the Philippine currency too high (two Philippine pesos for $1) for the East, thus making the price of its products so high that it could sell only to the United States and again establishing the pattern of dependence on the American market.

Powers Retained by the United States

Americans were also given special privileges in the Philippines. Section 341 of the Trade Act provided:

> The disposition, exploitation, development, and utilization of all agricultural, timber, and minerals, lands of the public domain, waters, minerals, coal, petroleum, and other minerals oils, all forces and sources of potential energy, and other natural resources of the Philippines, and the operation of public utilities, shall, if open to any person, be open to citizens of the United States and to all forms of business enterprise owner or controlled, directly or indirectly, by United States citizens.

This so-called parity provision has been a primary irritant in recent years. It has permitted the United States investors privileges equal to those of Philippine citizens, but not granted to other foreigners. It also required an amendment to the Philippine Constitution, and the Philippine leaders indicated that the people would resent its being imposed on them. They had proposed, following the U.S. State and Commerce Departments' suggestion, to provide such privileges by treaty. It was also pointed out that the same rights were not given reciprocally to Philippine citizens in the United States, and it was doubtful whether it could be done since this was in many cases a matter for the several states to decide.

In addition, United States citizens were given the right to return to the Philippines if they had resided there for three years during the 42 months ending 30 November 1941. This immigration of other Americans to the Philippines could not be restricted by the Philippine government to less than 1,000 a year for at least five years. Reciprocity was given to Philippine citizens with respect to the former, but not the latter, provision.

Military Bases

Toward the end of World War II, a joint resolution was passed:

> ... That it is hereby declared to be the policy of the Congress that the United States shall drive the treacherous, invading Japanese from the Philippines Islands ... and thereupon establish the complete independence of the Philippine Islands as a separate and self-governing nation.

But the resolution's subsequent clause was less generous to Philippine sovereignty:

> "Sec. 2. After negotiations with the President of the Commonwealth of the Philippines, or the President of the Filipino Republic, the President of the United States is hereby authorized by such means as he finds appropriate to withhold or to acquire and to retain such bases ... in addition to any provided for by the Act of March 24, 1934, as he may deem necessary for the mutual protection of the Philippine Islands and of the United States."[45]

In 1945 the Philippine Legislature had authorized by resolution the negotiation of the retention of bases by the United States in the islands in accordance with the joint resolutions. In 1947 the Military Bases Agreement was entered into by both governments.[46] Under it the United States retained, free of rent and for 99 years, a number of Philippine bases and was also given the right to use, on notice, many others. The duration of the agreement, 99 years, and the comprehensiveness of its provisions made it unusual, not in keeping with the pattern of military base agreements made by the American government with foreign countries.

The trade and military provisions have been the subject of frequent modification and negotiation, with the United States in general seeking continued reciprocity—parity—rights between Americans and Philippines for the exploitation of natural resources and other industries in the Philippine economy, and the Philippine government seeking to regulate and delimit the United States' involvement.[47] It has suggested divestment or at least transfer of American land holdings.[48]

Similarly, the extent and control of military bases in the Philippines has been a continuing subject of debate. The United States and the Philippines have signed not only the collective Southeast Asia Defense Agreement but a number of other military agreements under which the United States has been given the right to recruit Philippine citizens to serve in the United States Navy (2,000 per year) and Coast Guard (400 per year). In exchange, the United States has given economic and technical assistance to the Philippine armed forces.[49]

There have also been continuing discussions and major revisions made with respect to tariff and other barriers on trade between the United States and the Philippines. Thus, in 1955 the Philippines Trade Agreement Revision Act went into effect, authorizing the president to revise the 1946 agreement in certain respects to accommodate many of the Philippine objections. Under the revision, Philippine articles other than those with duty-free quotas would incur slightly lower tariffs than under the 1946 act and United States articles entering the Philippines would incur, in general, slightly higher tariffs. The year 1974 remained the date for the imposition of the full duty.

The absolute quotas on cigars, scrap tobacco, coconut oil, and buttons were changed to tariff quotas and the rate of decrease was lowered considerably. The absolute quotas on sugar and cordage remained the same "without prejudice to any increase which . . . Congress may allocate to the Philippines in the future."[50]

NOTES

1. Teodoro A. Agoncillo and Oscar M. Alfonso, History of the Filipino People, 2nd ed. (Quezon City: Malaya Books, 1967), p. 141.
2. A recent study covering the period is Peter W. Stanley, A Nation in the Making: The Philippines and the United States (1899-1921), (Cambridge: Harvard University Press, 1974).
3. Sec. 33, Act No. 136, (11 June 1901); Public Laws passed by the Philippine Commission (1900-1902), p. 257.
4. Toyota v. United States, 268 U.S. 402 (1924); Roque Espiritu de la Ysla v. United States (CA 9 1935) 77 F.2d 988, cert. den. 296 U.S. 575 (1935). It was not until the passage of Philippine Trade Act of 1946, P.L. 371 (30 April 1946); 60 Stat. 141, on the eve of independence, that naturalization of the islanders was permitted. It was limited to those who (1) were citizens of the commonwealth on 3 July 1946, (2) had entered the United States prior to 1934, and (3) had since their entry resided continuously in the United States.
5. P.L. 144 (9 May 1918); 40 Stat. 542.
6. P.L. 5 (5 August 1909); 36 Stat. 11. P.L. 7 (5 August 1909); 36 Stat. 130. It should be noted that when these acts were being considered the Philippine Assembly passed a resolution opposing them since they feared undue economic dependence would result, and this would be an obstacle to the eventual attainment of independence.
7. Sec. 5, Tariff Act of 1909.
8. Sec. 13, Tariff Act of 1909.
9. P.L. 16 (3 October 1913); 38 Stat. 114. This increased the free movement of goods between the two countries. It omitted the tariff

quotas imposed on some Philippine articles and eliminated the duty on Philippine rice. It also expressly repealed the export duties on all Philippine products regardless of the country of destination.

10. P.L. 318 (21 September 1922); 42 Stat. 858.

11. P.L. 361 (17 June 1930); 46 Stat. 590.

12. Testimony of the Hon. Manuel Roxas, Speaker of the House of Representatives of the Philippine Islands, Hearings Before the Committee on Insular Affairs on H.R. 7233 [hereinafter Hearings]—A Bill to Provide for the Independence of the Philippine Islands, House of Representatives, 72d Cong., 1st Sess., p. 54. This figure did not take into account the fact that 44 percent of the Philippine foreign trade was carried in American bottoms, nor the expenditures of the United States military forces in the islands.

13. The period is discussed generally in Joseph R. Haydn, The Philippines: A Study in National Development (New York: The Macmillan Company, 1942).

14. Also known as the Hare-Hawes-Cutting Act, P.L. 311 (17 January 1933); 47 Stat. 761.

15. Hoover veto message relating to Philippine Independence (13 January 1933); 14 House Documents, 72nd Cong., 2d Sess. (1932-33) Document No. 524.

16. Concurrent Resolution No. 46, adopted 17 October 1933; Vol. XXXII, No. 7, Official Gazette (1934) 118.

17. Philippines Independence Act of 1934, also known as the Tydings-McDuffie Act. P.L. 127 (23 March 1934); 48 Stat. 456.

18. Sec. 13.

19. Hearings, pp. 117, 119; see sec. 6 of the proposed Philippine bill, Hearings, pp. 137, 138.

20. Sec. 9 of the proposed Philippine bill, Hearings, p. 139.

21. Testimony of the Hon. Manuel Roxas, Hearings, pp. 82, 112, 139.

22. Sec. 8.

23. P.L. 213 (9 May 1934); 48 Stat. 670.

24. Revenue Act of 1934, P.L. 216 (10 May 1934); 48 Stat. 680.

25. Cordage Act of 1935, P.L. 137 (14 June 1935); 49 Stat. 340.

26. 1 Joint Preparatory Committee on Philippine Affairs (hereinafter Joint Preparatory), Report of 20 May 1938, p. 35.

27. 1 Joint Preparatory, p. 153.

28. 1 Joint Preparatory, p. 154.

29. P.L. 300, (7 August 1939); 53 Stat. 1226.

30. Quoted during testimony of Vicente Villamil, Philippine lawyer, Hearings Before the Senate Finance Committee on H.R. 5856, 79th Cong., 2d Sess., p. 114.

31. Testimony of the Hon. Paul V. McNutt, U.S. High Commissioner to the Philippine Islands, Hearings Before the Senate Committee on H.R. 5856, 79th Cong., 2d Sess., pp. 18, 109, 134. See also article by B. M. McKelway, associate editor of the Washington Star introduce ibid. at pp. 122-24.

32. P.L. 370 (30 April 1946); 60 Stat. 128.
33. P.L. 371 (30 April 1946); 60 Stat. 141.
34. Title I, Sec. 106(a).
35. Title II, Sec. 205.
36. Title III, Sec. 301.
37. S.1488, See <u>Hearings Before the Senate Committee on Territories and Insular Affairs on S. 1488</u>, 79th Cong., 1st Sess., p. 1. The Tydings Bill provided $100 million for war damage rehabilitation and $100 million transfer of surplus property. No free trade was provided prior to independence and normal trade relations (full duty) would take place in 1967.
38. Testimony of Hon. Millard E. Tydings, Senator from Maryland, <u>Hearings Before the House Committee on Ways and Means on H.R. 4185, H.R. 4676, and H.R. 5185</u>, 79th Cong. 1st Sess., p. 90. There was still discussion at this time concerning the possibility that the Philippines might want to reenter the United States as a protectorate if they found the going too rough.
39. Sec. 312.
40. Sec. 322.
41. Sec. 214(c).
42. See the memorandum introduced by Congressman Daniel A. Reed of New York, <u>Hearings Before the House Committee on Ways and Means, on H.R. 4185, H.R. 4676, and H.R. 5185</u>, 79th Cong. 1st Sess., 140-43.
43. Sec. 211.
44. Sec. 342.
45. S.J. 93, P.L. 380 (29 June 1944); 58 Stat. 625.
46. 61 Stat., Pt. 4, 4019. Signed at Manila, 14 March 1947, entered into force 26 March 1947. The military agreement is discussed in considerable detail in Julius W. Pratt, <u>America's Colonial Experiment</u> (Gloucester: Peter Smith, 1964), pp. 331-69.
47. For example, the Laurel-Langley Act of 1955. For criticism of the act's provision on this point and discussion of the 1972 Philippine Supreme Court decision restricting parity, see Pomeroy, <u>An American Made Tragedy</u> (1974), pp. 27, 100.
48. Sec. 231 and 331; "U.S.-Philippine Trade Talks Snagged," Washington <u>Post</u>, 11 August 1974, P.F.-1.
49. Treaty and protocol signed at Manila, 8 September 1954, came into effect 19 February 1955; 6 UST, Pt. 1, 81 [1955]. The other signatories were the United Kingdom, France, Australia, New Zealand, Pakistan, and Thailand.
50. P.L. 196 (1 August 1955); 69 Stat. 413.

CHAPTER 3
PUERTO RICO

    The status of Puerto Rico's relationships with the United States is a source of constant debate both within the Puerto Rican and the U.S. federal governments. With close economic ties, but with strong nationalistic feelings supported by a language and a heritage different from that of the United States, the commonwealth has developed its own rationale and objectives, building upon the Philippines experience but looking toward a permanent association.

    The Commonwealth of Puerto Rico is composed of four small islands (Puerto Rico, Vieques, Culebra, and Mona) located in the Caribbean, approximately 1,100 miles from Miami, 1,500 miles from New York, and 540 miles from Venezuela. The largest of them, Puerto Rico, is about 100 miles long (east and west) and 35 miles wide (north to south) with steep mountains running along its length and thus dividing it into a northern and southern half.

    Vieques, Culebra, and Mona are very sparsely populated. The island of Puerto Rico has one of the highest birth rates in the world, 30.6 per thousand, and a population density which is also unusually high, 768 persons to the square mile. The population growth has been rapid--there were 1.9 million people in 1940 and almost 3 million people in 1970, and it is projected that in 1985 the total population in Puerto Rico will be 4 million.

    The island has a mild, attractive climate with minimal seasonal rainstorms, the average mean temperature varying from $70°$ to $81°$ F. There is some good-quality land, although severe hurricanes have damaged its agricultural potential to a degree.

MAP 3

Puerto Rico

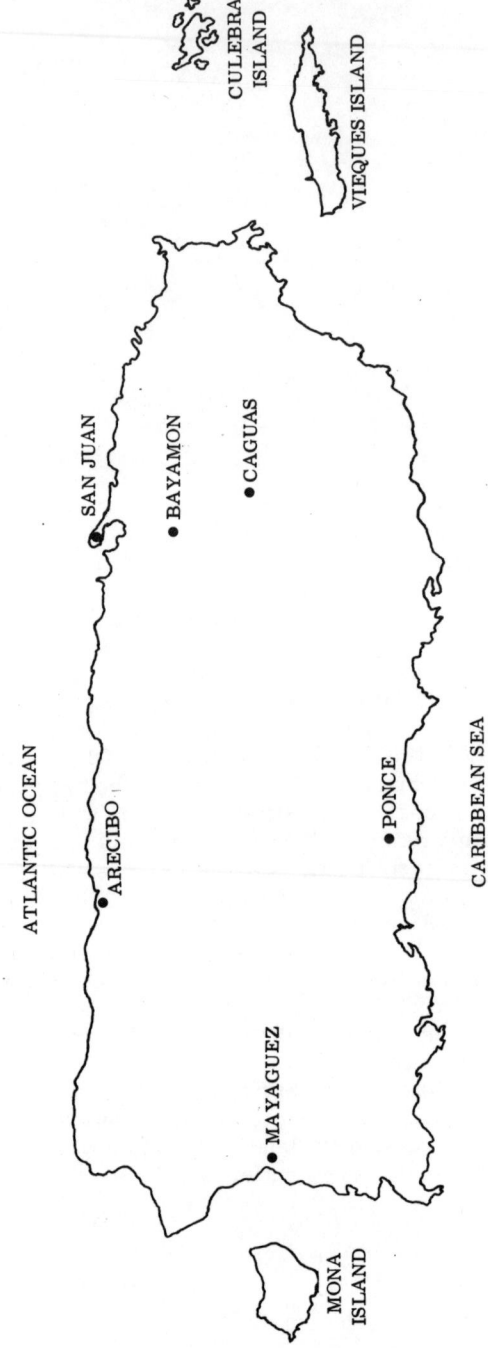

Source: Provided by the author.

PUERTO RICO

ECONOMIC STRUCTURE

The only major natural resource found on the island of Puerto Rico is cheap water power, although, in recent years, copper ore has been discovered and there has been a report of oil deposits in the waters surrounding the island. Puerto Rico's water resources are adequate but, because of poor drainage and lack of reservoirs, the southern section is generally dry and, by turns, subject to flooding and droughts.

Agriculture, historically, has been the economic base of Puerto Rico, primarily in the form of sugar cane, with coffee and tobacco also cultivated in some quantity. Since 1956, when the first hurricane in 25 years struck Puerto Rico and was followed by droughts in 1957 and 1958, the island's production of sugar cane has gone steadily downward. The exact reason for this is not clear, although it appears to be a combination of limited mechanization on the small farms and an unexplained drop in the sucrose yield of the cane. The soil in Puerto Rico is not particularly well suited for coffee and tobacco and, as a result, there have been attempts to diversify Puerto Rico's agricultural production in order to revitalize the industry.

In the late 1940s the Puerto Rican government made a decision to change its economy from an agricultural to an industrial one. This was to be done primarily on the basis of private investment from outside the island, making use of various U.S. federal benefits (the tax exemption, the exception to the federal minimum wage, access without tariff to the States) combined with Puerto Rico's own governmental efforts: a local tax exemption, governmental loan assistance, building constituted on speculation, and a highly skilled industrial promotional campaign. The effect of this change can be seen in the gross national product and per capita net income figures, which have risen sharply.

On the other hand, the high birth rate has meant that Puerto Rico, despite this major effort, has not been able to create sufficient jobs for its labor force. This has been exacerbated by efforts of the U.S. recession. In 1950 the island had a labor force of 686,000, an employment component of 596,000, and an unemployment rate of 13 percent. In 1972 the island's employed populace had grown to 795,000 but its labor force had increased to 906,000, resulting in little change in the rate or number of unemployed in the two decades. In July 1975 the employed figure had dropped to 724,000, and the unemployment rate was 19.2 percent.

Puerto Rico's major economic problem is to continue to create employment for its growing population, preferably jobs for men in higher-wage industries, which are less vulnerable to federal minimum wage changes. Further, there is concern that the centralization of industrialization in San Juan will result in excessive demands on public facilities in the San Juan area.

HISTORICAL BACKGROUND

Relationship with Spain: 1493-1898

For 300 years, following the discovery of Puerto Rico by Christopher Columbus in 1493 and the consequent forcible subjugation of the Indian—Taino—population, Spain treated Puerto Rico as a military outpost in the Western Hemisphere. Power was centered in a virtually omnipotent governor who not only was the chief executive but also promulgated decrees, headed the army and navy, was the chief fiscal official, and the supreme judge, and, as royal vice-patron, also participated in ecclesiastical authority. This total concentration of power in one official was coupled with a high degree of governmental control over human affairs, the Spanish white colonists being required to obtain permission before moving from town to town.

In the nineteenth century there was a major growth in population in Puerto Rico, from about 150,000 people in 1800 to a million people by the end of the century. This rapid rise was in part the result of the influx of Spanish royalists who fled the revolutions against the mother country which swept Central and South America. Its immediate significance was that it changed the balance in Puerto Rico between the Negro-Indian population and the Spanish population in favor of the Spanish. This burgeoning of the politically aware population gave rise to serious agitation by Puerto Ricans for increased participation in their own government. At various times reforms were promised by Spain but always Puerto Rican hopes were frustrated. In 1896 an agreement with the Spanish Liberal Party was effected by Puerto Rico's leaders, so that when this party came to power later that year it arranged for the declaration of an autonomous charter for the island.

The charter of 1897 was a substantial improvement. Under this Charter of Autonomy, Puerto Rico elected voting delegates to both houses of the Spanish Cortes (parliament). The island also elected all 35 members of the island's House of Representatives and 8 out of 15 members of the insular Administrative Council (which was equivalent to a senate). The governor general, appointed by Spain, chose the other seven senators. Although his powers were reduced by the initiatives allowed to the Puerto Rican Legislature, he retained the right to suspend civil rights and to refer insular legislation to the Council of Ministers of Spain if he felt it to be detrimental or unconstitutional. The Puerto Rican Legislature was generally given power to pass on all matters of purely insular importance: to fix the budget and determine tariffs and taxes. Commercial treaties were to be concluded by the home government but provision was made for Puerto Rican government concurrence.

PUERTO RICO 39

The Charter of Autonomy was decreed in November 1897, but was in actual operation for a very short time. In April 1898 the Spanish-American War was declared, and in July American troops occupied Puerto Rico.

The above brief history of the Puerto Rico-Spain relationship is significant for the perspective it gives to subsequent Puerto Rico-United States relations. The failure for many years of continental leaders to recognize that what to the United States was the beginning of a dialogue was to Puerto Rico the interruption of a long and continuous effort toward self-government at the moment when it seemed finally to be successful contributed to many ill-considered and deprecatory statements by mainland officials and to the impatience of Puerto Rican leaders.

Relationship with the United States: 1898-1950

Puerto Rico was ceded by Spain to the United States under the Treaty of Paris of 1898 with the provision that civil rights and political status of the native inhabitants of the territory should be determined by the Congress.[1]

The United States was a wealthy, democratic country and so in Puerto Rico there was considerable optimism at the transfer. Nevertheless, the islanders' expectations were varied. Some, like the Puerto Rican Federal Party, anticipated that the island would temporarily become a territory and that it would only be a matter of time before that transitional stage ended in full statehood. Others looked to greater autonomy for Puerto Rico, building upon the island's recent triumph in its status struggle with Spain.

General Nelson Miles in his first public speech raised these hopes even further:

We have not come to make war upon the people of a country that for centuries has been oppressed but on the contrary to bring you protection . . . to promote your prosperity, and to bestow upon you the immunities and blessings of the liberal institutions of our government.

But President McKinley's announcement of Puerto Rican policy, incorporated substantially in the Foraker Act of 1900, followed the views of General George Davis, the U.S. military governor and the Secretary of War, Elihu Root, rather than those of General Miles. He recommended a civil government in which the key roles would be given to Americans appointed by the president of the United States.[2]

In the Foraker Act, the U.S. Congress created a body politic called "the People of Puerto Rico," composed of neither American citizens nor citizens of an independent nation. There would be a governor appointed by the president of the United States, an 11-man Executive Council (with a majority of Americans), 35 elected Puerto Ricans in the House of Delegates (the laws of which were subject to Congressional veto), and an elected resident commissioner, who spoke for Puerto Rico in the U.S. House of Representatives but had no vote there.

The legal power of the U.S. federal government with respect to the territories was being tested in the courts at the same time. For the first time—Hawaii also had just been acquired—the United States was governing territories which were geographically separated from the mainland and inhabited by many people culturally distinct from the populace of North America. The legal debate centered about the shorthand question of whether the Constitution followed the flag. How much of the Constitution was available to protect the residents of Puerto Rico and to limit federal action? The issue was novel because when the Constitution was drafted, the territorial concern was the western lands (the Northwest Territory) already populated by migrants from the states.

The early cases dealt with relatively uninhabited, geographically contiguous territories and established that the governing power of the federal government stemmed not only from the territorial clause* but also from the inherent power to acquire territory. Federal power was extremely broad and, perhaps, unlimited† except where the civil rights of the inhabitants of the territories were involved.‡

The first full exploration of this civil rights issue arose in a series of cases,[3] the Insular Cases, which questioned whether territorial tariffs could differ from tariffs in the United States. The Supreme Court laid down the distinction, which continues today, between unincorporated and incorporated territories. The cases arose when the Collector of Customs attempted to collect duties on trade between Puerto Rico and the mainland United States. The first question presented to the Court was whether Puerto Rico was "part" of the United States. The Court held it was part of the United States. It was then argued that to collect duties

---

*"The Congress shall have Power to dispose of and make all needful Rules and Regulations respecting the Territory or other Property belonging to the United States . . ." (U.S. Const., art. IV, sec. 3)

†"Accordingly, we find Congress possessing and exercising the absolute and undisputed power of governing and legislating for the territory of Orleans." (Sere v. Pitot, 10 U.S. [6 Cranch] 332, 337 [1810]). "It [Congress] may make a void act of the territorial legislature valid, and a valid act void. In other words, it has full and complete legislative authority over the people of the Territories and all departments of the territorial governments." (National Bank v. County of Yankton, 101 U.S. 129, 133 [1879]).

‡The earliest case to suggest some limitations on federal actions in the territories affecting the personal liberties of the inhabitants was Murphy v. Ramsey, 114 U.S. 15 (1885) at p. 44.

PUERTO RICO   41

was contrary to Article I, Section 8 of the U.S. Constitution, which provides that "all duties, imposts, and excises shall be uniform throughout the United States." Although raised in a commercial law context, the cases involved the broader issue of what constitutional restrictions were imposed upon Congress in its treatment of the territories.[4]

The concurring opinion of Justice White in Downes v. Bidwell* is still the basic answer to this question.[5] White begins by stating that every function of government is derived from the Constitution and, therefore, the instrument is applicable everywhere potentially. The issue is, then, what particular provisions of the Constitution are applicable in a given situation to restrain the Congress.

To White, it was clear that the power of a government to acquire territories by discovery, treaty, or conquest must also bring with it the power to determine the status of the acquired territory. Automatic incorporation and extension of the Constitution would mean, he reasoned, that this power did not exist. He concluded that the Treaty of Paris, pursuant to which Puerto Rico was acquired by the United States, did not provide for incorporation but left Congress to decide the island's status. Since Congress had not acted positively, White concluded that Puerto Rico was an unincorporated territory.

The consequences of such a determination became significant since, White went on, to an unincorporated territory only the fundamental provisions of the Constitution applied—"the general prohibitions . . . in favor of the liberty and property of the citizen . . . which are an absolute denial of authority . . . to do particular acts."[6] Since the uniformity clause was not such a fundamental provision or general prohibition, it was held inapplicable to Puerto Rico.

Thus was formulated the basic distinction between an unincorporated and incorporated territory. To an unincorporated territory only the fundamental provisions of the Constitution apply, but to an incorporated territory the Constitution applies fully. Further, under the White formulation, it is left for the Congress to decide whether a territory is unincorporated or incorporated. "It must follow . . . that incorporation does not arise until in the wisdom of Congress it is deemed that the acquired territory has reached that state. . . ."[7]

---

*DeLima v. Bidwell arose prior to the legislation of 1900 when the importer sued for a refund of duties paid by him on sugar from Puerto Rico into the States. Downes v. Bidwell arose in a similar situation (oranges instead of sugar) but after the Foraker Act of 1900 had explicitly imposed such duties. It is of academic interest that the Court held in favor of the importer in the De Lima case and against the importer in the Downes case, with Justice Brown as the swing man in two 5-4 decisions.

This judicial action, confirming the executive and legislative approach, embittered the island's populace. The broadly based Union Party, which took power in 1904 (and held it for 30 years), made continuous demands for a plebiscite on alternative ultimate status preferences. Independence sentiment grew as Congress ignored these demands and the U.S.-appointed governors became increasingly unresponsive.

Matters were made worse when the United States-administered Department of Education tried to impose English as the language of instruction in the school system. Until 1943, when a Puerto Rican was finally appointed to head the Department of Education and Spanish became the language of instruction in all grades of the public schools, United States and Puerto Rican authorities were in constant strife over the degree of recognition to be accorded the English language in the Puerto Rican school system.[8]

Resistance to the Foraker Act was so strong by 1909 that the Puerto Rico House of Delegates refused to approve any legislation, including the next year's government budget. It sent a memorial to Congress and to President Taft, complaining of "the unjust law which makes it impossible for the people's representatives to pass the laws they desire." President Taft responded in a special message reviewing the history of the United States association with the island. He compared Puerto Rico's position to that of "favored daughter" upon whom the father has lavished his generosity. The president cited coastal surveys, harbor improvements, 2,400 new schools, 624 miles of newly paved roads, and mass inoculations of the population against smallpox and other epidemic diseases. His conclusion was: "There never was a time in the history of the Island when the average prosperity was higher, when opportunity was greater, or when liberty of thought and action was more secure." Taft cast doubt upon the wisdom of any extension of self-government by saying: "The present development is only an indication that we have gone somewhat too fast in the extension of political power to them for their own good."[9]

Before Woodrow Wilson took office, he announced that he favored extension of home rule for the island and the citizenship proposal put forth earlier by President Taft in the last year of his administration. His election, together with Democratic majorities in both Houses of Congress, led in 1917 to a revision of the organic act, the so-called Jones Act. It included a bill of rights, a collective conferral of citizenship, and provision for an elective Senate of 19 members. The majority of the department heads and the island magistrates were not to be appointed by the governor with the advice and consent of the elected insular Senate. This transfer of power from Congress and the U.S. federal government to the local officials was modest, since the attorney general, the commissioner of education, and the auditor were still appointed by the president of the United States, as were the members of the Puerto Rican Supreme Court.

The grant of citizenship, a turning point in U.S.-Puerto Rico relations, was made although Puerto Rican feelings on this issue at the time were divided. The Republican Party of Puerto Rico and the labor movement (which organized the Socialist Party in 1915) both favored statehood and were ardent supporters of American citizenship, but they constituted a minority in insular politics.

The majority Unionist Party of Puerto Rico favored increased autonomy and had expressed a preference for the designation of "citizen of Puerto Rico." They claimed that a substantial number of their fellow citizens would reject American citizenship if it were offered. During the floor debate, Resident Commissioner Munoz Rivera expressed this point of view, and suggested that a plebiscite be held to determine whether or not Puerto Ricans desired American citizenship. Independence partisans today continue to note the failure to have provided such an option and the fact that the granting of citizenship took place at the time of World War I so that the new citizens were also immediately eligible for conscription.

Although it was believed in some quarters (particularly among prostatehood Puerto Ricans) that this grant of citizenship implied the incorporation of Puerto Rico into the Union as a territory, the United States Supreme Court eventually decided that it did not. In Rasmussen v. United States,[10] the justices had found enough "implications" in the actions of Congress—primarily the grant of citizenship—toward Alaska to consider that the territory had been thereby incorporated. After the Jones Act, Puerto Rico had received from Congress all the concessions which, according to the legal formula set forth in the Insular Cases and elaborated upon in Rasmussen, were necessary to make it an incorporated territory. So it was declared by the U.S. District Court for Puerto Rico in In the Matter of Tapia[11] and by the Supreme Court of Puerto Rico in Muratti v. Foote.[12]

These cases, however, were reversed by the Supreme Court of the United States in a per curiam decision.[13] Then, five years later, in Balzac v. People of Porto Rico,[14] Justice Taft, delivering the opinion of the Court and continuing the approach he had adopted when he was president, indicated why the island had not been incorporated. His opinion noted cultural and racial differences in Puerto Rico:

> Alaska was a very different case from that of Porto Rico. It was an enormous territory, very sparsely settled and offering opportunity for immigration and settlement by American citizens. It was on the American continent and within easy reach of the United States. It involved none of the difficulties which incorporation of the Philippines and Porto Rico presents.
>
> We need not dwell on another consideration which requires us not lightly to infer, from acts thus easily explained on other grounds, an intention to incorporate

in the Union these distant ocean communities of a different origin and language from those of our continental people.[15]

Finally, the Jones Act authorized the governor to send to the president of the United States any bill that had been passed over his veto by a two-thirds vote in each house. If the president chose to uphold the veto, the bill could not become law. And two limitations on insular legislative authority were carried over from the organic act of 1900: the reservation of power by Congress to annul acts of the Puerto Rican Legislature (never exercised, however, either before or after 1917), and the declaration that Puerto Rico was subject to all federal laws of general application except the internal-revenue laws. The question of ultimate or final political status was left unanswered: Puerto Rico was still an unincorporated territory of the United States with an uncertain destiny.

The immediate result of the Jones Act was that the federally appointed governors found themselves more directly opposed to the Puerto Rican legislature. Every year the governor had to veto a large number of bills, many of which were passed merely for political effect without any hope or expectation that they would become law. In some years more bills were vetoed than were approved.

Despite the strains and uncertainties in the political relationship, there was considerable economic progress under the 1917 legislation until the late twenties when two hurricanes and the depression brought a virtual collapse.[16] The 1930s were terrible years; there was starvation and mass unemployment. Not surprisingly, these economic conditions brought with them an upsurge of nationalism among members of Puerto Rico's political and intellectual elite. Luis Munoz Marin, after a long stay in the United States as a journalist, returned to Puerto Rico. He and his followers were struck by the distortions in the insular economy: the excessive dependence on sugar production, the high prices Puerto Ricans had to pay for the imported staples of their diet and for commodities protected by the U.S. tariff, and the high cost of shipping. These, they argued, were products of American control and could only be rectified when Puerto Rico became an independent nation.

The literary intelligentsia also contributed to the nationalistic feeling. Antonio Pedreira wrote <u>Insularismo</u>, the most influential work of the depression period (published in 1934), essaying a construct of Puerto Rico's unique identity which remains the fountainhead of cultural and sociological thought on the island.

A more virulent form of nationalism characterized the attitude and activity of the revitalized Nationalist Party, headed by an exciting orator, Pedro Albizu Campos, a Harvard Law School graduate who had served as an officer in the American army. In the election of 1932 the Nationalist Party obtained less than 12,000 votes for the senator-at-large position (only 3 percent of the total vote), and the rest of the ticket received less than half that. After the election debacle Albizu

Campos turned the party toward direct action—violence, terrorism, and sabotage—and required all Nationalists to take military training in the party's so-called Army of Liberation. Then, on Sunday, 23 February 1936, two Nationalists assassinated Colonel E. Francis Riggs, the young and popular chief of the insular police. The assassins were immediately captured and taken to police headquarters where they were killed by the police. The incident triggered additional acts of violence even after Albizu Campos and seven of his followers were sent to prison.

The climax was reached the following year when the Nationalists obtained permission to hold a parade in the city of Ponce on Palm Sunday, 21 March. Governor Blanton Winship in San Juan revoked the permit but the Nationalists ignored the countermand. A group of young, black-shirted cadets assembled while the police, heavily armed, blocked all side streets. A large crowd had gathered. A shot was fired and soon there were 20 dead (including two policemen) and over 100 wounded, most of them peaceful bystanders. The governor called it "a nationalist riot"; but the American Civil Liberties Union, which investigated the matter, blamed the police and called it a "massacre." Today March 21 is remembered on the island as the anniversary of La Massacre de Ponce.

The official response in the United States was less sympathetic. Senator Millard Tydings (a close friend of Riggs), with the covert support of the Roosevelt Administration, submitted a bill providing for independence in four years, with tariffs rising 25 percent each year. It was designed to stem the independence movement by forcing their partisans to face a possible harsh economic reality.[17]

Munoz Marin, who favored independence in 1937, argued that it was America's moral duty to provide a more adequate transition period. The Tydings bill, and the subsequent Dorfman Report with its bleak prophecy of Puerto Rico's economic condition,[18] had the desired effect, causing Munoz Marin and other Puerto Rican leaders to undertake an agonizing reappraisal concerning the desirability of independence and to give priority attention to the economic problems of Puerto Rico. For, as the decade of the 1940s approached, economic conditions in Puerto Rico were critical. Per-capita income was $118 a year; farm work—the main source of employment—paid as little as 6 cents an hour. The labor class—construction workers—earned 22 cents an hour. Seven out of 10 persons were still illiterate and life expectancy was only 46 years.

Ironically, the Puerto Rico party then in power favored statehood and, therefore, Santiago Iglesias in 1937 introduced in Congress the first statehood bill by a resident commissioner from Puerto Rico. Bolivar Pagan was to repeat this action early in 1940, but then Munoz Marin's Popular Democratic Party gained control in Puerto Rico and status politics was to change radically.

In February of 1943 the Puerto Rican Legislature petitioned Congress for additional local autonomy and popular election of the governor. The next day Governor Rexford Tugwell supported this position and within a month President Roosevelt sent a special message to Congress endorsing the idea and naming the first joint Puerto Rican-U.S. committee to consider and recommend changes in the organic act. The committee, composed of an equal number of Puerto Ricans and continentals, reported legislation which provided the catalyst for major changes in U.S.-Puerto Rican relations in the next few years.

The chief recommendations were that (1) the governor was to be elected, and to have broadened administrative responsibilities in local affairs; (2) the governor was to appoint all Puerto Rican cabinet officers and Supreme Court justices; (3) Congress was to make no further changes in the organic act without the concurrence of the people of Puerto Rico or their elected representatives; (4) the power of the president of the United States to nullify Puerto Rican legislation was to be limited only to those cases where the security of the United States was threatened; and (5) a joint advisory council was to be named to advise the president and Congress on further changes.

Although the committee's report was accepted by President Roosevelt and legislation submitted promptly in accordance with its recommendations, congressional reaction was mixed and much more cautious. A series of bills and hearings, some quite critical of Puerto Rico but all reviewing U.S.-Puerto Rico relations in considerable detail, was the congressional response.[19]

In October 1945 President Harry Truman sent a special message to Congress with attendant legislation asking that the Puerto Rican people be allowed to settle for themselves their political future. The president listed four courses which he felt that the Congress might offer the island. These were (1) an elective governor and enlarged local autonomy; (2) statehood; (3) complete independence; and (4) dominion status. It was the first time that the federal government had suggested the last-named possibility.

When Governor Tugwell resigned in the summer of 1946, President Truman appointed as the new governor Jesus T. Pinero, then resident commissioner, the highest Puerto Rican official chosen at large in the preceding election. He was the first Puerto Rican governor of the island. The following year Congress passed the Elective Governor Act,[20] so that after the 1948 election, in which Munoz Marin was elected, the island possessed an entirely popularly elected government.

Almost since its foundation by Luis Munoz Marin in 1938, the Popular Democratic Party had been the dominant party in Puerto Rico. It had campaigned on the slogan that "status was not an issue"; that status politics should be temporarily set aside to address the more pressing economic problems of the island. The party's solution was to transform the island from an agricultural to an industrial society by increasing private investment from outside. The means used was primarily a tax exemption program which went in to effect in 1947. The provisions of the Fair Labor Standards Act, permitting Puerto Rico industries under certain circumstances to pay lower wages than those in the United States, Government Development Bank low interest loans, and special

PUERTO RICO

marketing studies were also used as inducements. In 25 years this conversion from an agriculturally based economy to one based on manufacturing was to take place;[21] and as a result, in 1970 the manufacturing and construction industries accounted for over 90 percent of the primary income generated in Puerto Rico, while in 1945 they accounted for only 40 percent.

Commonwealth: Public Law 600

The Populares had urged the end of status politics as it sought a consensus to deal with the island's economic and social problems. But by 1950 the Populares had returned status politics to Puerto Rico and began to evolve their own political status position: commonwealth.

In 1950, at the initiative of the Popular Democratic Party, the United States Congress passed Public Law 600 which authorized the island to draft its own constitution pursuant to a rather elaborate procedure. It provided for a referendum to be held in accordance with the laws of Puerto Rico. If a majority of the voters participating in the referendum were to approve Public Law 600, the Puerto Rican legislature could call a constitutional convention to draft a constitution for Puerto Rico. If this constitution were in turn approved by the people of Puerto Rico, it should be submitted via the president to Congress for approval. In addition, Public Law 600 repealed portions of the Jones Act of 1917, the basic federal law previously governing Puerto Rico, and renamed the remainder the Puerto Rican Federal Relations Act.

The people of Puerto Rico did vote and approved the law. Delegates were elected to a Constitutional Convention which drafted a Constitution and this, too, was submitted in a special referendum to the people of Puerto Rico for approval.[22] After the constitution was ratified,[23] it was sent to Congress which also approved it, conditional upon three changes: (1) deletion of a provision patterned after the United Nations' Universal Declaration of Human Rights recognizing the right to work, obtain an adequate standard of living, and enjoy social protection in old age or sickness; (2) addition of a provision assuring continuance of private elementary schools; and (3) addition of a provision requiring that amendments to the Puerto Rican Constitution must be consistent with the United States Constitution, the Puerto Rican Federal Relations Act, and Public Law 600. All three changes required by Congress were made by Puerto Rico and approved by the Puerto Rican Constitutional Convention and later by another referendum.

During the course of approving the constitution, violence, spurred by independence partisans, broke out in Puerto Rico and spread to the United States. The protesters were bitter at what they viewed as Nunoz's betrayal of their cause and the absence of the independence option on the referenda that had been submitted to the people of Puerto Rico.

During 30 October - 6 November 1950, 28 persons were killed and 419 wounded on various parts of the island; and on November 1, an attempt was made in Washington to assassinate President Truman.

With the establishment of commonwealth in 1950-52, Puerto Rico formally acquired the type of local governmental autonomy which in the U.S. federal structure is associated with the states of the Union. It now has its own constitution, pursuant to which it elects its governor and legislature; appoints its judges, all cabinet officials, and lesser officials in the executive branch; sets its own educational policies; determines its own budget; and amends its own civil and criminal code.

But the commonwealth has argued that more than local self-government was achieved by the 1950-52 legislation. It contends that a new legal entity was created with a unique status in American law: the commonwealth. The commonwealth at its stage of maximum development is conceived as a "permanent union between the United States and Puerto Rico on the basis of common citizenship, common defense, common currency, free market, and a common loyalty to the value of democracy" with the federal government retaining specifically defined powers "essential to the Union." Most important, in this view a commonwealth is not a "territory" covered by the "territorial clause" of the U.S. Constitution, nor, quite obviously, is it a state; rather, a commonwealth is sui generis and its judicial bounds are determined by a "compact" which cannot be changed without the consent of both Puerto Rico and the United States.[24]

Legal Interpretation of the Commonwealth

Comprehension of the compact argument and what it encompasses requires closer examination of the 1950-52 legislation.

In 1950, the United States Congress passed Public Law 600 which states in its preamble: "Fully recognizing the principle of government by consent this Act is now adopted in the nature of a compact so that the people of Puerto Rico may organize a government pursuant to a constitution of their own adoption."[25]

After the approval by Congress and the people of Puerto Rico of the Puerto Rican Constitution, the United States advised the United Nations that it would no longer report with respect to Puerto Rico under Article 73(e) of the United Nations Charter since Puerto Rico was now a self-governing territory.* After an extended debate the UN General Assembly

---

*Memorandum by the Government of the United States of America concerning the Cessation of Transmission of Information under Article 73(e) of the Charter with Regard to the Commonwealth of Puerto Rico, Annex II, U.N. Doc. A.Ac.35/L.121, at 8 (1953). The characterization

sustained the position of the United States.[26] Mason Sears, U.S. Representative to the Committee on Information from Non-Self-Governing Territories, characterized its status as follows:

> A most interesting feature of the new constitution is that it was entered into in the nature of a compact between the American and the Puerto Rican people. A compact, as you know, is far stronger than a treaty. A treaty usually can be denounced by either side, whereas a compact cannot be denounced by either party unless it has the permission of the other.[27]

Thus, the commonwealth argues, the language of the statutes and subsequent executive actions makes it clear that a "compact" was intended. In addition, the procedure set up by Public Law 600—a referendum, the drafting of the constitution, another referendum in Puerto Rico, and subsequent approval by Congress—is similar to the procedure often followed when an obligation is entered into by the federal government with a territory that is not unilaterally revocable by the federal government; namely, when territories become states or, as in the case of the Philippines, become independent.

With respect to the scope of the compact, the official commonwealth position is that it embraces both the Puerto Rican Constitution

of the status of Puerto Rico was as follows:

> ... Congress has agreed that Puerto Rico shall have, under that Constitution, freedom from control or interference by the Congress in respect of internal government and administration, subject only to compliance with applicable provisions of the Federal Constitution, the Puerto Rican Federal Relations Act and the acts of Congress authorizing and approving the Constitution, as may be interpreted by judicial decision. Those laws which directed or authorized interference with matters of local government by the Federal Government have been repealed.

and the Puerto Rican Federal Relations Act.* The argument is that this is what Public Law 600 refers to, and this is what was voted upon and accepted by the Puerto Rican people. Others see the compact as a grant of home rule, the boundaries of which are limited to the matters covered by the Puerto Rican Constitution. The changes made in the old organic acts which resulted in the Puerto Rican Federal Relations Act are viewed as draftmen's changes intended to remove from federal legislation provisions inconsistent with the Puerto Rican Constitution.

From the outset the minority parties in Puerto Rico, then the Statehood Republican Party and the Puerto Rican Independence Party, questioned the concept of commonwealth. They argued that although Congress may delegate powers to a territorial government, the broad powers granted to Congress under the territorial clause of the U.S. Constitution and the implied powers of the national government remain and may be excercised should the need arise. Further, they have pointed to the legislative history,[28] especially the testimony of Governor Munoz himself and the committee reports which emphasized this point.[29]

I think it fair to say that at this point the compact argument is of questionable validity. Congressional practice to the contrary has effectively nullified its significance whatever its legal validity was.† But

---

*The Puerto Rican Federal Relations Act includes the following provisions: (1) elimination of tariffs on trade between Puerto Rico and the United States; (2) equal tariffs for Puerto Rico and the United States on all items except coffee imported from abroad; (3) an exception from the Internal Revenue laws; (4) no export duties to be levied on exports from Puerto Rico; (5) bonds issued by the government of Puerto Rico to be exempt from federal taxation; (6) grant of U.S. citizenship to the people of Puerto Rico; (7) a provision that harbors, navigable streams, bodies of water and submerged land around Puerto Rico, not used by the U.S. for public purposes, be under the control of Puerto Rico; (8) a requirement that funds collected on exports—excise taxes—transported from the island to the states be returned to the Puerto Rican Treasury; (9) a provision for a resident commissioner; (10) an exemption for Puerto Rico from the Interstate Commerce Act and the Safety Appliance Acts; and (11) a statement of the jurisdiction of the U.S. District Court in Puerto Rico. The first two provisions result from Sections 2 and 3 of the Foraker Act of 1900 which are incorporated by reference in 48 U.S.C., Secs. 738 and 739 (1964).

†See amendment by Congress of Sec. 9 of Puerto Rican Federal Relations Act of 1955, Ch. 438, 69 Stat. 413; Int. Rev. Code of 1954, Sections 2208, 2501, as amended, 72 Stat. 1674 (1958) (changes in estate and gift tax provisions).

increasingly commonwealth as a status, as yet undefined but different from that of a territory or a state, is gaining acceptance within the American political system and in American law. This is seen in the Micronesia and Marianas negotiations (which are discussed in later chapters), statements by the executive, and, most importantly, the recent Supreme Court case Calero-Toledo v. Pearson Yacht Leasing Company, decided on 15 May 1974.30

The executive branch's affirmation of commonwealth has come in a series of presidential statements, the strongest of which was President Kennedy's:

> The Commonwealth structure, and its relationship to the United States which is in the nature of a compact, provide for self-government in respect of internal affairs and administration, subject only to the applicable provisions of the Federal Constitution, the Puerto Rican Federal Relations Act, and the acts of Congress authorizing and approving the constitution . . .
>
> All departments, agencies, and officials of the executive branch of the Government should faithfully and carefully observe and respect this arrangement in relation to all matters affecting the Commonwealth of Puerto Rico. If any matters arise involving the fundamentals of this arrangement, they should be referred to the Office of the President.31

The Supreme Court case arose when the Puerto Rican government seized without notice or hearing a yacht on which marijuana was found. The Puerto Rican statute was challenged as being unconstitutional, a taking of property without due process of law. The case was heard in the Puerto Rican Federal District Court by three judges who agreed that the statute was unconstitutional Puerto Rico, following the terms of the Three Judge Court Act, appealed directly to the Supreme Court of the United States, rather than to the Court of Appeals where normally appeals from the District Court are heard.

The Three Judge Court Act applies only to "state" statutes and, therefore, the first question presented to the Supreme Court was the breadth of the word "state" in the context of the Three Judge Court Act. Were Puerto Rican statutes "state" statutes requiring a hearing by a three-judge court before they could be declared unconstitutional? Earlier cases interpreting the Three Judge Court Act arising when Hawaii was a territory and in Puerto Rico prior to commonwealth (1919) held that the word "state" did not include a territory. In short, if the Three Judge Court Act applied to Puerto Rico, it now had to be because a commonwealth was different from a territory.

In the <u>Pearson Yacht</u> case the Supreme Court looked to see if there was sufficient sovereignty, sufficient local control, under commonwealth to require a three-judge district court, arguing that the Three Judge Court Act was intended to avoid judicial interference with state sovereignty. When, therefore, an area enjoyed local sovereignty, it was to be considered a state and the Three Judge Court statute should apply. The Court examined the powers of the island government as a result of the 1950-52 legislation. The Court emphasized the degree of commonwealth sovereignty over local matters and on that basis held that the commonwealth should be considered a state for the purpose of the Three Judge Court Act, thus sustaining the commonwealth argument that something of legal significance happened in 1950-52. Whether the Supreme Court would extend this commonwealth recognition to other areas is unclear.

The executive branch statements have, however, been filled with ambiguity, and litigation is too slow. The Populares have therefore sought a broad, specific, reaffirmation of the powers of the commonwealth from the Congress of the United States. In 1959 the Populares introduced comprehensive legislation to delineate the federal government-island relationship. But the bills died without being reported out of either the House of the Senate.*

Frustrated, the Populares appealed to the Congress once more in 1962, calling for a compact commission to draft the compact setting forth the relationship between the Commonwealth of Puerto Rico and the United States. Instead, Congress established the United States-Puerto Rico Commission on the Status of Puerto Rico, which was charged with studying "all factors . . . which may have a bearing on the present and future relationship between the United States and Puerto Rico."

This Commission held hearings and examined the economic, political, and cultural consequences of statehood, independence, and commonwealth. It affirmed the commonwealth as a third status alternative in addition to statehood and independence. It concluded as follows:

---

*The commonwealth introduced comprehensive legislation in both houses of Congress, S. 2023 and H.R. 5926, to improve the federal relationship. After hearings on S. 2023 were held late in the spring of 1959 by the Senate Committee on Interior and Insular Affairs, a substitute measure was introduced by Senator Murray, the chairman of the committee, and Dr. Fernos-Isern, the resident commissioner of Puerto Rico. These later bills (S. 2708 and H.R. 9234) were modifications of the original bills, having taken into consideration legislative and executive branch comment on the bills as first introduced. Extensive hearings were held in Puerto Rico on these later bills, but neither of them was ever reported out of either the Senate or House Committees. 105 Cong. Rec. (pt. 16) 1023 (1952) (S. 2708); ibid. at 1206 (H.R. 9234). Strangely, despite the extensive published commentary on commonwealth, there has been almost no discussion in legal periodicals of the Fernos-Murray legislation.

> [A]ll three forms of political status—the Commonwealth,
> Statehood, and Independence—are valid and confer upon
> the people of Puerto Rico equal dignity with equality of
> status and of national citizenship. . . .
> (4) All three status alternatives . . . are within the
> power of the people of Puerto Rico and Congress to
> establish under the Constitution. . . .
> The Commission does have views on the political
> character of the Commonwealth relationship created in
> 1950-52. . . . It constitutes a solemn undertaking,
> based upon mutual consent, between the people of the
> United States acting through their Federal Government
> and the people of Puerto Rico acting directly as well
> as through their established governmental processes.
> . . . A solemn undertaking of such profound character
> between the Federal Government and a community of
> U.S. citizens is incompatible with the concept of uni-
> lateral revocation. It is inconceivable that either the
> United States or Puerto Rico would, by an act of
> unilateral revocation, undermine the very foundation
> of their common progress: the fundamental political
> and economic relationships which were established
> on the basis of mutuality.[32]

The commission recommended a plebiscite to choose among state-hood, commonwealth, and independence and soon afterwards, following this recommendation, the Popular Democratic Party majority passed a bill calling for such a plebiscite on 23 July 1967.

The Statehood Republican Party decided to boycott the plebiscite, but one of its leaders, Luis A. Ferre, bolted the party to form the United Statehooders in order to compete in the plebiscite. The Independence Party also declared that it would refrain from participation; but again a university professor, Hector Alvarez Silva, formed a group to permit the Independentistas to be on the ballot.

The first plebiscite on status held since Puerto Rico became part of the U.S. federal system was hotly contested, with the various status positions putting forth the arguments still heard today in Puerto Rico. The plebiscite resulted in more than 60 percent of the 702,000 voters choosing commonwealth. The Statehooders polled nearly 39 percent and the Independentistas less than 0.6 percent.

It appeared that the issue might be put somewhat to rest and that the joint *ad hoc* advisory groups recommended by the Status Commission would now be selected to develop the commonwealth. But a division developed within the commonwealth camp between the incumbent Governor, Roberto Sanchez Villella, and the founder of the party, Munoz Marin.

As a result, on 4 November 1968, Luis Ferre, a statehood supporter, was elected governor of Puerto Rico with 44 percent of the 875,000 votes cast.

At Governor Ferre's initiative a joint Ad Hoc Advisory Group was appointed on 13 April 1970 to explore the desirability of extending the presidential vote to Puerto Rico, an issue of great importance to statehood advocates but one on which commonwealth partisans were divided. In August 1971 the advisory group recommended that the presidential vote be accorded the people of Puerto Rico, proposing that this recommendation be submitted to the people of Puerto Rico for approval or disapproval in a referendum. But no action was taken.

THE DEVELOPMENT AND GOALS OF THE COMMONWEALTH

In 1972 the Populares regained the governorship in Puerto Rico and a new Ad Hoc Advisory Group was appointed to develop further the framework of commonwealth. In 1975, as part of its charter, the group completed a major review of all aspects of the Commonwealth of Puerto Rico-U.S. relationship. Therefore, in examining more fully the Commonwealth of Puerto Rico relationship with the United States in key areas, we will note the situation as of 1975, the proposals put forth by the commonwealth government in its presentation to the Ad Hoc Advisory Group during its deliberations, and the recent recommendations of the Ad Hoc Advisory Group for a new "Compact of Permanent Union Between Puerto Rico and the United States." These recommendations require congressional approval before they go into effect.

Political Relations

The Compact

I noted above the lack of congressional practice supporting the compact theory. The recommendations of the Ad Hoc Advisory Group are for the reaffirmation of this concept by a "Compact of Permanent Union Between Puerto Rico and the United States." Under its terms, Puerto Rico is renamed the Free Associated State (rather than Commonwealth), of Puerto Rico* and a compact is freely entered into between the United

---

*The word "commonwealth" is the official translation of <u>estado libre associado</u> which literally translated would mean "free associated state." <u>P.R. Laws Ann.</u> (Vol 1, <u>Historical Documents</u>) Res. 22 (1952). The English translation was the subject of considerable debate in the constitutional convention, but the word "Commonwealth" was adopted

States and the Free Associated State of Puerto Rico. The United States is given the right to conduct Puerto Rico's foreign relations and the Supreme Court of the United States is stated to be final judge of the compact. Significantly, the Ad Hoc Advisory Group seeks the creation of a Joint Commission—three commissioners appointed by the president of the United States and three appointed by the governor of Puerto Rico—for five years to review the applicability of various federal laws and regulations and delegation of federal functions to Puerto Rico.

Participation in Political Process

The absence of state citizenship has prevented the United States citizen in Puerto Rico from voting for the president. There has been some discussion of a constitutional amendment similar to the recent one providing the vote for United States citizens residing in the District of Columbia, but this has met with mixed reactions in Puerto Rico.

At present Puerto Rico is represented in the U.S. Congress by a resident commissioner elected every four years pursuant to Puerto Rican law. He may not vote in Congress, but may do so in committee, and is paid the same as a congressman, receiving the same stationery allowance and franking privilege and the sum of $500 for each session of Congress he attends. But his staff allowance is considerably less than that of a congressman although this will likely be changed in the near future in the same way that his committee role has been gradually changed to equal that of a congressman. Under the proposed compact, Puerto Rico would have a representative in each House with "all the rights and privileges of [other] members which are compatible with the Constitution of the United States."[33]

General Applicability of Federal Law

Puerto Rico has sought for some time to restrict the applicability of federal law to Puerto Rico. Puerto Rico has urged that the present operating assumption that the statutory laws of the United States extend generally to Puerto Rico should be reversed. Unless Congress expressly extends a law to the island by specifically extending its applicability to Puerto Rico,* Puerto Rico will not be covered. This will avoid inad-

---

with only two dissenting votes. Diario de Sessiones de la Convencion Constituyente de Puerto Rico 883 (1956).

*Both because of the compact argument detailed earlier in the text and the various provisions of the Puerto Rican Federal Relations Act, the text puts the matter much too boldly. The issue is examined in detail in Leibowitz, Applicability of Federal Law to the Commonwealth of Puerto Rico, 56 Geo. L.J. 219 (1968).

vertent inclusion of Puerto Rico in legislation which should not be applicable according to the principles of association. In addition, the commonwealth has suggested that if the Congress does pass or is about to pass legislation covering Puerto Rico there may be a plebiscite on Puerto Rican initiative where the people themselves may directly voice their position.

The proposed draft prepared by the Puerto Rican side took a stronger position. It stated that congressional laws "shall not be applicable to Puerto Rico over the explicit and reasoned objection of the Free Associated State, provided such objection is formulated in any stage previous to the definite Congressional approval."

The final proposed compact is much weaker. Federal legislation would not apply to Puerto Rico unless the laws explicitly refer to the free associated state. In addition, the governor and resident commissioner would be entitled to submit objections to the Congress. If either committee considering the legislation agrees with the objection, the legislation would not apply.

It is somewhat unclear from the language what the significance of this is. The requirement of specific mention codifies a judicial decision and existing practice and the reference to the committee system may only connote political realities. The language suggests, however, that if there is a disagreement at committee level the legislation will not apply. If the compact is confirmed and ratified, this could be significant.

Military Presence

Puerto Rico is included under the provisions of the Universal Military Training and Service Act. In addition, under various federal statutes applicable to the mainland and Puerto Rico,[34] military departments may institute condemnation proceedings and acquire land upon payment of just compensation. Acting under these statutes the military has acquired approximately 23,352 acres on the island of Vieques and an additional 11,000 acres on the main island of Puerto Rico. (This figure is based on original condemnation. In some cases land once acquired has been exchanged for a different parcel. Thus, in one instance a parcel of 482,438 acres was exchanged for one of 12,600 acres.) Almost all of this land was acquired during World War II.

In recent years the U.S. military presence has been a major political issue. As a result, much of the land on the main island of Puerto Rico has been returned, and after a lengthy public and political struggle, the use of portion of Culebra for target practice has been discontinued. Puerto Rico wanted title to land in Puerto Rico to be transferred from the United States to the free associated state with necessary public use continued to be permitted by the federal government. They wished further that before new land was acquired for military use, the federal government would certify this need to the Governor of Puerto Rico who "shall proceed to acquire . . . the required property and place it at the disposal of the United States."

The proposed compact calls only for consultations. This would not limit substance and the language, which was face-saving, would not appear to limit the style and procedure of the military presence on the island very much either.

Immigration

As citizens of the United States, residents of Puerto Rico may migrate freely to the mainland. In the 1950s Puerto Rico experienced one of the greatest population outflows in modern history; 430,000 people (approximately 20 percent of the total population) left the island and moved to the United States. In the 1960s the net migration sharply declined, although there continued to be a large migration to the States and a substantial increase in the number of migrants returning to Puerto Rico.

In the early seventies there was a net migration to Puerto Rico (1971: 12,910; 1972: 33,656; and 1973: 34,381). This returning populace, in addition to the increase in the number of foreign citizens registered in Puerto Rico (55,888 in 1973, compared to 5,578 in 1960), and the persistent high rates of unemployment, caused a desire on the part of the commonwealth to control immigration to the island.

At present no alien may be admitted directly to Puerto Rico to fill a definite job opening until the secretary of labor issues a clearance to the effect that there is no American citizen willing and able to fill the position.[35] However, any foreign immigrant already residing elsewhere in the United States may travel freely to Puerto Rico. The commonwealth has urged a special visa permitting travel everywhere in the United States except to Puerto Rico. Those wishing to reside in Puerto Rico would submit a special application developed and processed by commonwealth authorities under the general responsibility of the attorney general of the United States and the Immigration and Naturalization Service.

The original Puerto Rican position went further and permitted the government of Puerto Rico "pursuant to its own laws [to] fix its own quota of aliens admissible to Puerto Rico." The proposed compact provides that the president and the governor may from time to time "in the light of economic and demographic considerations applicable to the Free Associated State" limit the number of aliens.

Puerto Rico's International Presence

As noted above, after the establishment of commonwealth in 1950-52, the United States advised the United Nations, and the General Assembly so voted, that Puerto Rico was "invested with attributes of political sovereignty which clearly identify the status of self-government attained by the Puerto Rican people as that of an autonomous political entity."[36]

Nevertheless, this has been continued to be questioned by independence parties within Puerto Rico and by various countries within the United Nations. The Special Committee on Decolonization—The Committee of 24—has reviewed the Puerto Rican case in the past few years with the Cuban delegation taking the lead in questioning the previous action by the General Assembly.[37]

Even assuming the broadest validity to the UN action, the consequences with respect to the commonwealth role in international law is unclear. Puerto Rico has suggested before the Ad Hoc Advisory Group that as a result of commonwealth it has the legal right to be admitted to the UN as a "state" in addition to associate membership in a variety of international organizations where this kind of membership is permitted. The World Health Organization, for example, specifically provides for membership by "territories which are not responsible for the conduct of their international relations."[38]

Puerto Rico has played some role in relations with foreign countries, most notably as a member of the Caribbean Organization and in the Joint Dominican Republic-Puerto Rican Economic Commission.[39] The State Department has been cautious in this regard even where legal capacity appears not to be an issue. Thus, while membership in various international organizations appears increasingly likely, the capability of Puerto Rico to evolve its own independent foreign policies in areas not affecting the national security of the United States or to sign international agreements has not been encouraged. Puerto Rico has regarded this issue as one of great importance relating to its own image in the world and will continue to press for a stronger international presence.

Role of the Federal Judiciary

Since commonwealth, Puerto Rico has sought to upgrade the status of the Federal District Court while at the same time limiting its jurisdiction and establishing its uniqueness. Thus, after commonwealth, it succeeded in getting the federal district judge appointed for life as in the United States, rather than for the previous term of years, and eliminating a special diversity jurisdiction established in 1900. It has recently introduced legislation into the Congress to have proceedings in the District Court normally conducted in Spanish and the proposed compact adopts a similar position.[40]

Appeals from the Supreme Court of Puerto Rico now are direct to the U.S. Supreme Court rather than to the First Circuit Court of Appeals, as previously was the case. The governor, after the U.S. Supreme Court's abortion decision in 1973, suggested the inapplicability of Supreme Court decisions to the commonwealth, but this view was not urged before the Ad Hoc Advisory Group.

Economic Aspects of the Relationship

The Commonwealth of Puerto Rico has based much of its economic growth on special provisions in federal law for Puerto Rico within a common market relationship which permits free transportation of goods and persons to and from the United States. We shall note key elements of this economic relationship.

Taxation

Section 14 of the Foraker Act of 1900, which in substance is Section 9 of the Puerto Rican Federal Relations Act today, treated Puerto Rico specially in two major respects for the purposes of United States taxation. First, it excepted Puerto Rico from the federal "internal revenue laws." Second, it provided that Puerto Rican manufactured goods entering the United States would incur duties and tax equal to the internal revenue tax imposed on similar articles in the United States. The funds so collected would be returned to the Puerto Rican treasury.[41]

The original exception to the internal revenue laws arose prior to the income tax when the internal revenue laws meant only various excise taxes and a special wartime levy. The section granting the exception, however, has been carried forward and reenacted with minor changes in the succeeding years when there were no longer any duties levied on Puerto Rican goods entering the United States and the internal revenue laws included the income tax.

This exception from federal income tax, combined with the fact that "possession" income is treated specially under the internal revenue laws[42]—deferring any tax on income from these sources until that income is received in the States—has been a major selling point in Puerto Rico's industrialization program, Operation Bootstrap. In 1959 Puerto Rico suggested that it would begin to pay taxes when its per-capita income was equal to that in the state of the Union in which the figure was lowest. (As of the mid-1970s it was about one-half that.) There was considerable discussion of a contribution before the Ad Hoc Advisory Group; but after the suggestion of various alternatives, the issue was left for a joint commission to "study, with the highest priority . . . a system of contributory payments."

Tariffs and Trade: United States-Puerto Rico Trade

Since 25 July 1901, federal law has provided that trade between Puerto Rico and the United States shall be free of tariff duties (although constitutionally this is not required).[43] In fact, this trade has been almost completely unrestricted. The one major exception is a quota limiting imports on sugar into the United States from the island. The proposed compact affirms the common market between the United States and Puerto Rico and requires it to continue.

Tariffs and Trade: Foreign Country-Puerto Rico Trade

Section 2 of the Foraker Act of 1900, which is valid today as a result of Section 58 of the Puerto Rican Federal Relations Act, provides that the same tariff rates be imposed on all imports from foreign markets entering the United States or Puerto Rico.

Following the hurricane of 12 September 1928, the coffee industry in Puerto Rico suffered losses estimated at 75 percent. Congress, therefore, in June 1930 empowered the Legislature of Puerto Rico to set a duty on coffee imports entering Puerto Rico although no such duty was to be imposed on imports into the United States.[44]

Thus, present federal law requires that the same tariff rates be imposed on all imports from foreign countries entering the United States or Puerto Rico, with the single exception of coffee. Coffee may be imported duty free into the United States, where very little coffee is grown (except for small quantities in Hawaii); but a tariff, the rate of which is determined by the Puerto Rican Legislature,* is imposed on imports into Puerto Rico, where a significant amount of coffee is produced.[45] The proposed compact continues the coffee exception but would also permit Puerto Rico to set other tariffs, should it wish to do so, after coordination with United States officials. All tariffs collected on imports into Puerto Rico from abroad or into the United States from Puerto Rico shall be remitted to Puerto Rico, as they are at the time of writing.

Minimum Wage Laws

The Fair Labor Standards Act (FLSA),[46] which sets minimum wages, fixes maximum hours and overtime premium pay, prohibits the use of child labor, and, in certain circumstances, forbids discrimination on the basis of sex, now contains special provisions permitting some employers in Puerto Rico to pay less than the minimum wage.[47]

In 1938, when FLSA was first passed,[48] it was fully applicable to Puerto Rico.[49] Since the minimum wage established by that law (25 cents an hour and phased increases to 30 and 40 cents an hour within seven years) was generally below the prevailing wages in the United

---

*The Puerto Rican Legislature redelegated this power to the Puerto Rican Secretary of Agriculture. Act of 21 June 1955, Act No. 95, Sec. 1 (now P.R. Laws Ann., Tit. 13, Sec. 2201 (1962), as amended, [1966 Supp.]). The congressional delegation has even been held valid since commonwealth, but the redelegation by the Puerto Rican Legislature was overturned. Pan American Standard Brands, Inc. v. United States, 177 F. Supp. 769 (U.S. Cust. Ct. 1959). The Puerto Rican Legislature recently redelegated part of this power to the Puerto Rican executive in a more restricted fashion. P.R. Laws Ann., Tit. 13, Sec. 2201 (1964), as amended, (1966 Supp.). This redelegation has not been tested in the courts.

PUERTO RICO 61

States, the effect in the United States was rarely disruptive. In Puerto Rico, however, where the prevailing wage scale in the needlework trade was about 4 cents an hour and in manufacturing about half the newly established minimum, there were immediate repercussions. Needlework exports, for example, declined from $20 million in 1937 to $5 million in 1940.[50] As a result, in 1940, by a separate amendment to the Fair Labor Standards Act,[51] Puerto Rico was excepted from the minimum wage established for the stateside laborer and instead a special committee was appointed to set wages for Puerto Rico and the Virgin Islands.[52] Since the 1961 amendments to FLSA,[53] the Puerto Rican and stateside minimum wages have been related more closely. In the 1961 law, the same percentage increases which were applied to stateside minimum wages were required for Puerto Rican-covered industries. However, the secretary of labor could appoint review committees which had the power to except a particular industry on the island from the automatic percentage increases.[54]

Puerto Rico argued that as a developing economy it was unable to pay the wages paid in the developed economy present in the United States without large-scale unemployment and decreased economic development.[55] The eastern textile industry and labor unions, on the other hand, feared unemployment and loss of the industry from Puerto Rico's low-cost competition. The final arrangement was a compromise of these views. The theory behind the 1961 act was that maintaining the same relative wage scales prevented Puerto Rico from gaining competitive advantage without being unduly harmful to the island's economy. Furthermore, the review committee procedure could act as a safety valve if automatic percentage increases would result in undue hardship in certain industries. The later amendments,[56] including those passed in 1974, follow the practice of providing for automatic percentage increases in the prevailing wage scale in Puerto Rico while retaining the possibility of exceptions via the review committee procedure.

The industry committee approach has been attacked by labor groups in Puerto Rico and the United States as being unduly conservative and a means to delay increases in the minimum wage. These groups urge automatic percentage increases with no exceptions. Others, however, emphasizing Puerto Rico's different economic circumstances and the ability of the commonwealth government to regulate wages itself, urge the complete removal of Puerto Rico from the coverage of FLSA.

The government of the Commonwealth of Puerto Rico has urged the continuation of the exemption, based upon the need to attract labor intensive industry to the island. It has pointed out that prior to 1956 the U.S.-Puerto Rican relationship between average factory wages and average per-capita incomes remained relatively stable. Since then, even with the exemption for Puerto Rico under FLSA, average hourly factory earnings in Puerto Rico have been pushed up much more rapidly and they are now over half the U.S. average, while average per-capita income in Puerto Rico remains at 39 percent of the U.S. average.

Manufacturing profits in Puerto Rico have declined as of 1975, to about the U.S. average. The Puerto Rican government argues that the slowdown in industrial development in Puerto Rico since 1969 is in considerable part a reflection of this loss of competitive advantage.

The proposed compact would give the Free Associated State of Puerto Rico "exclusive jurisdiction over all matters pertaining to labor-management relations" except for shipping, aviation enterprises and those enterprises whose products are sold substantially in the States." The minimum wage exception would be continued although the attempt would be to have the two minimum wages be equivalent "as soon as economic conditions in Puerto Rico so permit."

Federal Financial Assistance

At the present time Puerto Rico receives a little more than $1.2 billion, a little less than 20 percent of its total gross income, from federal expenditures in Puerto Rico. This gross flow of federal funds has more than tripled in the decade preceding 1975, from $391 million in 1964. The largest component of this increase, the federal grant program, increased from $96.1 million to $446.2 million and federal aid payments to individuals increased from $59.7 to $401.6 million in a similar period of time.[57]

There is no consistent pattern for this federal grant assistance; in some cases Puerto Rico is treated like a state, in others it is accorded special treatment, usually to its detriment.[58] Thus, until recently the Elementary and Secondary Education Act of 1965 treated Puerto Rico differently from a state under a formula distinctly less advantageous to Puerto Rico. The matching grant-in-aid highway program formula does not treat Puerto Rico as favorably as a state,[59] and the commonwealth was excluded from participation in the general revenue-sharing program, the State and Local Fiscal Assistance Act of 1972.

Similarly, under the Social Security Act and Medicaid there is an absolute limit on payments to Puerto Rico, which means that Puerto Rico's share of aid to families with dependent children and other welfare payments is substantially less than in the case of a state. On the other hand, many of the major matching grant-in-aid programs, such as the air pollution control program, the slum clearance and urban renewal program, the medical facilities program, and the program grants on aging under the Older Americans Act of 1965, do not single out Puerto Rico for special treatment; but treat it as a state of the Union.

A three-judge District Court decision has held unconstitutional—as contrary to the equal-protection clause of the Fourteenth Amendment—restricting social security payments to United States citizens in Puerto Rico.[60] The case is now on appeal to the Supreme Court of the United States.

Puerto Rico has lobbied for equal treatment with a state under various categorical grant formulas and has begun to have some success, most notably under the recent amendments to the Elementary and Secondary Education Act. Before the Ad Hoc Advisory Group, Puerto Rico has urged a block grant system to be negotiated yearly between the federal government and Puerto Rico to eliminate the regulating aspects and distortion of local priorities which is linked to program funding. It has suggested a higher matching share for Puerto Rico as a trade-off for the greater commonwealth taxing ability because of the inapplicability of the federal tax laws.

NOTES

1. Art. II, Art. IV, Treaty of Paris, 30 U.S. Stat. 1754 (1899)
2. Kal Wagenheim, Puerto Rico: A Profile (New York: Praeger Publishers, 1970), p. 67.
3. De Lima v. Bidwell, 182 U.S. 1 (1901); Downes v. Bidwell, 182 U.S. 244 (1901); Dooley v. United States, 182 U.S. 222 (1901); Armstrong v. United States, 182 U.S. 243 (1901).
4. For contemporaneous legal discussion of the problems, see Randolph, Constitutional Aspects of Annexation, 12 Harv. L. Rev. 291 (1899); Baldwin, Constitutional Questions Incident to the Acquisition and Government by the United States of Island Territory, 12 Harv. L. Rev. 393 (1899); Lowell, The Status of Our New Possessions--A Third View, 13 Harv. L. Rev. 21 (1899); and Palfrey, The Growth of the Idea of Annexation and Its Breaking Upon Constitutional Law, 13 Harv. L. Rev. 371 (1899). The problem is discussed in retrospect by one of the participants in Coudert, The Evolution of the Doctrine of Territorial Incorporation, 26 Col. L. Rev. 823 (1926).
5. Granville-Smith v. Granville-Smith, 349 U.S. 1 (1955), p. 5.
6. Downes v. Bidwell, at p. 295.
7. Ibid., at p. 339.
8. Arnold Leibowitz, Educational Policy and Political Acceptance: The Imposition of English as the Language of Instruction in American Schools (Washington, D.C.: Center for Applied Linguistics, 1969), pp. 81-104. More detailed histories of U.S. educational policies in Puerto Rico are Cebollero, A School Language Policy for Puerto Rico (1945) and Osuna, A History of Education in Puerto Rico (1949).
9. U.S. Congress, S. Doc. 40, 61st Cong., 1st Sess., Affairs in Porto Rico: A Message from the President Inviting the Attention of Congress to the Legislative Difficulties in Porto Rico (10 May 1909), p. 3.
10. 197 U.S. 516 (1904).
11. 9 P.R. Fed.R. 452 (1917).
12. 25 P.R.R. 527 (1917).
13. People of Porto Rico, et al. v. Tapia, 245 U.S. 639 (1917).
14. 258 U.S. 298 (1922).
15. Ibid., at pp. 309, 311.

16. One of the early, now classic, studies of the Puerto Rican economy was conducted under the auspices of the Brookings Institution at the onset of the depression: Victor Clark and Associates, Porto Rico and Its Problems (Washington, D.C.: Brookings Institution 1930).

17. S. 4529, 74th Cong., 2d Sess. (23 April 1936). For a detailed discussion of the assassination of Col. Riggs and the reactions in Washington and in Puerto Rico, see Mathews, Puerto Rican Politics and the New Deal (1960), pp. 249-63.

18. U.S. Tariff Commission, The Economy of Puerto Rico (1946), esp. pp. 18-20.

19. The response is discussed in some detail in Hunter, Historical Survey of the Puerto Rico Status Question, 1898-1965, Selected Background Studies Prepared for the United States-Puerto Rico Commission on the Status of Puerto Rico (1966).

20. Act of 5 August 1947, Ch. 490, Sec. 6, 61 Stat. 772, amending Act of 2 March 1917, Ch. 145, Sec. 49(b), 39 Stat. 967.

21. The Puerto Rican industrialization program has had many chroniclers. Perhaps the most thorough is Henry Wells, The Modernization of Puerto Rico (Cambridge: Harvard University Press, 1969). An administrative study focusing on the personalities of the Marxist critique is to be found in Manuel Maldonodo-Denis, Puerto Rico: A Socio-Historic Interpretation, (New York: English trans. Vintage Books, 1972). A broader study also favorable to independence is Gordon Lewis, Puerto Rico: Freedom and Power in the Caribbean (New York: Monthly Review Press, 1964).

22. Act of 3 July 1950, Ch. 446, 64 Stat. 319; Act of 3 July 1952, Ch. 567, 66 Stat. 327. The laws are quoted in full in Documents on the Constitutional History of Puerto Rico (2d ed., 1964).

23. The care with which the Puerto Rican Constitution was drafted can be seen in Escuela de Administracion Publica, La Nueva Constitucion de Puerto Rico (1954). The debates are reported in P.R. Legislative Assembly, Diario de Sesiones, Procedimientos y Debates de la Convencion Constituyente, 1951-52, vols. 1-4. For an analysis of the new features of the constitution, see Franquil and Wells, The Commonwealth Constitution. Annals 285 (1953).

24. Both sides of the compact argument and the subsequent discussion in the many cases are presented in Leibowitz, Applicability of Federal Law to the Commonwealth of Puerto Rico, 56 Geo. L. J. 219 (1967). The argument in favor of compact is excellently presented by the former secretary of justice and present governor of Puerto Rico, Hernandez Colon, in The Commonwealth of Puerto Rico: Territory or State?, 19 Rev. C. Abo. P.R. 207 (1950). See also The Power of The Congress to Enter Into a Compact with the People of Puerto Rico; and the Legal Status of the Compact Under Existing Legislation and Under S. 2023 and H.R. 5926, Hearings on S. 2023 Before the Senate Comm. on Interior and Insular Affairs, 86th Cong., 1st Sess. 90 (1959), in 22 Rev. C. Abo. P.R. 341 (1962).

25. P.L. 600 (3 July 1950), Ch. 446, 64 Stat. 319 (emphasis added).

26. G.A. Res. 748, 8 U.N. GAOR Supp. 17 at 25, U.N. Doc. A/2630 (1953).

27. United States Mission to the United Nations, Press Release No. 1741 (28 August 1953), at 2.

28. Stern, Notes on the History of Puerto Rico's Commonwealth Status, 30 Rev. Jur. U.P.R. 33 (1961); Helfeld, Congressional Intent and Attitude Toward Public Law 600 and the Constitution of the Commonwealth of Puerto Rico, 21 Rev. Jur. U.P.R. 255 (1952).

29. H.R. Rep. No. 2275, 81st Cong., 2d Sess. 3 (1950); see S. Rep. No. 1779, 81st Cong., 2d Sess. 3 (1950). See also Statement of Munoz Marin, Governor of Puerto Rico, in Hearings on H.R. 7674 and S. 3336 Before the House Comm. on Public Lands, 81st Cong., 2d Sess. (1950); Statement of Irwin W. Silverman, Chief Counsel, Office of Territories, Dept. of Interior, in Hearings on S. J. Res. 151 Before the Comm. on Interior and Insular Affairs, 82nd Cong., 2d Sess. 40 (1952). At one point in the congressional debate on the House version, Congressman Meader offered an amendment which would have made clear the revocable nature of the federal law (98 Cong. Rec. 6183 [1952]). The amendment was rejected but it is unclear whether for technical reasons or because it was unnecessary (Ibid. at 6168.)

30. 416 U.S. 663 (1964).

31. Memorandum of 25 July 1961, from President Kennedy to all heads of the executive departments and agencies, 26 Fed. Reg. 6695.

32. Report, United States-Puerto Rico Commission on the Status of Puerto Rico, pp. 5-13. But see Ibid. at 21 (supplemental views of Senator Henry Jackson).

33. Sec. 11, Proposed Bill to Establish the Compact of Permanent Union Between Puerto Rico and the United States.

34. 10 U.S.C.A. 2663; 33 U.S.C.A. Sec. 591; 40 U.S.C.A. 255.

35. P.L. 79-911, Sec. 203, 166-A.

36. General Assembly Resolution 748 (VIII), 27 November 1953.

37. The issue is briefly discussed in Reisman, Puerto Rico and the International Process (American Society of International Law 1975).

38. The issue is explored extensively in ibid.

39. Agreement for the Establishment of the Caribbean Organization (21 June 1960); 2 U.S.T. 1297, T.I.A.S. No. 4853.

40. See Hearings on S. 1724 Before the Subcomm. on Improvement of Judicial Machinery of the Senate Judiciary Comm.

41. Section 3 of the Foraker Act of 1900 continued today in Int. Rev. Code of 1954, Sec. 7652(a).

42. Int. Rev. Code of 1954, Secs. 7651(3), 7701(c). But see Sec. 931(c). See also United States v. Rexach, 185 F. Supp. 465 (D.P.R. 1960). This amendment arose in 1921, partly as a result of the general desire not to tax foreign source income in order to permit domestic companies to compete more readily abroad, and partly because of the

refusal of a number of domestic companies doing business in the Philippines to pay taxes to the U.S. Government after having paid taxes to the government of the Philippines.

43. Proclamation No. 8, 32 Stat. 1884-85.
44. 19 U.S.C., Sec. 1319 (1964).
45. This situation is specifically mentioned in the GATT protocols. General Agreements on Tariffs and Trade, 30 October 1947, Schedule XX, Pt. 1, § 1654, 61 Stat. A3 (1947), T.I.A.S. No. 1700 (effective 1 January 1948).
46. 29 U.S.C. §§ 201-19 (1964).
47. Fair Labor Standards Amendments of 1974, PL 93-259 (8 April 1974), § 5.
48. Act of 25 June 1938, Ch. 676, §§ 1-19, 52 Stat. 1060.
49. Ibid, § 3(c).
50. Hearings on Amendments to the Fair Labor Standards Act (Puerto Rico) Before the Subcomm. on Labor of the Senate Comm. on Labor and Public Welfare, 89th Cong., 2d Sess. 1531 (1966). (Statement of Ramon F. Calderon, executive director, Puerto Rico Mfrs. Ass'n.)
51. Emergency Relief Appropriations Act, Fiscal Year 1951, Ch. 432, §§ 1-41, 54 Stat. 611.
52. Ibid, § 3(c).
53. Act of May 5, 1961, P. L. 87-30, 75 Stat. 65.
54. Ibid, § 5.
55. Reynolds, Wages and Employment in a Labor-Surplus Economy, 60 Am. Econ. Rev. 19 (1965). See generally Reynolds and Gregory, Wages, Productivity and Industrialization in Puerto Rico (1965).
56. 29 U.S.C. § 206 (1964).
57. The figures are from the testimony to the Ad Hoc Advisory Group on Puerto Rico by Richard Cappalli, special assistant to the governor (27 April 1974).
58. A detailed discussion of the various federal grant programs, their formulas, and their applicability to Puerto Rico is to be found in Richard Cappalli, Federal Aid to Puerto Rico (Rio Piedras: Institute of Urban Law, University of Puerto Rico, 1970). See also Arnold Baker, A Study of Federal Public Assistance Payments to Puerto Rico.
59. See 23 U.S.C. Sec 103(d) (1964).
60. Jesus Rodriguez Cintron v. Richardson,___F. Supp.___(Civ. A.1099-72, D.C.P.R. 1975).

CHAPTER

4

**TRUST TERRITORY
OF THE
PACIFIC ISLANDS**

Puerto Rico pioneered the commonwealth concept in the United States federal system. It was born of necessity, midwifed by guile, and grew as an orphan looking for guardians who would remove the question concerning its legal validity.

In the case of the Trust Territory of the Pacific Islands (TTPI), the United States had to negotiate in truth because it was dealing with a territory which had been gained not in conquest but in trust. During the negotiation the federal government began to view the Puerto Rican Commonwealth not as a product of unique circumstances of questionable constitutionality but as a precedent for association within the United States federal structure. It was also in the Trust Territory negotiations that the ramifications of commonwealth were explored, and found acceptable in one case, (the Marianas) and in the other (the rest of the Trust Territory which we shall call Micronesia) found wanting. And it was in the Trust Territory also that the key issues of United States military power and local control of land were to be explicitly joined.

The Trust Territory of the Pacific Islands encompasses 2,000 tiny islands. Only two (Ponape and Babelthaup) are greater in area than 100 square miles.

The territory stretches for more than 2,700 miles from east to west and 1,300 miles from north to south and includes approximately 3,000 square miles of ocean area. The approximate geographic center of the Trust Territory—Truk in the Carolines—is 5,000 miles from the continental United States and 2,000 miles from the Philippines.

Only about 100 of these islands are inhabited, with a total population of 115,000. There is no one culture that embraces all the peoples of this area. Instead, there is great linguistic and cultural diversification, with the peoples of the islands speaking nine distinct languages. Adding further to the diversity are the differing effects resulting from recent contacts with Americans and Japanese.

MAP 4

Trust Territory of the Pacific Islands

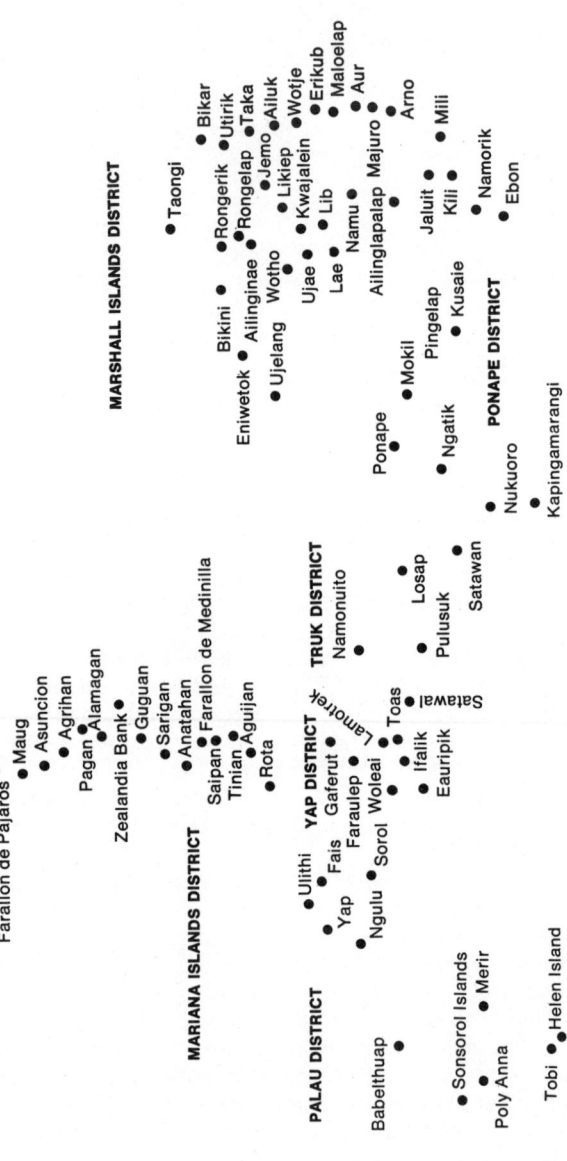

Source: Bank of America National Trust and Savings Association, Tokyo, Japan.

TRUST TERRITORY 69

The major island groups within the Trust Territory are the Marshalls, the Carolines, and, of particular interest here, the Marianas. The Marianas are a string of volcanic islands stretching southward from Japan towards New Guinea with Guam at its southernmost point. However, because of historical accident—Guam, as we shall discuss in more detail in Chapter 5, was transferred to the United States after the Spanish-American War—Guam does not come within the Trust Territory but rather is a territory of the United States. Since at various times, including the present, an association between Guam and the rest of the Marianas has been discussed, some comparisons are worth noting.

The total land area of the Marianas District of TTPI is 183 square miles, that of Guam 225 square miles. Two-thirds of the Mariana Islands land area is made up of the three principal islands: Saipan, Tinian, and Rota. Only these and three other islands are inhabited. The total population is approximately 14,000, of whom almost 11,000 live on Saipan. Guam's population is slightly more than 100,000. Chamorro is the native language spoken throughout the Marianas District and is the native language in Guam.

The Trust Territory is divided politically into six districts, the Marshalls and the Marianas each comprising a separate district, and the Carolines being divided into four districts paralleling the geographic assemblages of islands—Ponape, Yap, Truk, and Palau.

HISTORICAL BACKGROUND

Spanish explorers under Ferdinand Magellan were the first Europeans to come in contact with these islands when they stopped at the Marianas in 1521. Although the agreement for colonial exploitation between Spain and Portugal, the Treaty of Toresillas in 1495, gave the Spanish claim to all of them, early Spanish colonial efforts in the Pacific Islands centered almost exclusively in the Mariana Islands, particularly Guam. The remainder of TTPI—with the exception of modest Spanish outreach efforts into Yap and Ponape in the Carolines—was relatively unaffected by Spanish suzerainty.

The growth of whaling and copra interests in the Pacific during the nineteenth century subjected the Pacific Islands to the rivalries of Western powers. The islands' population, which some have estimated may have been 200,000 or more, was reduced sharply as a result of exposure to European diseases in the latter half of the nineteenth century. About the same time that Spain was succumbing to the United States the island of Guam, Spain sold its other Pacific islands to Germany for $4.5 million. The islands remained under German control only until World War I when they fell under Japanese sovereignty.

Japan had declared war against Germany in October 1914 and shortly after this captured the islands without any major resistance. At the

Peace Conference in Paris, Japan was awarded the islands as a class "C" mandate of the League of Nations. Under the League mandate, similar to the current UN trust territory category, Japan did not acquire the sovereign right over the territory but held it in trust under the supervision of the League of Nations. Unlike the terms of the current status, Article 4 of the mandate directed that "no military or naval bases shall be established or fortifications erected in the territory." Whether or not Japan fortified these islands prior to World War II has been much disputed.[1]

During the years of Japanese control, great agricultural development occurred. While opinions differ as to the negative or positive effects this foreign investment and development had on the islanders,* the fact remains that the Japanese turned the islands into a net exporter of agricultural commodities. Much of this agricultural activity centered in the Saipan district which, while only half the size of Guam, registered agricultural exports valued at four times that of the United States territory.

During World War II the strategic value of the islands became increasingly important; and in the minds of the United States strategists, the islands were viewed as essential to American security and peace in the Pacific. In November 1943 the meeting among President Roosevelt, Churchill, and Chiang Kai-shek concluded that "Japan shall be stripped of all the islands of the Pacific which she seized or occupied since the beginning of the First World War in 1914."[2]

At the conclusion of the war many in the United States government urged outright annexation although there were a few who rejected further colonial relations, urging instead that the islands' status be decided by the United Nations.[3] In response to various international pressures against outright territorial acquisitions and fear of Soviet territorial ambitions elsewhere in the world, the United States acquired the Pacific Islands as a strategic trust territory, a unique UN relationship. (The United Nations established ten other trust territories but no other was a strategic trust.)

This strategic trust territory status, as distinguished from the more customary trust relationship, allowed the United States to establish military bases, station troops in the territory, control fully the admin-

---

*Only one writer has personally visited Micronesia during both the Japanese and United States administrations and attempted a comparison: Willard Price, America's Paradise Lost (New York: John Day, 1966). Price notes that per-capita income of Micronesia in 1964 was only one-fifth of what it was at its Japanese peak. Although he is highly critical of U.S. economic effort, his comparison between the United States and Japan is that the United States is "better and worse."

istration of the islands, and report not to the General Assembly, but to the Security Council, where the United States retained veto power. Further, the United States as administering authority could prohibit UN supervision in any areas specified as "closed for security reasons."[4] In return, the United States agreed to promote the economic self-sufficiency of the territory, encourage agriculture, industry, and education, and promote the "development" of the inhabitants of the trust territory towards self-government or independence as might be appropriate to the freely expressed wishes of the peoples.[5] In sum, the United States assumed that it could accommodate its national security interests with its obligations to the Micronesians to help them achieve economic and social betterment and full self-determination.

UNITED STATES ADMINISTRATION

Since the trusteeship agreement gave the United States "full powers of administration, legislation, and jurisdiction over the territory," the United States could establish its own precedents and governing structure for the territory.[6] While the United States was responsible for the promotion of self-government, there was no UN guideline which directed how this would be carried out or how soon the islanders would be brought into the political process. Quite naturally, perhaps, the United States followed its own colonial administration precedents; most notably, that of Guam. And although the Appellate Division of the High Court of the Trust Territory tried to dignify the territory as "quasi"-sovereign, TTPI seems to have no status in American law except that of an occupied territory.[7]

The islands were initially governed by naval orders and proclamations. When civil administration was established in 1947, the Department of the Navy continued to be the governing agency;[8] and thus the form of central authority changed very little. Admiral Louis E. Denfield, serving as high commissioner, continued the pattern of issuing regulations to serve as legislation for the territory; and when the responsibility for civil administration was transferred to the Department of the Interior in 1951,[9] the high commissioner continued the practice of legislating by executive decree.

Organic act legislation which would have established various legislative, executive, and judicial offices, while proposed at various times,[10] was never enacted by the Congress of the United States. During the entire period when the Trust Territory was under United States administration, the Congress of the United States has allowed the president of the United States to delegate all executive, legislative, and judicial functions to whatever agencies he deemed fit.[11] Even after the president vested governmental functions with the Department of the Interior in 1951, military concerns for the Marianas after the

Korean War led to the reinstatement of naval control in Saipan and Tinian in 1952[12] and the remainder of the Northern Marianas, except Rota, likewise reverted to naval control in 1953.[13] Not until 1962 did the president once again transfer control of these islands to the Department of the Interior.[14]

Thus, during most of the years of administration by the United States, the Trust Territory has been governed by the plenary powers of the secretary of the interior or the Navy Department. Under the present political structure, which calls for the appointment of the high commissioner by the president of the United States with the advice and consent of the Senate,[15] the secretary of the interior still retains ultimately all legislative, executive, and judicial power over the territory.[16] Federal programs can be extended to the territory only if the secretary gives approval.

The secretary, until recent years, generally found it appropriate to delegate his plenary administering powers to the high commissioner. While the high commissioner periodically held territorial-wide conferences with islanders to discuss current issues, no legislative power was delegated to a body of elected TTPI representatives until the establishment of the Congress of Micronesia in 1965.[17]

This was a significant although limited breakthrough. The legislative power of the Congress of Micronesia extends to "all rightful subjects of legislation."[18] The language, which is standard in most United States organic acts, is perhaps somewhat broader than that of the legislative power set forth in the Guam organic act, which is limited to "all subjects of local application."[19] The limitation found in the language may restrict the legislative authority where the legislation has extraterritorial effects or does not "grow out of the needs of the Island." Further, the Congress of Micronesia cannot enact laws which are inconsistent with executive orders of the president of the United States, orders of the secretary of the interior, treaties or international agreements of the United States, laws of the United States applicable to the Trust Territory, or the "bill of rights" sections of the code of the Trust Territory promulgated by the secretary.[20] This last is something of a sore point. The first section of the Trust Territory code was explicit in requiring a separation of church and state. Prohibiting the Congress of Micronesia from amending the bill of rights upset a number of the Micronesian leaders who wished governmental support of religious institutions.[21]

The secretary's order establishing the present political structure also prohibits the Congress of Micronesia from taxing any property of the United States or taxing the property of nonresidents at a higher rate than that of residents.[22] Further, any legislation which is passed by the Congress of Micronesia can be vetoed by the high commissioner.[23] If the Micronesian Congress then overrides this veto by two-thirds and the high commissioner again refuses to approve the legislation, the U.S. secretary of the interior can still disapprove the bill and prevent any enactment.[24]

All executive authority over the Trust Territory is vested with the high commissioner. This includes both executive authority over the internal government of the Trust Territory and the responsibility for carrying out the international obligations undertaken by the United States.[25] In addition, the high commissioner alone determines how moneys appropriated by the United States are to be spent in the territory. The original Department of the Interior draft of the Congress of Micronesia's legislation gave the Congress a formal review function over the high commissioner's budget, but the legislation which passed did not go that far. The budget is presented to the Congress in a joint session with no required action by that body.[26]

The Congress of Micronesia has legislative authority only over those moneys raised within the territory.[27] In recent years this has been approximately 5 percent of the territorial budget. Thus, if the Congress of Micronesia enacts legislation requiring substantial funds for implementation, the high commissioner's concurrence is needed.

Judicial authority has been delegated to a High Court, the chief justice and associate justices of which are appointed by the U.S. secretary of the interior.[28] To insure greater independence from the executive and legislative branches, although no greater responsiveness to local concerns, the chief justice submits his own budgetary requests to the secretary of the interior.

Political development within the Trust Territory during the years of United States administration, considered by some to be exemplary,[29] is certainly the area within which American administrators take pride for having "scored their greatest success."[30] U.S. policy has been to build the TTPI government from the bottom up. Beginning in 1947, the United States began to regularize local municipal government so as to begin the orderly political development of the territory. Municipal government was institutionalized and elections were held to replace the hereditary chiefs. Often such revision was accepted without enthusiasm, as many preferred their own system of government. At the same time, district governments were being established. Palau established the first regional legislative body in 1947 and in 1949 an all-Marshall conference was held. The Northern Marianas formed a governing body for that district in 1950. After periodic territorial-wide conferences had been held, the Council of Micronesia was formed in 1961. Finally, in 1965, the Congress of Micronesia was established.[31]

Nevertheless, even sympathetic commentators consider the overall quality of the United States administration as at best mediocre. "Whatever the cause, the certainty is that the United States has not, at any point since its association with the Trust Territory began in World War II, governed it admirably."[32] The cause of this is clear. The military role overwhelmed all others; and since land was scarce, its use and control not only involved major conflict in principle which exacerbated matters but also caused relatively little energy to be directed toward the nonmilitary area.

The U.S. priorities—the lack of balance—did not go unnoticed by the Micronesians:

> . . . the [Micronesia] Coalition realizes that America is sincere in its expressed interest in the people of Micronesia themselves and their long-term welfare and that the United States, as administering authority, has certain moral and legal obligations to Micronesia. However, behind these generous intentions we know there lies America's overriding, strategic interest in Micronesia. If this were not true, then how is one to explain the millions of dollars spent by the United States testing nuclear bombs at Bikini and Eniwetok and missiles in Kwajalein Atoll. And, further, how is one to explain the United States Central Intelligence Agency training complex built on Saipan in the late 1950's at a cost of $30 million when the total Trust Territory budget hovered around $5 million annually. As I said, the paramount nature of America's strategic interest in Micronesia has been recognized by the Coalition . . .[33]

Further, United States officials were not particularly subtle. In late 1968 and early 1969 inspection teams from all branches of the United States military service toured the six administrative districts. The assistant marine corps commandant, who visited several districts around this time, found many of the islands exceptionally suitable for military use. By the time he got to the Palau District, he indicated that he regarded Palau as a possible additional marine training site and the island of Rota, in the Marianas, as suitable for practicing assault tactics for establishing a beachhead.

The Palau Legislature, on the assistant commandant's departure, adopted a resolution recalling the destruction of World War II and rejecting any projected U.S. military presence. Matters rapidly reached a head. The Department of the Interior took steps for military acquisition of land, the Micronesian Congress passed a law giving Micronesia a greater determination in the use of land taken by eminent domain, the high commissioner vetoed the bill without explanation, the Peace Corps volunteers petitioned the high commissioner for reconsideration, and a major brouhaha resulted in a case where negotiation perhaps would have been possible.[34]

On key islands such as Saipan, more than 50 percent of the land was set aside for use by the military. The military attitude kept out the foreign investor, a policy which was specifically criticized by the United Nations.

> The Mission hopes for a change in this general policy towards foreign private capital, as it considers that along with investments of internal capital and development

projects to be undertaken by the Government, the investment
of foreign capital in selected projects may have much to offer
the Territory by way of advancing its economy.[35]

But it was the psychological impact of the military role which was
to be the most offensive and also the most difficult to handle. Critics
of the military's presence in TTPI base their reasoning on past experience under both Japanese and American control. The activities of
World War II, including the prewar occupation by the Japanese and the
United States taking of the islands, brought great destruction to the
Pacific Islands. The United States negotiated the settlement of war
damage claims against Japan for damages sustained by the islanders
during the war, and in 1969 the Japanese agreed to make a payment in
commodities and services equivalent to $5 million for the islanders'
welfare. A similar amount would be paid by the United States.[36] Many
within the TTPI consider this $10 million figure inadequate and are
especially disturbed because of the limited amount of input they had
in the negotiations. Also, the settlement conceded to the Japanese
the right to open two ports in the Trust Territory.

Complaints against American military activities in Micronesia
under United States administration include the failure to disable live
bombs remaining on the islands after World War II and the use of
Bikini Atoll for hydrogen bomb tests (which necessitated the forced
movement of territorial inhabitants off their island and were accompanied by questionable precautions to protect the islanders from
radioactive fallout). Speculations on future military use of the TTPI
include fears that H-bomb and/or toxic gas storage facilities will be
built in the islands, particularly on Babelthaup.

By 1961 the military priority accorded the islands was becoming
an embarrassment. Except for New Guinea and Nauru, all of the
trusteeships were ended. The economy of the islands was worsening,
partly due to the population boom which increased the population from
54,843 in 1950 to 75,836 in 1960 (with a population distribution which
made matters worse); and partly to the absence of concern with development of what economic potential the islands had.

Unlike the Japanese, who aggressively developed the agricultural
potential of the islands,[37] the United States has not taken a great
interest in developing self-sufficiency in the Trust Territory as a
whole. Much of the economy and infrastructure of the islands which
was destroyed during the war was not rebuilt because of the financial
costs. The UN Visiting Mission in 1961 noted that economic development of the territory would entail heavy infrastructure outlays by the
administering authority.[38] Such heavy expenditures were not forthcoming from the United States. Appropriations for the trust territory
were small during the 1950s and most of this was absorbed as part of
the operational administrative costs and not as capital improvements.

In 1963 the United States began to become more interested in the economic issues. This resulted partly from the above-mentioned criticism and partly as a result of the recommendations of the Solomon Report, the survey mission established in May 1963 to "make recommendations leading to the formulation of programs and policies for an accelerated rate of development." The goal was to obtain a long-term relationship "so that the people may make an informed and full choice as to their future in accordance with U.S. responsibilities under the Trusteeship Agreement." The headquarters of the territory were moved from Hawaii to Guam and then to Saipan. The annual appropriation for Micronesia, which ranged between $4 and $6 million between 1952 and 1962, shot up to $15 million and increased rapidly after that to $25 million in 1967, $35 million the following year, and $50 million in 1970.

Initially the funds were utilized for education and social concerns so that the economy continued to founder. The 1967 UN Visiting Mission expressed the opinion that

> [the] economy is virtually stagnant. Agricultural development is hampered by the lack of an efficient system of marketing and of adequate extension services. The fishing industry lacks certain essential facilities such as boats, docks, ice plants and cold storage installation. Indigenous small industries and handicrafts receive little help in their development . . . the need for a vigorous programme of economic development cannot be overstressed.[39]

The great dependence on financial grants was deemed the principal dilemma of the islanders by the 1970 UN Visiting Mission. The United States contribution to the territorial budget for 1968 amounted to 95 percent of all funds and the Visiting Mission saw no signs of

> significant progress in the economy of the Territory as a whole. In particular, the basic infrastructure is still in a lamentable state, agriculture is stagnant and seems to be threatened by the movement of population to the towns, the adverse trade balance is increasing and, apparently, some pressure is beginning to be felt on prices.[40]

Many of the economic difficulties of the territory stem from the great distances between islands, which make communication and transportation among the islands extremely difficult and costly. It is estimated that roughly one-fourth of all United States federal funds spent on administration of the territory during the 1950s was expended solely to keep airplanes and vessels moving within the islands to carry goods and persons.[41] The geographic isolation of the islands,

TRUST TERRITORY NEGOTIATIONS

Mounting UN pressure for the United States to expedite its responsibility to promote the progressive development of Micronesia toward self-government or independence, plus a petition from the islanders to President Johnson in 1966 to establish a joint status commission to study political alternatives open to Micronesia, led President Johnson to ask the Congress in August 1967 to select a presidential commission to consider future status for the Trust Territory. When the U.S. Congress did not act on the president's proposal, the Congress of Micronesia established its own status commission. This was a key step. From this point on the initiative passed to the territory, where it was to remain.

The Micronesian Future Political Status Commission went about its business very carefully, without the sense of urgency that one might have thought likely under the circumstances. First it prepared an interim report in 1967 after exploring a variety of political possibilities, including joining a polity other than the United States and associating with other island territories. It noted four broad options: (1) independence; (2) a "free associated state" or protectorate status; (3) integration in some form of relationship with a sovereign nation, most probably the United States; and (4) remaining a trust territory. Its conclusion was that a substantial amount of research remained to be done before the territorial populace would be in a position to make an informed choice regarding its various political options. The interim report did, however, find the following:

1. Expansion of Micronesia geographically was out of the question, except for possible integration with Guam.
2. "Fragmentation" of the Trust Territory was also not a valid consideration and was against the public policy of both the United States and the United Nations.
3. Whatever status eventually chosen, prime consideration would be given to the sources of funding of governmental and development programs and control over the Islands' economy.

In September 1969 the United States and the Congress of Micronesia's Joint Committee on Future Status began their status negotiations in Washington, D.C. The Micronesians presented 11 topics for discussion and the United States agreed to all except the one relating to land, where it had been proposed that the Micronesians will be assured that there will be no confiscation of their land, and no military bases will be established in the islands without full consultation and consent of the government of Micronesia and fair compensation; that land currently held, controlled or possessed by the United States under lease or other arrangements will be renegotiated.[42]

The economic-military conflict over land utilization had been exposed immediately.

The talks continued through 1969 and into the following year. In May 1970, the United States proposed a draft agreement which offered TTPI representatives a status similar to that of the Commonwealth of Puerto Rico. This was rejected by the TTPI delegation as falling below the minimum acceptable standards of self-government.

On 14 August 1970 the Congress of Micronesia adopted House Joint Resolution No. 87, which directed the following:

1. Sovereignty in Micronesia resides in the people of Micronesia and their duly constituted government.
2. The people of Micronesia possess the right of self-determination and may therefore choose independence or self-government in free association with any nation or organization of nations.
3. The people of Micronesia have the right to adopt their own constitution and to amend, change, or revoke any constitution or governmental plan at any time.
4. Free association should be in the form of a revocable compact, terminable unilaterally by either party.

These principles looked to powers not present in the Commonwealth of Puerto Rico, and specifically item 4 incorporated the unilateral option first initiated in the New Zealand-Cook Islands association. The corollary of sovereignty listed in item 1 (control over eminent domain, immigration, and military activities) also went far beyond the powers of the commonwealth status enjoyed by Puerto Rico.

In order to help ease the developing impasse in the status negotiations between the United States and TTPI, in March 1971 President Nixon appointed Franklin Haydn Williams as his own personal representative, with the rank of ambassador, for the purpose of negotiating the future political status with the Trust Territory.

The third round of status talks took place in Hawaii in October 1971. This session saw increased interest in independence among members of the TTPI delegation. In response, the United States, to the surprise of many, was very forthcoming. It gave precise figures on the amount of lands in TTPI (except for the Marianas Islands) then reserved or used for military purposes by American forces, and precise future projections of United States defense needs in the islands. This

TRUST TERRITORY   79

specification of future military needs marked a significant departure
from the consistent withholding of projected United States defense and
security requirements. The result was that the negotiating parties
reached tentative agreement on the amount of land which the United
States would require and in which specific lands and waters of TTPI
these rights would be exercised:

(a) Pursuant to Sections 302 and 303 of the Compact, the
parties agree that the rights and uses of the United States
in the lands and waters of Micronesia include:

   (1) <u>Marshall Islands</u>
       a) Within the Kwajalein Atoll, continuing rights for
          the use of those lands and waters associated with
          and currently controlled as part of the Kwajalein
          Missile Range, the land portion of which encom-
          passes approximately 1,320 acres.
       b) In the Bikini Atoll, continuing rights for use of
          1.91 acres of Ourukaen and Eniman islets, and to
          use the pier, airfield and boat landing on Eneu
          Islands.
       c) In the Eniwetok Atoll, retention of such use rights
          as may be negotiated, upon return of the atoll.
   (2) <u>Palau Islands</u>
       a) Access and anchorage rights in Malakal harbor
          and adjacent waters, together with rights to
          acquire 40 acres for use within the Malakal harbor
          area, composed of submerged land to be filled and
          adjacent fast land.
       b) Rights for the joint use of an airfield capable of
          supporting military jet aircraft (the proposed airfield
          at Garreru Island reef, or Babelthuap airfield/
          Airai site), the right to improve that airfield to
          meet military requirements and specifications and
          the right to develop an exclusive use area for air-
          craft parking, maintenance and operational support
          facilities.
       c) On the island of Babelthuap the right to acquire
          2,000 acres for exclusive use, along with the right
          for non-exclusive use of an adjacent area encom-
          passing 30,000 acres, for intermittent ground force
          training and maneuvers.
   (3) Continuing rights to occasional or emergency use of
       all harbors, waters and airfields throughout Micronesia.
   (4) Agreements for lands and waters specified in paragraph
       (a) above are listed below. All agreements for the use
       of lands and waters concluded after the effective date

of this Compact, and all modifications to any agreement under this Title, shall conform to the provisions of this Compact and shall be listed in this Annex.[43]

In other respects, however, the United States military role was conceived as quite far-reaching. Under this tentative agreement the United States would acquire responsibility for and authority over all matters which relate to defense in Micronesia. It would be able to conduct all activities and operations necessary for the exercise of its authority in order to prevent third parties from using the territory for military purposes. Finally, it would use its military bases in Micronesia to support its responsibilities for the maintenance of international peace and security.[44]

On the key point of future land acquisition there was lack of clarity. Should the United States government require additional land for military use in TTPI, the government of TTPI agreed to establish suitable procedures to provide prompt response to such requests and to negotiate in "good faith" to achieve agreement on reasonable terms.[45]

While the status talks in the fall of 1971 brought out further inclinations toward independence for TTPI, the Marianas District broke with their fellow islanders and expressed a desire for a close and permanent political association with the United States. During the fourth round of the TTPI status negotiations in Koror, Palau in April 1972, the representatives of the Marianas officially requested separate status negotiations with the United States.

In December 1972 Ambassador Williams recognized and met with the Marianas Future Political Status Commission to initiate separate talks. The United States then embarked on parallel sets of negotiations, those with the five remaining districts (Micronesia) moving towards some sort of loose "associated state" status and those with the Marianas moving towards a closer "commonwealth" relationship. The Congress of Micronesia did not recognize these separate talks, going so far as to initiate a lawsuit to prevent them. The United Nations also opposed the separate U.S.-Marianas discussions. It had consistently been against division of colonial entities along regional, tribal, or ethnic lines; and, as far back as 1963 when the headquarters of the Trust Territory had been moved to Saipan, had warned of the dangers of fragmentation.

MICRONESIAN NEGOTIATIONS

Rather than presenting a United States blueprint for the future political status of the Trust Territory, the United States delegation headed by Ambassador Franklin Haydn Williams sought to concentrate on specific issues important to the island delegation. This approach was based on the United States assumption that both delegations had pretty much agreed on a general political status of "associated state" for TTPI. These specific issues centered on control over laws applicable to the new associated state control over land, and control over any future change in status. At the same time, the United States set forth its own interests in the Trust Territory against which it would test any future agreement: (1) the United States' general concern for the long-term welfare of the peoples of the islands; (2) the United States' legal and moral obligations as the administering authority under the UN agreement; and (3) the United States' larger Pacific role and other commitments with respect to the peace and stability of the Pacific.[46]

Before the negotiations of the sixth round held in Hawaii in September 1972, the Congress of Micronesia adopted Senate Joint Resolution No. 117, which directed the Joint Committee on Future Status to conduct negotiations with the United States regarding the establishment of TTPI as an independent nation, while continuing negotiations toward free association. This two-pronged approach did not go down well with the United States delegation, which believed that "it will be somewhat more difficult for the United States to consider the status negotiations under that format."[47] Ambassador Williams was more explicit about the unwillingness of the United States to consider independence.

> I cannot imagine, for instance, that my Government would agree to termination of the trusteeship on terms which would in any way threaten stability in the area and which would in the opinion of the United States endanger international peace and security.[48]

The TTPI delegation asked again for details of United States land requirements in the Marianas, which had not yet been forthcoming:

> We have asked, and ask again, that the United States provide to our subcommittee on land the details of its requirements in the Marianas. As you are aware, the mandate received by this Committee from the Congress of Micronesia requires that our consideration and negotiations encompass the entire Trust Territory and not only five out of the six districts. The unilateral action of the United States in accepting separate negotiations with the Marianas does not, obviously, relieve this Committee from the obligations with which the Congress has entrusted us.[49]

To a degree this represented the unwillingness of the island Congress to recognize the separate Marianas negotiation. But there were other issues as well, including financial support by the United States, the power of eminent domain by the military and the power of termination.

The TTPI delegation stressed the urgency of completing the draft compact of free association which was tentatively adopted in very rough form in July 1972. The islanders threatened that unless a draft compact of free association were completed promptly, the pressures of the status of independence might become "irresistible."[50] However, the elections held in TTPI in the fall of 1972 weakened the independence movement, since the leader of the independence coalition was very badly defeated.[51] Thus, when the seventh round of negotiations finally resumed in Washington, D.C. in November 1973, the negotiations toward a compact of free association continued.

The primary reason for the great length of time between the sixth and seventh negotiation sessions was the fact that the TTPI delegation had preconditioned the resumption of the talks upon the return of "public lands" in the islands to their rightful owners. Over the years, under Spanish, German, Japanese, and finally United States administration, much of the land of the Trust Territory had been acquired by the administering authority. With land a premium item in the Trust Territory and only a small proportion of these public lands being used for any public purpose, the islanders urged the United States to return control to the local districts or traditional leaders before any ultimate political status could be decided. Calculations showed that over 60 percent of the Territory's land was being held by the administering authority, with the district breakdown being Palau, 68 percent; Yap, 4 percent; Truk, 17 percent; Ponape, 66 percent; Marshall Islands, 13 percent; and Mariana Islands, 90 percent.[52] The land included tidelands, marine lands, and property seized from the Japanese at the end of World War II.

The United States agreed to transfer title to the district governments and their people as soon as the Congress of Micronesia passed enabling legislation to properly safeguard legitimate interests.[53] All land currently in active use by the trust administration would be retained as well as those lands specifically identified as needed for capital improvement projects covering the next five years. Any leases or homestead agreements entered into by the trust administration would remain in effect and any public land planned to be used to meet United States defense needs under the terms of the proposed status arrangements would pass with an interest retained by the United States or administering authority. The Trust Territory government also retained the right to control activities in the tidelands, filled lands, submerged lands, and lagoons, although "title" would be held by the district governments. The Trust Administration would retain the power of eminent domain to acquire lands to meet subsequent needs if negotiations with property titleholders should fail in the future. All other surplus land would be turned over to the district governments to be held in trust for the people of the districts. The districts could then dispose of the land by traditional means: leasing, homesteading programs, or any other method locally determined.

TRUST TERRITORY 83

The Micronesian delegation found this commitment adequate enough to at least allow resumption of status negotiations, but argued that the United States power of eminent domain should be severely curtailed; that agreement to the lease of lands to the United States military could not be a precondition to the return of title to public lands; and that possession of all land leased to the military which was not currently being used should be terminated immediately. Leases made by the Trust Territory government should be kept in force only if leased for public purposes and all negotiations for military land requirements must be made through the Congress of Micronesia and not solely with a landowner.

In addition, the islanders asked for special representation at the Law of the Sea Conference and put forward a claim to the exclusive control of the 3,000 miles of water within the islands area based on the extension of the archipelagic theory of territorial waters. In a well-written legal brief prepared by Micronesian attorneys, the Micronesian delegation relied on the <u>Norwegian Fisheries</u> case decided by the International Court of Justice which held that the sea between the islands off the coast of Norway and Norway itself was territorial waters and belonged to Norway. The delegation argued that a similar rationale meant that the 3,000 miles connecting the various islands were not open sea but belonged to the Trust Territory, a result which unfortunately proved too great a request to be taken seriously.

Negotiations on the associated state status continued; and in July 1974 a tentative agreement was made between the United States and the Joint Committee on Future Status of the Congress of Micronesia. While many issues were still left open by the draft compact, if approved by the people of the Caroline and Marshall Islands in a free plebiscite and by the Congress of the United States, the compact would establish a new political relationship with the United States and terminate the trusteeship agreement between the United States and the United Nations. This new status relationship would be one of free association. We shall analyze this association, although there has been no approval of the compact in Micronesia as of this writing, and negotiations have been stalled.

Political Relations

Military Presence and Foreign Affairs

Under the proposed compact the United States would retain full power over the "foreign affairs" and "defense" of Micronesia. The United States would be able to make and extend treaty provisions to Micronesia unilaterally unless the treaty related "exclusively or predominantly to Micronesia," in which case it would have to be consented to by the government of Micronesia.

The United States would have the authority to prevent third parties from entering Micronesia for military purposes and could establish its own military bases within the islands. The United States would have specific control over designated lands for military use and the government of Micronesia would agree to establish prompt procedures by which further military needs could be fulfilled by good-faith negotiations. Should either party ever wish to properly terminate the relationship, the United States would have the right to good-faith negotiations for concluding a security agreement which will keep intact all United States military land and use rights in Micronesia.

Micronesians would be able to volunteer for United States military service, but would not be subject to any involuntary induction into the armed forces of the United States. The United States would also extend diplomatic protection to Micronesians traveling outside the United States and Micronesia.

The Compact

The government and people of Micronesia would have the full right to establish and alter their own constitution and their political institutions as long as these amendments are consistent with the compact. (This parallels the Puerto Rican language.) However, unlike Puerto Rico, no provisions are made which would establish representation for Micronesia in the United States Congress. The government of Micronesia would have full authority over all "internal affairs" of Micronesia.

Before the compact can go into effect, it must be approved by the United States "in accordance with its constitutional processes." The most that this will require is the majority vote of both houses of the United States Congress and the signature of the president of the United States. The compact will be considered approved by the people of Micronesia if a majority of at least 55 percent of those people voting support the compact. Further, the compact will not take effect in any district of Micronesia where two-thirds of the people vote against it. Such a district, such as the Marianas, will be given "an immediate opportunity to negotiate with the United States with respect to that district's future political status."

The approval process envisions legislative approval by the United States and a direct plebiscite in the islands, a distinction of some validity given the respective size of the two entities and the relative importance of the issue to the area's inhabitants. But the process also envisioned, indeed expected, the rejection by the Marianas and fragmentation of the Territory.

Immigration

Micronesia would be able to control immigration of persons not citizens of Micronesia. It would agree to allow citizens and nationals of the United States free entry, but not the right to establish residence in Micronesia without the consent of the government of Micronesia.

Micronesia's International Presence

The government of Micronesia would be allowed to join the United Nations' specialized agencies and establish representation of Micronesian trade or commercial interests in foreign countries as long as they did not conflict with United States international commitments. However, the United States would retain full control over foreign consulates being established in Micronesia and could prevent Micronesian international memberships which conflicted with United States international commitments.

Citizenship

Generally, all persons who are now citizens of Micronesia would become nationals, not citizens, of the United States upon adoption of the compact. The reason for this is that American Samoa is the one island territory which controls immigration and restricts land ownership to Samoans. The fact that Samoans are nationals rather than citizens has been mentioned as a justification for what otherwise would be regarded as an unconstitutional discrimination against other U.S. citizens. It is doubtful whether the distinction is what legally permits these actions, but the U.S. Congress appears to regard it so; hence the Micronesian position.

The compact would allow Micronesians, as nationals, free entry into and exit from the United States, but they would be unable to establish residence in the "territories and possessions" of the United States except with the consent of the United States. It appears that this term "territories and possessions" of the United States is used in its most precise sense and would not prevent free emigration of Micronesians to the fifty states of the United States. Only a Micronesian wishing to emigrate to Guam, the Virgin Islands, American Samoa, or some other territory or possession would need the consent of the United States government. Persons now living in Micronesia wishing to preserve island citizenship or acquire foreign citizenship would be able to do so and would not become nationals of the United States.

Economic Aspects of the Relationship

Taxation

United States federal property and personnel engaged in administering federal programs in Micronesia would be exempt from taxation by the Micronesian government and Micronesia would agree to protect the property, personnel, and information of United States government programs in Micronesia.

Tariffs and Trade

Micronesia would be able to control import duties. Both Micronesia and the United States would agree to accord products of the other no less favorable treatment than like products of any other foreign country. Also, under the "most favored nation" trading arrangement, United States citizens would be accorded the same trading privileges as any other foreign government.

Federal Financial Assistance

The proposed compact itself specifies the level of funds which would be supplied by the United States during the first 15 years of the compact.* In addition, the president's personal representative announced that during the transition period before the compact became effective, the United States would provide to the Trust Territory continuing financial support in the amount and on the terms which follow:

a. There are two transition stages. The first stage covers that time needed to approve the compact by plebiscite and to draft and adopt

---

*The level of appropriations authorized by the U.S. Congress for the Trust Territory has risen eight-fold since the early 1960s. The appropriations ceiling began at $7.5 million in 1954 (Act of 30 June 1954, c. 423, §1, 68 Stat. 330). This was raised to $15 million for 1963 and $17.5 million for fiscal years thereafter (Act of 19 July 1962, P.L. 87-541, 76 Stat. 171). By successive steps the level was raised again to $25 million for 1967, $35 million for 1968 and 1969, and $50 million for 1970 (Acts of 10 May 1967, P.L. 90-16, §1, 81 Stat. 15 and 21 October 1968, P.L. 90-617, 82 Stat. 1213). Further, legislation raised the level to $60 million for years 1971, 1972, and 1973 (Act of 24 December 1970, P.L. 91-578, 84 Stat. 1559) and to $60 million plus up to an additional $10 million to offset reduction in or the termination of federal grant-in-aid programs or other funds made available to the Trust Territory by other federal agencies for years 1974 and 1975 (Act of 21 September 1973, P.L. 93-111, §1, 87 Stat. 354).

by popular referendum a constitution for Micronesia. This is expected to take until about the end of fiscal year 1976. The second stage is to commence at the beginning of the first fiscal year following the end of Stage I and will end with the effective date of the compact. By the wording of the compact, this will not occur until the president issues a proclamation announcing a date mutually acceptable to the government of the United States and Micronesia. During this period, Micronesia will move toward full internal self-government under its own constitution in preparation of termination of the trusteeship agreement. It is expected that Stage II will begin in fiscal year 1977 and end in fiscal year 1980.

    b. The projected amounts cover either the present six districts of Micronesia as a whole or Micronesia sans the Marianas in case the Marianas District negotiates a separate status or administration of that district.

    c. The amounts shown will be adjusted annually to reflect changes in the value of the dollar as determined by the official United States consumer price index (or the Guam retail price index).

    d. The United States agrees to provide both annual funding for government operations and funding for capital improvement programs.

The projected breakdown is as shown in Table 1.

TABLE 1

Proposed U.S. Financial Support of Micronesia, 1976-80
(millions of dollars)

Fiscal Year	Government Operations		Capital Improvement Programs		Total	
	With Marianas	Without Marianas	With Marianas	Without Marianas	With Marianas	Without Marianas
Stage I						
1976	55	48	25	22	80	70
Stage II						
1977	54	47	30*	26*	84	73
1978	52	46	35	30	87	76
1979	50	44	20*	18*	70	62
1980	45	39	15	14	60	53

*In the event Stage I is delayed to fiscal year 1978, these figures for capital improvements will be averaged; that is, either $25 million (with the Marianas) or $22 million (without the Marianas) for both fiscal year 1977 and fiscal year 1979.

The United States has tentatively agreed to provide the following once the compact becomes effective:

1. The United States shall provide without compensation the services of:
   (a) U.S. Postal Service
   (b) U.S. Weather Service
   (c) U.S. Federal Aviation Administration
   However, land needed for these purposes must be supplied at no cost to the United States government.
2. An annual grant shall be made of:
   (a) $35 million for the first five years
   (b) $30 million for the next five years
   (c) $25 million for the next five years thereafter.
3. Annual capital improvement grants shall be made of:
   (a) $12.5 million for the first five years
   (b) $11.0 million for the next five years
   (c) $ 9.5 million for the next five years thereafter.
4. The United States shall provide annual loans for the first 15 years of $5 million.
5. An amount not yet agreed upon shall be paid for the fair market value of the land and water areas used for military purposes.

These grants and loans are subject to change to reflect the change in purchasing power of the United States currency, and after five years the level of loans, grants, and support of the Postal Service, Weather Service, and FAA are subject to "review."

The United States has tentatively agreed to cover the costs of relocating the present capital to a new site as part of the Micronesian status agreement. The president's personal representative for Micronesian status negotiations has agreed, subject to the approval of Congress, that the United States will contribute an undetermined sum to the government of the Trust Territory to cover in part the costs of relocating the present capital to the new site in Micronesia to be chosen by the people of Micronesia.

Unresolved Issues

Many specific areas are either still left open to further negotiations between the two governments or are unclear and will necessitate interpretations of the compact provisions. A primary concern will be the interpretation placed upon those areas deemed to fall within either the "defense and foreign relations" responsibility of the United States or the "internal affairs" responsibility of the government of Micronesia. While the United States clearly retains final authority in these defense and foreign areas, it has agreed to "consult" with the government of Micronesia on matters of mutual concern.

This concept of consultation, agreement and good faith is the hallmark of the compact. The compact has made no provisions for judicial review of any conflicts arising out of the interpretation of the compact but instead specifically states that it does not subject either party to the courts of the other. All disputes arising over the interpretation are subject to "good faith negotiations."

Another area where interpretation may become crucial stems from the provision which allows the United States to negotiate and extend treaties without the consent of the government of Micronesia except where the treaty relates "exclusively or predominantly to Micronesia." Further, while it appears that the United States will lose its all encompassing power of eminent domain in the islands, the government of Micronesia has tentatively agreed to "establish suitable procedures to provide prompt response" to any request by the United States for additional land needed for military use. The parties will negotiate in "good faith to achieve on reasonable terms an agreement for the use of such areas."

Possibly more important is the provision which requires the government of Micronesia to negotiate in good faith and enter into a mutual security agreement should either government intend to terminate the compact at some later date. This assures the United States that its existing leases and rights in the lands and waters of the islands used for military purposes will remain in effect even if the compact should be terminated unilaterally by Micronesia.

A critical item still unresolved is the amount of compensation which Micronesia will receive from the United States for the use of lands in the islands for military purposes. Further, at five-year intervals beginning five years from the effective date of the compact, the level of loans, grants, and United States support for the Postal Service, Weather Service, and the Federal Aviation Administration "will be reviewed by the government of Micronesia and the government of the United States . . . and adjusted as appropriate taking into account changes in economic conditions."

Mutual agreement has not yet been reached on the legal status which United States military and civilian personnel engaged in federal programs will have in the islands; nor have the parties agreed to the particular procedures for periodic general audit of all grants, loans, and funds expended for federal service and programs.

Termination

Negotiations have foundered on the issue of termination. The Micronesians proposed that the compact could be terminated at any time by "mutual consent" of the government of Micronesia and the government of the United States. Presumably this would not necessitate a referendum or plebiscite on the question in Micronesia, although the government of Micronesia could certainly so provide.

In addition, after the first 15 years of the compact, which would be no sooner than 1995, the compact could be terminated unilaterally by either party. This provision, modelled after the Cook Islands constitution, was outside the U.S. territorial experience and the U.S. negotiators refused to countenance it. According to the Micronesian proposal, either party would have to furnish notice of such intention at least two years before termination could be effective. The United States could terminate merely by the same constitutional process needed for adoption, no more than approval and the House and Senate and the president of the United States. However, the people of Micronesia could terminate only if at least two-thirds of the people in two-thirds of the districts voted for termination. If we assume there would be only five districts in Micronesia, the requirement of two-thirds of the districts would effectively mean four-fifths. Thus, if two districts favored the status quo or did not disapprove by at least a two-to-one margin, the compact would remain in effect. Further, any district which voted two to one against termination would not be bound by the action of the rest of Micronesia and would be given the opportunity to negotiate its own future political status with the United States.

MARIANAS NEGOTIATIONS

The Trust Territory administered by the Department of the Navy was transferred to the Department of the Interior in 1951. Only the Marianas were returned to naval administration in successive transfers in the years of 1952 and 1953. (The single exception was the island of Rota, which was not returned to naval control and remained administratively isolated as the only island of the Marianas not under naval control.) Not until 1962 were these islands returned to the jurisdiction of the Department of the Interior and unified administration with the rest of Micronesia achieved.[54] United States strategists prize the military potential of the Marianas greater than that of any other district in the Trust Territory and, as noted above, have been hesitant to disclose future military projections in the Marianas—unlike plans for the other five districts—to the Micronesian Joint Committee. Further, United States holdings of "public lands" in the Marianas have been calculated at 90 percent, which is significantly higher than the average throughout the Trust Territory.[55] The location of the office of the high commissioner and the headquarters for the government of Micronesia on Saipan since 1962 has resulted in particularly heavy United States influence in the Marianas.

In the past the Marianas have expressed a desire for reunification with Guam, which geographically and ethnically is part of the Marianas chain. The people of Guam, however, rejected this idea in 1969. When the rest of Micronesia began moving toward a looser relationship of free association with the United States in the summer of 1970, the Marianas representatives asked for a different status arrangement for themselves. At first the United States rejected this request, saying that it was committed to discussions on a territory-wide basis.

Then, at the second regular session of the Fourth Congress of Micronesia, during January and February 1972, the territorial Independence Coalition grew to include half the membership in the Congress. In August of that year, the House and Senate of the Congress of Micronesia directed the Micronesian Status Committee to negotiate the possibility of establishing Micronesia as an independent nation.[56] In this climate, when the Marianas reaffirmed their request for a closer relationship and separate talks with the United States in April 1972, the United States responded affirmatively.

In response to this potential separation and loss of an "inestimable value to the Trust Territory," the Congress of Micronesia resolved that it was the only lawmaking body duly empowered to authorize a separate political future for the Mariana Islands District. The Congress of Micronesia offered to authorize such a separate political future for the Marianas on the promise of the United States to pay $200 million to the government of Micronesia.[57] Despite this action and considerable UN criticism because of fragmentation of the territory, the United States began the first round of status talks with the Marianas in December 1972. This session was characterized by warm expression from both sides in favor of a close and permanent affiliation between the United States and the Marianas.[58] During the second round of talks in the spring of 1973, the parties concentrated on particular issues such as the applicability of the U.S. Constitution and federal laws, national security considerations, representation in Washington, citizenship and nationality, features of a Marianas constitution, and the extent of self-government possible for the Marianas.[59] The fourth (May 1974) and fifth (December 1974) sessions formalized the details of the relationship, and the tentative covenant was signed by both sides in Saipan on 15 February 1975.

Political Relations

The Covenant

The parties have agreed that the political arrangement to be worked out would be that of "commonwealth," following the model of the Commonwealth of Puerto Rico, effective in the year 1981.

"Sovereignty" over the Marianas would be vested in the United States and the territorial clause of the U.S. Constitution would apply to the Marianas. Past interpretation of the territorial clause of the U.S. Constitution has given the U.S. Congress an almost unrestricted hand in legislating for the territories.[60] Because of its plenary powers, Congress may legislate for territories in purely local affairs and can also modify the organic legislation establishing the territorial government. In fact, Congress could dissolve and replace the territorial government if it so chose.

To meet this problem, at the third session of negotiations in December 1973 the parties tentatively agreed that the "fundamental" provisions of the status agreement cannot be amended or repealed except by the mutual consent of both parties. To this extent, United States authority in the Marianas would not be plenary. Once the status agreement has indicated the respective powers of the two governments, the U.S. Congress could not alter the relationship unilaterally, an explicit commitment in an area where Puerto Rico had at best only an implicit one.

The following are the "fundamental provisions" which may not be modified without the consent of the Marianas government:

1. The people of the Northern Mariana Islands have the right of local self-government with respect to internal affairs and will formulate a constitution which will provide for three branches of government, an elected governor, and a bill of rights.

2. The United States will have complete responsibility and authority over matters of "foreign affairs and defense."

3. The people of the Marianas will be granted U.S. citizenship, unless they take steps to preserve their foreign citizenship, and will be entitled to the same "privileges and immunities" of citizens in the several states.

4. Various U.S. constitutional guarantees—the Bill of Rights and personal protections of habeas corpus (generally those applicable to Guam under Section 5(u) of the organic act, 48 U.S.C. § 1421(u))—will apply to the Marianas as if it were a state.

5. The government of the Northern Mariana Islands may, for a period of 25 years after termination of the trusteeship agreement, restrict the acquisition of land to persons of only Northern Mariana Islands descent.

The "fundamental" provisions of the covenant will not be subject to unilateral termination or revocation by either party. The people of the Marianas are willing to enter into a binding, permanent relationship with the federal power, and have insisted on no clause such as the provision for unilateral termination after a 15-year period discussed in the course of the Micronesian negotiations.

Adoption of the status agreement will require the approval of the Marianas people in a plebiscite held as an act of self-determination. Ratification by the United States will involve the usual U.S. constitutional process of congressional approval in both the House and Senate. The new government of the Commonwealth of the Marianas will take office after a constitutional convention has been held to draft a local constitution, the constitution has been ratified by the people of the Marianas by another ballot, and new representatives have been elected pursuant to general election.

Any disputes arising out of the interpretation of the covenant will be reviewable in the federal courts.[61]

Participation in Political Process

Unlike citizens of a state, the people of the Marianas will have no vote in the election of the United States president and will not possess voting representation in the U.S. Congress. The United States delegation to the negotiating sessions has agreed to "support" a request by the Marianas for their own nonvoting delegate in the U.S. Congress.[62] The covenant leaves open the question of Washington representation, stating only that "the Northern Mariana Islands may provide for the appointment or election of a Resident Representative to the United States," a person outside the Congress, similar to the present Washington representative to American Samoa, rather than a representative, but with some congressional privileges as in the case of Puerto Rico and Guam.

General Applicability of Federal Law

As mentioned above, the covenant recognizes the sovereignty of the United States government over the Mariana Islands. Certain powers, such as the right to control immigration* and the power of eminent domain,† are generally considered inherent in sovereignty and the covenant does not alter this concept. There is, however, an attitude of greater cooperation and conciliation. For example, the immigration and nationality laws may be extended to the Northern Marianas to the

---

*"It is admitted that sovereign states have inherent power to deport aliens, and seemingly that Congress is not deprived of this power by the Constitution." Tiaco v. Forbes, 228 U.S. 549, 556 (1913).

†"The right of eminent domain inheres in the Federal Government by virtue of its sovereignty and thus it may, regardless of the wishes either of the owners or of the States, acquire the lands which it needs within their borders." James v. Dravo Contracting Co., 302 U.S. 134, 147 (1937).

"extent made applicable by the U.S. Congress . . . after termination of the Trusteeship Agreement" (Art. V, § 503) but until such action is taken, the brunt of the immigration laws will not apply. The same presumption of nonapplicability also includes the coastwise shipping laws (such as the Jones Act) and the minimum wage provisions of the Fair Labor Standards Act.

The covenant categorizes federal laws of general applicability and presumes that each either does or does not apply to the Marianas. Congress retains the power to unilaterally alter any of these presumptions and extend or retract coverage; but until such action is taken, the presumptions will be effective (that is, once Congress approves the covenant).

The following is a breakdown of various federal laws and their presumed applicability to the Marianas under the covenant:

Presumed to Apply to the Marianas
1. federal services and financial assistance: to the same extent as they apply to Guam
2. banking laws: to the same extent as they apply to Guam
3. Social Security Act:
   a. Section 228 of Title II (42 U.S.C. § 428)—benefits at age 72 for uninsured individuals who are residents of the United States: to the same extent as if the Marianas were a state. Currently, these benefits are not extended to Guam citizens, or to those of the Virgin Islands or Puerto Rico (see 42 U.S.C. § 428 [e]).
   b. Title XVI (42 U.S.C. § 1381 et seq.)—supplemental benefits for those over 65, blind, or disabled: to the same extent as if the Marianas were a state. Currently, these benefits are not extended to Puerto Rico or the Virgin Islands (see 42 U.S.C. § 1382 [e]).
   c. Social security laws now in effect in the Marianas will continue to apply and can only be modified so as not to create any additional differences between the social security laws of the Trust Territory and those of the United States which impose excise and self-employment taxes to support benefits: to the same extent as they apply to Guam.
4. Public Health Service Act (42 U.S.C. § 201 et seq.): to the same extent as it applies to the Virgin Islands. Guam, unlike Puerto Rico and the Virgin Islands, is not considered a state for all purposes of this act (see 42 U.S.C. § 201 [f]), yet is eligible for certain grants and services (see 42 U.S.C. § 246 [g] [4] [B]—grants and services to states, comprehensive health planning and services; and 42 U.S.C. § 291b—state allotments for construction and modernization of hospitals and other facilities).
5. Micronesian War Claims Act (50 App. § 2018 et seq.; see also the Agreement with Japan concerning the Trust Territory of the Pacific Islands, 18 April 1969, 20 U.S.T. 2654, T.I.A.S. No. 6724): to the same extent as it applies to the rest of Micronesia.

6. Those other laws which are applicable to Guam and are of "general application to the several states": to the extent they are applicable to the states.
7. The activities of the United States government and its contractors in the Marianas will be covered by the federal laws regarding coastal shipments and conditions of employment, including the wages and hours of employees.
8. Immigration and Nationality Act only to the extent it bestows U.S. citizenship upon residents of the Marianas and their relatives: to the same extent as applicable to the states.
9. The income tax laws: to the same extent and manner as applicable to Guam (that is, as a territorial income tax).
10. All bonds or other obligations issued by the Marianas government will be exempt from taxation by the United States, any state, or political subdivision.

Presumed Not to Apply to the Marianas
1. The remaining portions of the Immigration and Nationality Act, except as they apply under Item 8 above.
2. The coastwise laws (such as the Jones Act), except as they apply to the United States government and its contractors (Item 7 above).
3. Any prohibition in the laws of the United States against foreign vessels landing fish or unfinished fish products in the United States.
4. The minimum wage provisions of the Fair Labor Standards Act.
5. The Marianas will not be included in the customs territory of the United States, and may itself levy duties on goods imported into its territory from any area outside the United States. (However, this authority must be exercised in a manner consistent with the international obligations of the United States, including the General Agreement on Tariffs and Trade.)

After the covenant becomes effective, the president of the United States will appoint a Commission on Federal Laws to survey the laws of the United States and to make recommendations to the U.S. Congress as to which laws should apply to the Marianas. This is not unlike procedures used in Guam where a commission provided the same review and recommendations after passage of the 1950 organic act (Organic Act Sec. 25, 48 U.S.C. § 1421 [c]). The parallel is hardly comforting to the Marianas since in a number of key matters its recommendations had no effect.

Powers of the Government of the Marianas

The government of the Marianas is to exercise the "maximum amount of self-government"[63] consistent with the U.S. Constitution and federal law. Presumably, this would give the commonwealth powers as extensive as those of a state; and unlike those of a mere territory, these powers cannot be revoked by the U.S. Congress.

The covenant vests in the Marianas Legislature the powers over "all rightful subjects of legislation." This is the same wording used in most organic acts establishing territorial governments and has been found to be as extensive as the police powers of a state. Thus, the Virgin Islands Legislature's powers extend to "all rightful subjects of legislation,"^{64} while Guam's extends over "all subjects of local application."^{65}

Various provisions of the United States Constitution will restrict the full power of the Marianas government in legislating for the commonwealth just as the Constitution restricts the powers and actions of a state. Generally, these are the same restrictions now placed upon the government of Guam, under Section 5(a) of the organic act, to guarantee rights to its citizens. Notwithstanding these constitutional guarantees, the government of the Marianas has the right to restrict the acquisition of real property to persons of Northern Mariana Islands descent for 25 years after termination of the trusteeship agreement.

The extension of the privileges and immunities clause to the territory of Puerto Rico before commonwealth and to the territories of Guam and the Virgin Islands has been held to prevent taxation of nonresidents (statesiders) at a rate higher than residents and to guarantee to all United States citizens—including the corporations of any of the United States—rights of national citizenship when residing in or entering the territories. These include the right of appeal in proper cases to the national courts and the right of protection abroad.*

If the United States does not extend the immigration laws to the Marianas, then presumably the Marianas government could set barriers to the entrance of aliens. The constitutionality of such action would largely depend on congressional intent, since Congress can certainly delegate this power.

It is unlikely, however, that the commonwealth could create barriers to free entry by U.S. citizens. Since the commonwealth relationship is intended to bring the Marianas within United States sovereignty and vest self-government only so far as not inconsistent with the relevant portions of the U.S. Constitution, United States citizens could expect the rights to travel to, and engage in interstate and foreign commerce with, the commonwealth. Any power to restrict the entry of United

---

*In discussing the proposed extension of the privileges and immunities clause, the due process clause, and the equal protection clause of the U.S. Constitution to Guam, Harry R. Anderson, assistant secretary of the interior, noted that: "This will guarantee to all U.S. citizens in or entering Guam—including the corporations of any of the United States—rights of national citizenship such as the right to engage in interstate and foreign commerce, the right to appeal in proper cases to the national courts, and the right to protection abroad." H. Rpt. No. 1521, 90th Cong., 2d Sess. 14 (1968).

TRUST TERRITORY   97

States citizens would seemingly conflict with the rights of national citizenship.

Other restrictions on the power of the Marianas government will stem from its own constitution, which must be consistent with relevant provisions of the U.S. Constitution, the final covenant, and relevant federal laws.[66] The parties envision that the commonwealth constitution will contain a bill of rights, provide for a separation of powers, and provide for a popularly elected chief executive.[67] These are "fundamental" provisions of the covenant and cannot be altered by the people of the Marianas. Future amendment may be made by the people to their constitution, but such changes must be consistent with the covenant and relevant federal laws.

Rights of U.S. Citizens in the Marianas

Concern by the people of the Marianas over the alienability of their scarce lands has resulted in special provisions giving the people of Marianas ancestry special protection and rights to lands in the Marianas.* Since these rights can be established along blood lines, U.S. citizens coming to the Marianas will effectively stand in the same position as non-U.S. citizens and aliens. The amount and extent of lands which will be so protected is unclear. In other areas, extension of the privileges and immunities clause of the U.S. Constitution would guarantee U.S. citizens the rights of national citizenship in the new commonwealth: the right to engage in interstate and foreign commerce, the right to appeal in proper cases to the national courts, and others. Thus, except for limitations on land acquisitions, U.S. citizens would have the same rights in the Marianas as anywhere under United States sovereignty.

Rights of Citizens of the Marianas in the United States

Generally, all persons born in the Marianas prior to commonwealth will become U.S. citizens and be eligible for all the benefits of such citizenship, including free entry into the 50 states.[68] As citizens, they will presumably owe military service to their country if called.

---

*"The question of how to implement the prior agreement that the Marianas Government will have the authority to prohibit the alienation of land to persons not of Marianas descent was also referred to the Joint Drafting Committee. This Committee will consider as well limitations on the amount of public lands which might be made available to or held by any one individual." Joint Communique, Marianas Political Status Negotiations, 4th Sess. at 3.

Military Presence

Retention of "public lands" by the United States for military and administrative purposes, calculated at 90 percent of the total area,[69] was a crucial item during the negotiations. Like the Micronesian negotiators, the Marianas Political Status Commission expressed its general satisfaction with the United States policy statement of November 1973 on the return of public lands to the Marianas government.[70] Implementation of the policy statement will return surplus lands to district control with appropriate safeguards to allow the United States to retain rights over those lands currently being used by the trust administration, land identified as needed for capital improvement projects, and public land to be used for defense purposes.

Legislation to accomplish this goal has not been passed by the Congress of Micronesia and as of 1975 no lands have been returned in accordance with the policy statement. However, since both sides have tentatively resolved their disagreements, these lands may soon be returned by executive action.

Throughout the status negotiations the Marianas delegation resisted efforts by the United States to acquire land outright in the islands. Eventually, the United States agreed to a 50-year lease, with an option for another 50 years, of 18,118 acres (7,557 hectares) or about 15 percent of the total land area of the Marianas for defense purposes. The negotiations tried to reconcile the possible need for further U.S. military landholdings and the United States' power of eminent domain with the desirability of keeping as much land as possible in the hands of private persons and the Marianas government. Eventually the parties agreed that in the future the United States would be able to exercise the power of eminent domain to the same extent as if the Marianas were a state. First, however, the United States must attempt to acquire the land through negotiation and voluntary means. If this fails, then the United States may take the land subject only to the due process clause of the U.S. Constitution.

Total compensation for this full 100-year period will be a lump sum payment of $19.5 million to be made by the United States at the time the lease is executed. Since current plans do not anticipate a need by the United States military for all of this land, the United States has provisionally agreed to lease back 6,592 acres (2,666 hectares) to the Marianas government for the nominal sum of $1.00 per year. The United States may cancel this lease-back at any time it deems the situation urgent.

A summary of the agreements reached on land requirements follows:

Tanapag Harbor. Approximately 177 acres (72 hectares) in Tanapag Harbor will be leased by the United States for 50 years, with an option for an additional 50 years for the lump sum amount of $2 million. Currently this land is under military retention and could be made available for future contingency use by the United States. However, there are no such plans at this time. Most of this land, 133 acres (54 hectares) will be developed into an American Memorial Park which can serve as a recreation area for the people of the Marianas. The cost of upkeep will be paid by the interest on the $2 million payment which will be placed in trust for this purpose. Preliminary plans call for cleared beaches, an amphitheatre, a family picnic area, an arboretum, a swimming pool, and other athletic facilities in addition to the monument. The other 44 acres (18 hectares) will be leased back to the Marianas government for possible sublease for civilian harbor-related activities.

Isely Field. During most of the negotiations, the United States expressed a desire for approximately 485 acres (196 hectares) in the Isely Field area. At the fifth negotiating session, the United States withdrew this proposal.

Farallon de Medinille. This unused, uninhabited island of approximately 220 acres (90 hectares) will continue to be made available to the United States as a target area. The lump sum for this land will be $20,600.

Tinian. Originally, the United States desired approximately 18,700 acres for the development of a joint service military base on Tinian. This figure was reduced to 17,475 during the negotiations and finally readjusted upwards at the fifth session to 17,799 (7,203 hectares). The lump sum payment for the 50-year lease for these lands, and option for an additional 50 years, will be $17.5 million. The United States agreed to permit the government of the Northern Marianas to retain control over the nine acres of valuable land at San Jose Harbor for civilian harbor purposes and agreed to carefully reevaluate its military needs in the area to make as much of this leased land as possible available for agricultural and other purposes compatible with planned military activities. During the fifth session, the United States agreed that this land use arrangement would take the form of a lease-back of approximately 6,458 acres (2,648 hectares) to the government of the Marianas for a fee of $1.00 per year:

1. Approximately 1,335 acres south of West Field and at the harbor will be leased back at such time as the 50-year lease is entered into;

2. 4,010 acres north of West Field and east of Broadway now being used by the Micronesian Development Corp. will be allowed to continue in accordance with its terms;

3. 1,113 acres north of West Field and west of Broadway presently under grazing leases or homesteaded by individuals.

The length of these lease-backs are for relatively short terms, generally five years, in comparison to the total lease time available to the United States of 100 years. The acreage south of West Field (number 1 above) will be leased for 10 years and the remainder will run for five years. While the Marianas have an "option" to renew, the United States must agree to the renewal. The United States may cancel any lease-backs, upon payment of fair compensation, upon one year's notice or without any notice in the event of urgent military requirements or a national emergency. Planned uses for this land to be compatible with military activities are agricultural and grazing; permanent construction will not be permitted without United States approval.

Role of the Federal Judiciary

Federal courts will be "competent to pass on the consistency of such amendments."[71] Like a state, the new Marianas commonwealth will have the right to establish local courts to handle cases arising under local laws and the jurisdiction of the U.S. District Court in the Marianas will be at least the same in the Marianas as it would be in a state.[72] However, the U.S. constitutional requirements of indictment by grand jury and of a jury trial in civil cases need not be made applicable.[73]

Economic Aspects of the Relationship

Tariffs and Trade

Unlike that of a state, the government of the Marianas will be able to establish its own customs laws and lay duties on imports and exports, as long as these measures are consistent with United States international obligations.

Federal Financial Assistance

The financial benefits to the Marianas are quite attractive although not up to the $51 million over eight years requested by the Marianas initially. The two delegations agreed on an initial seven-year financial program to begin following the establishment of the commonwealth, which could come as early as 1976.[74] Under the program, the United States will provide roughly $17 million of assistance with $13.5 million coming in the form of direct financial grants:

1. $8 million per year for general operations of the Marianas government
2. $1.75 million per year for funding of economic development loans with $500,000 reserved for small loans to farmers, fishermen, and agricultural and marine cooperatives, and $250,000 reserved for housing loans to low income families

3. $4 million per year to fund capital improvement projects with $500,000 a year to be reserved for Rota and another $500,000 to be reserved for Tinian
4. approximately $3 million per year to be spent by the United States in providing a wide range of services and assistance under regular United States federal programs
5. $250,000 per year for special education in connection with the change in political status

To protect against inflation, United States assistance will be provided in constant 1975 dollars. In addition, the United States has tentatively agreed to pay the transitional costs for the necessary constitutional convention,[75] plebiscite, and election of the necessary government to implement the status agreement. Additional expenses, including social and economic planning and research, will increase the costs of planning and implementing the political status change to about $1.2 million.

Funding after this seven-year initial period is still open, with the hope that the commonwealth will be able to achieve greater self-sufficiency and fulfill the demand for capital improvement programs.

NOTES

1. For a recent discussion of this point, see P. Haigwood, "Japan and the Mandates," in Wm. Roger Louis, ed., National Security and the International Trusteeship in the Pacific 97 (Annapolis, Md.: Naval Institute Press, 1972) (hereinafter National Security).
2. U.S. Dept. of State Bulletin (4 December 1943), Vol. 9 at 393.
3. Dorothy E. Richard, United States Naval Administration of the Trust Territory of the Pacific Islands (Washington, D.C.: U.S. Office of Chief Naval Operations, 1957), 3: 6-19.
4. Trusteeship Agreement for the Former Japanese Mandated Islands, 61 Stat. (Pt. 3) 3301, art. 13, approved by the Security Council of the UN on 2 April 1947 and approved by the U.S. Congress by J. Res. 18 July 1947, c. 271, 61 Stat. 397 (hereinafter referred to as Trusteeship Agreement).
5. Ibid., art. 6.
6. Trusteeship Agreement, art. 3. A broad review of various aspects of the United States administration from a number of points of view is found in a collection of papers published in Francis M. Smith, ed., Micronesian Realities: Political and Economic (Santa Cruz: University of California Center for South Pacific Studies, 1972) (hereinafter referred to as Micronesian Realities).

7. Alig v. Trust Territory, 3 Trust Territory Rep. 64 (1965). The Trust Territory does have rights under the Trust Agreement People v. Saipan ___ F. 3rd ___ (C.A. 9th Cir., 16 July 1974).
8. Ex. Order No. 9875, 12 F.R. 4837 (18 July 1947).
9. Ex. Order No. 10265, 16 F.R. 6419 (29 June 1951).
10. For example, S. 2992 and H.R. 7427 introduced in the 82d Congress and H.R. 5381 introduced in the 83d Congress. See Norman Meller, The Congress of Micronesia 188 (Honolulu: University of Hawaii Press, 1969).
11. 48 U.S.C. § 1681.
12. Ex. Order No. 10408, 17 F.R. 10277 (10 November 1952).
13. Ex. Order No. 10470, 18 F.R. 4231 (17 July 1953).
14. Ex. Order No. 11021, 27 F.R. 4409 (8 May 1962).
15. U.S.C. § 1681[a].
16. U.S.C. § 1681.
17. Dept. of the Interior Order No. 2882, 29 F.R. 13613 (28 September 1964).
18. Dept. of the Interior Order No. 2918, pt. III, § 2, 34 F.R. 157 (27 December 1968).
19. Granville-Smith v. Granville-Smith, 3 U.S. 1 (1955). The issue is discussed in Leibowitz, The Applicability of Federal Law to the Territory of Guam, 16 Va. J. of International Law 1 (1975).
20. Dept. of the Interior Order No. 2918, Pt. III, § 2.
21. Meller, Congress of Micronesia, p. 205.
22. Dept. of the Interior Order No. 2918, Pt. III, § 2.
23. Ibid., Pt. III, § 13.
24. Ibid.
25. Ibid., Pt. II, § 1.
26. Dept. of the Interior, draft order, Recommendations for Territorial Legislature, presented by the Working Committee of the Territorial Legislature Committee, Council of Micronesia (9 January 1963). The order is discussed in Meller, Congress of Micronesia, pp. 197-221.
27. Dept. of the Interior Order 2918, Pt. III, § 4.
28. Ibid., Pt. IV.
29. Van Cleve, The Office of Territorial Affairs 137 (New York: Praeger Publishers, 1974).
30. Meller, The Congress of Micronesia 21 (1968).
31. Dept. of the Interior Order No. 2882, 29 F.R. 13613 (28 September 1964).
32. Van Cleve, The Office of Territorial Affairs 123 (1974).
33. Representative Hans Wiliander, "Independence as a Political Alternative," in Micronesian Realities.
34. Kaleb Undi, "America's Dilemmas in Carrying Out Its International Trusteeship Obligations in Micronesia," in Micronesian Realities.
35. UN Visiting Mission, Report of the Trust Territory of the Pacific Islands, Trusteeship Council, 27th Session, Supplement No. 2 (New York, 1961), p. 20, in Micronesian Realities, p. 182.

36. Agreement with Japan concerning the Trust Territory of the Pacific Islands, 18 April 1969, 20 U.S.T. 2654, T.I.A.S. No. 6724.
37. J. Lincoln, "The Mariana Islands," in National Security.
38. Report of the U.N. Visiting Mission to the Trust Territory of the Pacific Islands, 27th Sess., U.N. 7003 (1961) at 12.
39. Report of the U.N. Visiting Mission to the Trust Territory of the Pacific Islands, 34th Sess., T/1658 (1967) at 18.
40. Report of the U.N. Visiting Mission to the Trust Territory of the Pacific Islands, 37th Sess., T/1707 (1970).
41. Van Cleve, The Office of Territorial Affairs 129 (1974).
42. Report of the Political Status Delegation of the Congress of Micronesia, 3d Cong., 3d Sess., at 2 (1970).
43. Draft Compact of Free Association, Annex B, 12 July 1974 (hereinafter cited as Draft Compact).
44. Draft Compact, § 302.
45. Draft Compact, § 303(c).
46. Wiliander, in Micronesian Realities, at 3.
47. Statement by Ambassador Williams during the Proceedings of the 6th Round of Negotiations, Micronesian Status Negotiations (28 September-6 October 1972), at 28.
48. Ibid.
49. Ibid., at 33.
50. Ibid., at 34.
51. Hearings to Hear Progress Report on Negotiations Concerning the Future Status of the Trust Territory of the Pacific Islands Before the Subcomm. on Territorial and Insular Affairs of the House Comm. on Interior and Insular Affairs, 93rd Cong., 1st Sess., ser. 93-4, at 9 (1973).
52. U.S. Policy Statement of 2 November 1973, Transfer of Title of Public Lands from the Trust Territory of the Pacific Islands Administration to the Districts: U.S. Policy and Necessary Implementing Courses of Action (printed in Micronesian Status Negotiations, Proceedings of the 7th Round 25 [1973]).
53. Ibid.
54. Ex. Order No. 11021, 27 F.R. 4409 (8 May 1962).
55. U.S. Policy Statement of 2 November 1973, Transfer of Title of Public Lands from the Trust Territory of the Pacific Islands Administration to the Districts: U.S. Policy and Necessary Implementing Courses of Action (printed in Micronesian Status Negotiations, Proceedings of the 7th Round 25 [1973]).
56. Congress of Micronesia, S.J. Res. 117 (30 August 1972).
57. Congress of Micronesia, S.J. Res. 114 (25 August 1972).
58. Hearings to Hear Progress Report on Negotiations Concerning the Future Status of the Trust Territory of the Pacific Islands Before the Subcomm. on Territorial and Insular Affairs of the House Comm. on Interior and Insular Affairs, 93d Cong., 1st Sess., ser. 93-4 at 6 (1973).

59. Joint Communique, <u>Marianas Political Status Negotiations</u>, 2d Sess., at 7-11 (4 June 1973) (hereinafter cited as Joint Communique, 2d Sess.).
60. <u>Downes</u> v. <u>Bidwell</u>, 182 U.S. 244 (1901).
61. Joint Communique, 2d Sess. at 7.
62. Joint Communique, 2d Sess. at 8.
63. Ibid.
64. 48 <u>U.S.C.</u> § 1574(a).
65. 48 U.S.C. § 1423(a). See <u>Granville-Smith</u> v. <u>Granville-Smith</u>, 349 U.S. 1 (1955).
66. Joint Communique, 2d Sess., at 8.
67. Ibid.
68. Joint Communique, <u>Marianas Political Status Negotiations</u>, 3d Sess. (12 December 1973) (hereinafter cited as Joint Communique, 3d Sess.).
69. U.S. Policy Statement of 2 November 1973, op. cit.
70. Joint Communique, 3d Sess.
71. Joint Communique, 2d Sess., at 8.
72. Ibid.
73. Ibid.
74. Joint Communique, <u>Marianas Political Status Negotiations</u>, 4th Sess., at 4 (31 May 1974).
75. Ibid.

CHAPTER 5

GUAM

Guam represents the more "normal" United States colonial territory. Its "unincorporated" constitutional status is the same as that of the Virgin Islands and American Samoa and in degree of political participation the same as that of the Virgin Islands (American Samoa's is somewhat less). For some time political status evolution was rarely, if ever, discussed for Guam; but it seemed to be assumed if a major status change were ever to occur, the Hawaii precedent of integration—statehood—was in accord with the Guamanian desires and this was the only option envisioned (however dimly) at the federal level. The possibility of commonwealth was rarely discussed in Guam. But the Micronesia-Marianas negotiation changed all that. Guam has now begun to survey its political status evolution more broadly, exploring a number of alternatives; and, more importantly, some United States decision makers have begun to realize that a distinct change is required.

Guam is the largest island in the Northern Pacific: the largest in a broad expanse of ocean stretching from Hawaii to the Philippines and from Japan to Papua New Guinea. Guam lies at the southern end of the Marianas Chain of 15 islands. The distance from north to south along this chain covers 420 miles. Guam, like the Marianas, because of its size and location, has been viewed by larger countries—to its misfortune—as an area of prime military importance.

The island itself is about 30 miles long, between 4 and 9 miles wide, with a pinched waist which, as a number of writers have said, gives it a peanut shape. The northern part of the island is a high plateau, while the southern half is high and mountainous, with numerous streams cutting across the terrain. The climate is tropical with generally a rainy season during the last half of the year which sometimes brings with it violent storms. Among the worst of these was Hurricane Karen, which in November 1962 almost completely devastated the island.

MAP 5

Guam, Showing Communities
and Military Installations

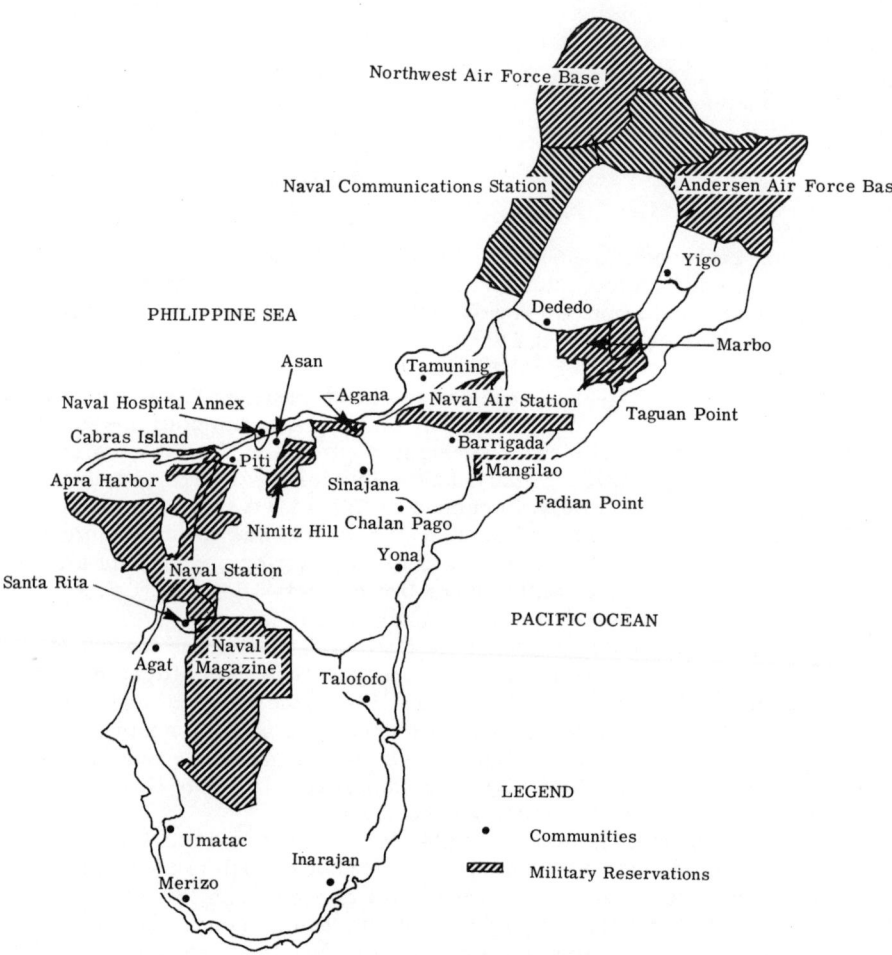

Source: James H. Webb. Micronesia and U.S. Pacific Strategy: A Blueprint for the 1980s (New York: Praeger, 1974), p. 67.

GUAM

The islands were originally occupied by the Chamorros, a Malaysian people, but there has been considerable ethnic mixing in the last two centuries so that the present day Guamanian is composed of many racial strains. Chamorro is still spoken as the native tongue at home although the official language in Guam is English.

ECONOMIC STRUCTURE

The Guam economy is dominated by military expenditures and tourism. Agriculture was once of great importance, but since the war, as a result of both Japanese occupation and the subsequent seizure of the land by the United States military immediately after the war, the agricultural life of the island has stagnated and has not regained its former importance.

In recent years Guam's economy has undergone a tremendous expansion based on the military presence of the United States and the opening up of Guam to the Japanese tourist. The statistics alone are startling. The civilian population in Guam increased by 61 percent from 1960 to 1970 and an additional 14 percent, from 66,507 in 1970 to 75,699, in 1973. There has been a similar parallel increase in the military population, from 18,489 in 1970 to 30,952 in 1973. The growth in business income more than tripled during 1967-73, from $148.2 million to $499.1 million, and bank deposits grew from a modest $42.8 million in 1967 to $271.1 million in 1973. In 1974 Guam was host to over 250,000 visitors, a figure to be contrasted with the fewer than 5,000 visitors in 1967.

The strain on Guam of this economic expansion has been very great. Building construction, which increased more than six times between 1967 and 1973, caused a labor shortage on the island, resulting in workers being brought to Guam from either the States or the Philippines. These temporary employees and the increased military presence total almost one-third of the island's population. The large numbers of transients raise a significant problem, because their vantage point may be quite short-range and opportunistic.

HISTORICAL BACKGROUND

Relationship with Spain: 1521-1898

Guam's first contact with the West occurred when Ferdinand Magellan landed there in 1521 during the course of his journey around the world. The island had been settled about 3,000 years before by

Malaysian people from Southeast Asia; and by the time Magellan landed, there was a population of between 50,000 and 100,000, organized into a clan and district government and supporting themselves by agricultural activities and fishing.

From the outset relationships with the Spanish went badly, with various houses being burned and seven Chamorros being killed during the initial encounter. Shortly after that, in 1526, the Spanish claimed Guam as a possession of Spain. Serious colonization began almost a century and a half later in 1668 when Father Diego Luis de Sanvitores led Jesuit missionaries under the authority of the Spanish Crown. From this point until the end of the century there was open rebellion by the Chamorros against the Spanish. Fierce battles, coupled with typhoons and European diseases, reduced the Chamorron population to less than 5,000. During the course of this campaign many fled to the northern Mariana islands. As a result, the tie with those islands was reinforced.

After the decimation of the Chamorron population, matters settled down. The only important historical incident worth mentioning here is the Spanish defeat by Napoleon at the beginning of the nineteenth century which resulted in the locus of imperial Spanish administrative control of Guam being shifted from Mexico to the Philippines.[1]

Relationship with the United States: 1898-1950

In 1898 the Spanish-American War broke out. During the course of that war, American naval cruisers sailing to the Philippines in June 1898 were ordered to stop and capture Guam; and did so almost without firing a shot. Six months later, when the Treaty of Paris was signed ending the war with Spain, Guam was ceded to the United States,[2] with its political status and civil rights to be determined by the United States Congress.[3]

Two weeks later President McKinley issued an executive order placing Guam under the Department of the Navy to be ruled at the discretion of naval superiors by orders and proclamations. The naval governors were a mixed bag. Most were content to preserve order, treating Guam as basically a military post serving U.S. national security interests. A few concerned themselves with the wishes of the local inhabitants of the island; but in general they did so as benevolent despots rather than attempting to obtain political participation by the Guamanians.

Perhaps worst of all was the short tenure of the governors of Guam, almost all of whom lasted only one tour of duty, so that within two years or so there was a new man whose views toward Guam were very short-term.

The initial actions of naval governors were undertaken with an unusual vigor and confidence. Captain Richard P. Leary, the first governor of Guam, received the following instructions from President McKinley:

> It should be the earnest and paramount aim of the naval administration to win the confidence, respect, and affection of the inhabitants of the island of Guam, by securing to them in every possible way that full measure of individual rights and liberties which is the inheritance of all free peoples, and by proving to them that the mission of the United States is one of benevolent assimilation, substituting the mild way of justice and right for arbitrary rule. In the fulfillment of this high mission, supporting the temperate administration of affairs for the greatest good of the governed, there must be sedulously maintained the strong arm of authority. . . .[4]

Within a month Leary issued proclamations transferring all Spanish-owned land to the United States, abolishing peonage, voiding all contracts for personal labor, abolishing political rights of the clergy, and establishing freedom of religion. He also forbade religious processions in the streets and public celebration on village saint days. Shortly after this proclamation, most of the priests were deported. Every adult was required to be able to write his own name and was urged to adopt the English language.

Through a series of orders at the turn of the century the government of Guam was organized into ten departments. The Guam government, however, was nonexistent. The local populace realized this and as early as 1902 petitioned the United States government for increased political participation, arguing that "fewer permanent guarantees of liberty and property rights exist now than when under the Spanish domination." To his credit, Captain Leary endorsed this petition, noting its "propriety and urgency." But Washington did not respond.

The Guamanians continued to petition for increased political participation with little result. The Guam Congress was finally established in 1917 but it was advisory only, serving without pay and made up solely of appointees of the governor. That same year universal military training went into effect and the Guam militia was prepared in case of a call to action.

In 1930 Governor Willis Bradley attempted to open up the political system. He called for an elected Guam Congress, although its power was still to be advisory. He issued a proclamation setting forth fundamental rights for the people of Guam but this proclamation was disapproved by the secretary of the Navy and was revoked.

Under the *Insular Cases*, as noted above, the fundamental provisions of the Constitution applied: "the general prohibitions . . . in favor of the liberty and property of the citizen . . . which are an absolute denial of authority . . . to do particular acts" applied even to an unincorporated territory.[5] But the applicability of the <u>Insular Cases</u> to Guam, even in theory, was not clear since Congress did not legislate for the Territory of Guam until passage of the organic act in 1950.

The <u>Insular Cases</u>, decided at the turn of the century, emphasized the importance of congressional action and suggested that the military might continue to rule a territory—that a territory might not even have the protections of an unincorporated territory—without legislation:

> . . . it is not open to serious dispute that the military arm of the government of the United States may hold and occupy conquered territory without incorporation for such length of time as may seem appropriate to Congress in the exercise of its discretion. The denial of the right of the civil power to do so would not, therefore, prevent the holding of territory by the United States if it was deemed best by the political department of the government, but would simply necessitate that it should be exercised by the military instead of by the civil power. . . .
>
> The Civil government of the United States cannot extend immediately, and of its own force, over territory acquired by war. Such territory must necessarily, in the first instance, be governed by the military power under the control of the President as Commander-in-Chief.[6]

The executive branch supported an anomalous status for Guam.

> The political status of these Islands (Guam and Tutuila) are anomalous. Neither the Constitution nor the laws of the United States have been extended to them and the only administrative authority existing in them is that derived mediately or immediately from the President as Commander-in-Chief of the Army and Navy of the United States.[7]

The effect of this anomalous status was to justify plenary power for the military authority unchecked by civilian, constitutional limitations:

> . . . the continuance in force of the municipal laws of the territory (Guam) was not intended as more than a recognition of what would have been presumed in the absence of instructions and cannot be regarded as intended to deny the power of the governor to alter the laws. They were continued in force as to the inhabitants among themselves, but not to control the governor; that is to say, the government itself. His power as military

> governor was intended to be plenary. He had authority to do what the exigencies of military government required, and held the supreme legislative, executive, and judicial authority of the Island. At that time, in that distant and little known Island, the President could not do otherwise than leave him a large discretion, and his acts should not be held void upon strictly technical reasoning.[8]

Whether this was legally the correct situation was unclear in theory, since there was no judicial test of the military rule. What was important was the practice which, backed by the attorney general's opinions, resulted in complete discretion of the military governor until 1950.

Their continuing limited political role so disturbed the Guamanians that in 1933 twelve seats of the Guam Congress could not be filled by the elective process. Governor Root then decided to remove all commissioners from the elected list and appoint them himself.

The Guamanians turned their political energies to obtaining American citizenship. On 19 December 1933 a petition for American citizenship was sent by 1,965 Guamanians to President Roosevelt and three years later the Guamanian Legislature unanimously petitioned for citizenship. The Guamanians raised money by popular subscription to send their spokesmen to Washington to personally argue the cause of American citizenship after the governor had refused the use of public funds for this purpose. The first legislation to grant citizenship to Guam was introduced in July 1936 but the Navy Department opposed the bill, as did the secretary of state, and it did not pass. The naval position was this:

> Guamanians are afforded passport privileges, have no Federal taxes or tariffs to pay, receive free medical and educational services, and are, in general, a particularly privileged people. The naval island government carefully guards them from exploitation by outsiders and protects their islands. . . . The general policy of the naval government with reference to educational activities has been to enlighten the minds of the people and to stimulate their development through training and self-discipline. Emphasis is placed on industrial and agricultural training in order to improve the capacity of the native population for self-maintenance and economic independence. However, as attested by the fact that they are not self-supporting and require not only Federal economic assistance but careful training and supervision from the paternal island government, there is every indication that these people have not yet reached a state of development commensurate with the personal independence, obligations, and responsibilities of United States citizenship.[9]

The most traumatic event in the life of Guam was World War II; and in many ways the shock of that event still determines the attitude of both Guam and the United States toward the relationship. A political/military judgment was made by the United States government between 1935 and 1938 not to have an arms buildup on Guam; and in case of attack, to retreat to Hawaii. And in fact that is what happened. Japan attacked Guam the day after Pearl Harbor; and within a few days, Governor McMillan surrendered the islands and the Japanese occupation began. It was a particularly brutal occupation, especially in the last days of 1943 and early 1944. Forced labor and starvation were quite common. In the summer of 1944 the Americans recaptured Guam.

The war had had its effect on the United States military thinking. Almost immediately, major military fortifications were initiated on the island, a program which was spurred on even more by the war in Korea and later by the Vietnam war. The buildup had two major effects: (1) the restriction by military order of the movement of all persons, United States citizens or not, to and from the island until 25 August 1962; and (2) the seizure and occupation by the military in Guam of one-third of the island. These military actions are still remembered with considerable bitterness on Guam. Their history and background is, therefore, worth relating.

Military Control of Entry Into Guam After the 1950 Organic Act

Upon the outbreak of World War II, President Franklin Roosevelt promulgated Executive Order No. 8683 which designated the three-mile limit around the Island of Guam as a Naval Defensive Sea Area and an Airspace Reservation.[10] No person, other than those persons on public vessels of the United States, was to be allowed entry without authorization of the secretary of the navy.

Prior to the promulgation of this executive order, Guamanian law (promulgated by the naval governor) gave the military control over the entry and exit of civilians anyway. "Residents of Guam shall not be permitted to leave Guam without a passport issued by the Governor or a certificate of identification issued by the Department of Records and Accounts."[11] The Navy had adopted the policy of preventing non-Guamanians from entering the island for business purposes unless there were no local people qualified or financially able to supply the particular service. This policy was enforced mainly through restrictions on the issuance of business licenses required by the government code of Guam, a code subject to change by the order of the naval governor.[12]

After the war and congressional passage of the organic act in 1950 transferring administration of Guam governmental affairs from the Navy to the Department of the Interior, there were indications that Executive Order No. 8683 might be obsolete. But less than three months after passage of the organic act, before the new civil government could act to remove the statutory control of entry into Guam, the Navy reinstituted the security clearance program.[13]

Worse, the postwar enforcement of Executive Order 8683 went far beyond that envisioned by the original presidential directive. The intent of the 1941 order was to prevent the entry of potentially dangerous aliens. The military on Guam in peacetime, however, used this authority to exclude persons who would not contribute to the "strategic development" of Guam.[14] Navy regulations discriminated against those citizens who did not work for the military. Civil service employees, military dependents, and those Guam citizens who became citizens of the United States by passage of the organic act did not require security clearances. Others, aliens and stateside citizens traveling to Guam, were required to get military clearance.

Under the statutory authority by which Executive Order 8683 was promulgated, enforcement of the naval security clearance program was to be by criminal prosecution. However, despite acknowledging that it had no power to exclude anyone from the island, the Navy issued notices to many persons and their employers that clearance had been revoked and they were to return to their countries. By this mechanism, the military could achieve one objective—control of the labor supply of the island—at the same time preventing a legal test of the constitutional validity of the program.* Employers were forced to cooperate with the Navy's wishes because the Navy could prevent the future importation of labor by refusing security clearances. The effect of this was to limit the availability of skilled personnel, especially in the civilian construction market, at a most critical time: just when the island was attempting to rebuild, to recover from the destruction of World War II. This lack of skilled persons, plus the high cost of materials, prevented, for example, the development of modern housing, and the effects of this setback still are felt today.[15]

Public opinion against this program intensified after the Korean War had receded in public memory and the peace and prosperity of the 1960s were upon us. The denial or revocation of a security clearance appeared more clearly as an unjustifiable, unconstitutional deprivation of liberty.[16] Finally, on 21 August 1962, President John Kennedy discontinued the Defensive Sea Area and Airspace Reservation by Executive Order No. 11045. The enabling congressional legislation remains, however;[17] and under recent judicial interpretation of these statutes, the president may declare defensive sea areas for the purposes of national defense even in peacetime and in the absence of a threat of war.[18]

---

*In 1961, the District Court of Guam held that the organic act did not repeal Ex. Order 8683 (<u>United States</u> v. <u>Angcog</u>, 190 F. Supp. 696 [D. Guam 1961]).

Military Control of Guam Land

The military role in Guam also involves the question of land use and control. At present, with land in short supply, the military occupies approximately one-third of the island. Part of this stems again from World War II and part from the initial transfer of the island to the United States.

Uncertainty of Land Titles. When the United States took control of Guam from the Spanish, the only recorded means by which original title was taken in Guam was by the practice of claiming ownership by occupation. As no surveys were made before May 1914, land disputes were numerous and longstanding.

The order of the secretary of the navy to the first American governor and military commander of Guam directed him to assume control of "all Crown Lands, fortifications and public buildings on the Island."[19] Precisely what lands were included was, however, unclear. Because the "conditions of tenure of land thus have been uncertain," a cadastral survey of Guam was begun in May 1914. The hope was that all property in Guam would eventually be physically defined, charted, and recorded within a few years, but this survey never reached the success which had originally been envisioned.

In reviewing the land situation in 1950 for Governor Skinner, the Division of Land Utilization of the Department of the Interior noted that prior to World War II surveys were very inadequate, adding greatly to the confusion incidental to military land-taking, and that by the best estimates at least 20 percent of the island remained unsurveyed as of that time.[20]

But the major responsibility for the land confusion rests with the military. Until 1950 the naval government supervised all transfers of real property and the operation of the land survey and registration. No land could be transferred without the governor's consent. The island's attorney general appeared in the hearing of land registration proceedings in order to "protect the rights and interests of the Naval Government of Guam."[21]

Further, upon reentry in 1944, the American forces turned the island into a major military base, taking and converting farm land and remaining villages into airfields in accordance with military needs. Little or no attention was paid to land ownership or to compensation for land taken during this period. Thus, Admiral Forrest P. Sherman stated: "When we recaptured Guam we proceeded with the development of the island without regard to ownership for the most effective and rapid prosecution of the war."[22]

Compensation. It has been charged that in the decade after the war when the military government and its agencies possessed the only legal force on the island, the commission used "threats, coercion, appeals to patriotism, and fear of military reprisal" to pressure Guamanians to turn their land over to the federal government for inadequate consideration.[23] The military government also artificially depressed the market value of the land it acquired by its orders and regulations. This point was acknowledged by Acting Secretary of the Navy H. Struve Hensel in August 1945:

> Private owners of land in Guam will not usually sell their holdings. Even if they would sell, it could not be desirable to open the real-estate market at the present time when money is plentiful as a result of the current construction program, since this would result in unwarranted inflation in real estate. For this reason, the military government of Guam has prohibited private transfer of property.[24]

After World War II, the United States enacted the Meritorious Claims Act,[25] special legislation in order to compensate victims of war damage and injury. Payments were to compensate for loss or destruction of all public and private property resulting from either the Japanese occupation, the hostilities of war, or noncombat activities of the United States armed forces. The program was to be administered by the Navy Department.*

Records of what happened—the period of land-taking went on from 21 July 1944 to 13 March 1957—are lacking. Hearings held prior to passage of the Meritorious Claims Act indicated that the military authorities expected to pay $12 million for claims under the act,[26] and claims in about this amount were actually filed.† A supplementary

---

*"Since Guam is at present an integral part of combat operations, it is not feasible to have other Government agencies operating within the island. For that reason it is proposed that the Navy be authorized to settle the damage claims referred to." (Letter from Acting Secretary of the Navy H. Struve Hensel to the Hon. Sam Rayburn, 9 June 1945, contained in H. Rpt. No. 1135, 79th Cong., 1st Sess.) See also Letter from the Commander of Naval Forces Marianas, 18 October 1949, reprinted in Information on Guam Transmitted by the United States Secretary to the Secretary-General of the United Nations pursuant to Article 73(e) of the Charter, June 1950.

† The Summary of Information Transmitted by the Government of the United States of America for the Year 1946 for Guam, prepared by the Navy Department, U.N. Doc. A/320 (25 July 1947), states that to date "there are claims in the total amount of $10,427,403.55 for loss and damage to real and personal property; and 711 injury and death claims in the total amount of $1,396,005.00." (at 25). Examination of subsequent reports to the United Nations by the United States makes no reference as to what claims were actually paid.

report of the United States War Claims Commission states that as of 1953 an aggregate of only $1,440,076.70 had been paid to residents of Guam.[27]

Various bills have been introduced into Congress to rectify the inequities of the postwar land-taking. However, the Departments of Justice and Navy have consistently opposed these attempts to right the injustice. In early 1973 the Department of the Navy was asked by the House Subcommittee on Territorial Affairs to prepare background material showing exactly what property was acquired after the war, how it was transferred, and the price paid as "just compensation."[28] Such information has not been forthcoming.

Civilian Government

After the war, Guam continued to press for a civil government and for United States citizenship. In July 1946 the first legislation providing an organic act for Guam was introduced into Congress. Since it would transfer jurisdiction from the Navy Department to the Department of the Interior, the issue of self-government for Guam became tied to the irrelevant question of an evaluation of the effectiveness of the Navy's past administration. As a result, there was further delay.

In January 1947 the Guam Legislature asked the naval governor to give it the right to take action on revisions, amendments, and enactments of local laws before they became law on the island. In August, the governor announced that the Guam Legislature was to have legislative authority, subject to his veto (or, if a bill were repassed by a two-thirds vote, to the ultimate decision of the Secretary of the Navy). The governor retained the right to legislate by decree if, in his opinion, time were "of the essence."

The demand for citizenship and an organic act was renewed by resolution of the Guam Legislature in December 1948 and unanimously the next year. The year 1949 also brought a direct conflict between Governor Pownall, then the federally appointed naval governor, and the elected Guam Legislature. The issue, the power of the legislature to subpoena witnesses, led to a major confrontation before it was resolved; the Guam Legislature refused to meet and the governor attempted to declare the seats vacant and to appoint substitutes.

To break the deadlock, on 7 September 1949 President Truman transferred the administration of Guam from the secretary of the navy to the Department of the Interior[29] and before the month was out appointed the first civilian governor—a non-Guamanian—for Guam. Within a week of this appointment the Committee on Public Lands authorized hearings in Guam on the proposed organic act and the following year reported out a bill establishing Guam as an unincorporated territory of the United States with a civil government. It created a legislature with full lawmaking powers, established a District Court of Guam, enacted a bill of rights for the people of the territory,

GUAM

and granted them United States citizenship. The new government consisted of three branches: executive, legislative, and judicial. Its relations with the federal government were required to be supervised by a civilian department or agency of the government of the United States.

Organic Act: Political Representation

The most notable omission in the Guam organic act was the absence of any political representative in the U.S. Congress. The people of Guam were required to press the issue themselves. In 1964 the Guam Legislature, after unsuccessfully urging the Congress to permit political representation, created the office of a Washington representative.[30] Antonio B. Won Pat, the present residential delegate, was then elected to fill the position. His duties were similar in private corporate terms to those of a lobbyist, but his own effectiveness and the Congress's embarrassment brought forth the desired result. In 1972 Guam was accorded the right of representation in Congress in a manner similar to that of the Puerto Rican resident commissioner (with no voting privileges on the floor, but participation with voting rights and seniority in various committees in the House of Representatives). No formal representation was permitted in the Senate.

The organic act created a unicameral (one-house legislature that was to consist of not more than 21 members. All persons who had established residence in Guam and had lived there for at least two years were eligible to vote. A most significant restriction on the Guam Legislature was the veto power of the governor, who was still appointed by the president. A bill vetoed by the governor could be passed a second time by a two-thirds vote of the legislature. Then it would be sent to the president of the United States, who would make the decision as to whether it would become law. Two bills were sent to the president during the first decade of civilian government. The president in each case upheld the governor's veto.

Elective Governor

In 1972 further autonomy was granted. The Elective Governor Act provided that the governor was to be elected, and the presidential power to finally uphold vetos of legislation by the Guam governor was also repealed.

THE DEVELOPMENT AND GOALS OF THE TERRITORY

During the 1970s Guam has been affected by the general trend toward self-government throughout the world and by the events in

Micronesia and the Marianas, where a commonwealth government has been negotiated with the United States under very favorable financial conditions. As a result, Guam, for the first time, began to consider seriously its own status situation. The Twelfth Guam Legislature established a Political Status Commission to examine all aspects of Guam's relationship with the United States. Its conclusions and recommendations, although not necessarily endorsed by the legislature as a whole or by the executive, reflect the first serious study of the problem and are an indication for the need of some movement in this area. We shall consider these recommendations in the context of the existing political situation.

Political Relations

As of 1975 Guam is a territory of the United States and is non-self-governing as defined by the United Nations. Within Guam there is a general consensus that this status should change. The issue is whether it should move toward a commonwealth status or toward statehood. In the past, statehood had been viewed as the direction for the territory and there had been much discussion about an island state coupled in some fashion with the Marianas (a position similar to that of the Hawaiian Islands).

The Legislative Political Status Commission, without taking a position on the ultimate status, suggested a short-run status of commonwealth, with a future plebiscite to determine ultimate direction.

> The Commission recommends the development by the people of Guam of a Constitution for the governing of Guam, those matters not covered by the Constitution to be covered in a Guam Federal Relations Act.
> The Commission recommends a referendum in which the people of Guam could indicate whether they wish to go forward with a Constitution rather than the existing Organic Act.

This would permit the people of Guam to obtain the autonomy required to meet the economic and social problems that are now upon the Island and to participate more fully and effectively in the Federal decision-making process.

The Commission regards this as a short-term, immediate response to Guam's problem so that the longer-term issue can be handled more at its leisure and with the proper degree of local control. It is the Commission's view that this interim position would be similar to the Commonwealth status granted Puerto Rico and that which is being discussed for the Marianas. But this interim position is not necessarily the longer term status goal. It may be that Commonwealth would continue to develop and grow but it could also be the people of Guam would wish closer association with the United States through statehood or a more distant one similar to that being discussed with Micronesia at present.[31]

The delegate from Guam, A. B. Won Pat, has, in several annual reports, suggested commonwealth as an alternative without necessarily favoring it.

The emphasis in the Status Commission's report on a constitution drafted by Guam from which local authorities would gain their legislative sanction is appropriate if Guam is to gain local self-government. The need had been recognized by Guam and the first constitutional convention in Guam was convened in 1970—three years before the Status Commission—but was unable to agree on a final product. Guam's resident commissioner has introduced legislation in the U.S. Congress requesting congressional authorization for the drafting of a constitution. It failed to pass either house in the last Congress, but has, in 1975, passed in the House of Representatives.

At present one major federal control exists through the post of the government comptroller—appointed by the secretary of the interior—and who, in addition to the normal auditing powers, is given quasi-judicial powers under the organic act. He can summon witnesses, administer oaths, and make determinations. He can also make recommendations for action by the territorial legislature; and, in fact, he has done so.*

Guam has been sensitive to this intrusion on its authority. It resisted the control's inclusion in the original organic act at considerable length and the first Guam constitutional convention proposed to remove Interior Department supervision[32] and make the comptroller only an arm of the comptroller general of the United States.[33] This would still insure proper accounting and discharge of congressional responsibility for federal funds.† Other suggestions made at the

---

*For example, the amendment of P.L. 9-131 which removed the requirement that the Hospital Administration certify that the debtor had the capability to pay the bill before legal action could be taken; and the enactment of a system of public accountability, P.L. 12-34. Hearings on Appropriations for 1975 Before the Subcomm. on Dept. of the Interior and Related Agencies of the House Comm. on Appropriations, 93rd Cong., 2d Sess., Pt. 1, at 671-72 (1974).

† In supervising federal funds in Puerto Rico, a federal auditor was established by the Foraker Act to keep full and accurate accounts showing all receipts and disbursements (Act of 12 April 1900, § 23

constitutional convention would make the comptroller answerable to the people of Guam by making him an appointee of the governor subject to the advice and consent of the Guam Legislature. This would be in accordance with the standard provisions in state constitutions and in that of the Commonwealth of Puerto Rico, creating an auditor to insure supervision of state fiscal action.[34]

The other federal controls revolve about the secretary of the interior and establish his position as the intermediary between locally elected Guam officials and the Congress or the federal executive branch. Thus, the governor at present must make an annual report to the secretary of the interior which is then transmitted by the secretary to the Congress.

Finally, the local legislative and executive authority is somewhat limited as a result of organic act sanction. Under the organic act, all laws passed by the legislature must be reported by the governor to the secretary of the interior, who must forward them to the Congress of the United States. Congress has the power to annul any law passed by the Guam Legislature, even one concerned solely with local issues. Only if Congress fails to annul such a law within one year after receiving it is the law deemed to have been approved. In addition, the Guam Legislature does not have plenary authority but is limited to "subjects of local application," a phrase which is somewhat unclear but which may be used to limit the legislature further.

Participation in the Political Process

As in Puerto Rico, the absence of state citizenship prevents Guam from voting in the presidential election, although the territory has representation in the Congress through a nonvoting delegate similar to that mentioned and discussed in connection with Puerto Rico.

Interestingly enough, although Guam has been concerned with the applicability of federal laws in specific areas, the general applicability of federal law which Puerto Rico has worked so hard to limit has not been a major issue in Guam.

---

ch. 31 Stat. 82). When provisions creating an elective governor were passed in 1947, Congress installed a coordinator of federal agencies to coordinate all federal civilian functions (Elective Governor Act, 5 August 1947, ch. 490, § 6, 61 Sta. 772). The coordinator reported to the secretary of the interior and advised the secretary respecting all appropriation estimates. When Puerto Rico achieved commonwealth, control of the comptroller, whose responsibilities were to audit all revenues and expenditures, was placed directly in the hands of the governor (P.R. Const. art III, § 22).

Military Presence

The Political Status Commission of Guam looked to a continuing dialogue with the military, especially on the question of land. It said:

> The Commission recommends there be immediately constituted a Joint United States-Guam Ad Hoc Committee composed of private and public members appointed by the President and an equal number of members appointed by the Guam Government to review fully the military presence on the Island of Guam.
>
> We have noted earlier the significant land holding of the military in Guam in addition to the military's activity in importation of labor and developmental operations. We believe it is important to the people of Guam and the greatest urgency to assure the long-term harmony between Guam and the United States that a thorough review of this military presence be conducted with a view to seeing that land holdings not necessary to the national security interest be returned for use by the people of Guam.
>
> This recommendation is not motivated by any desire to intrude upon U.S. military policy or to acquire military information nor in its implementation is it expected that this will occur. We are aware that in the course of the Micronesia and Marianas negotiations discussions of the present and potential future military needs of the United States took place, making available documents only administratively secured. This permitted the people of those Islands to plan more effectively their future development. We would expect this Commission to examine the existing situation and to have available to it similar information on future projections.[35]

Attempts to implement this recommendation have been futile. So far there has been little response on the part of the executive branch. Although the report's recommendation is modest, especially when compared to activities in Puerto Rico or Micronesia along the same lines, the Defense Department has taken a negative view and has not been responsive at all to the Legislative Political Status Commission's recommendation.

On the broader question of the military's role on Guam, there has also been considerable discussion on the island. The Political Status Commission's conclusion may be worth noting here:

> The United States military presence has played an unduly large role in the life of Guam in areas not affecting the national security but of critical importance to Guam.

> No area within the United States has proved itself more willing, both in times of war and peace, to assist the national security needs of the Federal government. Guam is aware that because of its geographical location it can be, and has been, important to this national security. It is proud of this fact and does not desire, even if it could, to change it.
>
> But the military in Guam in recent years, as when Guam was under naval rule, has been unwilling to meet a corresponding obligation: to consider the problems of the Island's inhabitants. The continued maintenance of large tracts of land on Guam beyond the needs of national security, the importation by the military of foreign laborers, and the restriction of migration into Guam until 1962 are examples of military actions of questionable legality and singularly bad grace. This has been combined with an unwillingness to be forthcoming on matters which may affect our destiny although they do not involve the national security interests of the United States.
>
> These practices, policies and operating style of the military must change.[36]

This represents the strongest local official challenge to the military to date. Local political officials have been aware of the economic advantages of the military presence on Guam, and also of the strong patriotic sentiment on the island, but the power of the military and its unrestrained use require some curbing and it appears that Guam officials are beginning to put up some resistance to the military.

In 1972 under the Sella Bay agreement the governor of Guam executed a land exchange agreement transferring lands and interests in the Sella Bay area for use by the Department of the Navy in return for various joint-use rights to permit Guam to become eligible for an airport grant. The agreement was challenged in Bordallo v. Camacho procedurally on the grounds that both the governor and the Guam Legislature had to approve the agreements. (The substantive issue was the increased land to be utilized by the military under the agreement.) The Ninth Circuit agreed,[37] requiring the legislature to give its approval. The Guam Legislature's Committee on Resources, Development and Agriculture denounced the agreement as "contrary to the best interests of the people of Guam" and charged that the Navy had included in the agreement land that was surplus to the needs of the Department of Defense and therefore, under the statutes, policies, and regulations governing surplus federal land, should have been returned to the government of Guam independently of any exchange. The committee also concluded that the Navy's offer to lease 29 acres at the Masso Reservoir was related to the government of Guam's

questioning of the military's recreational use of the Fena Reservoir.*
The issue is still being negotiated as of this writing.

Immigration

Perhaps of all the issues the question of immigration is the most sensitive, because it points up the fragility of life on the island, where the presence of a very few additional persons can make a major change. The Legislative Political Status Commission concluded as follows:

<u>Immigration to Guam is threatening to change the way of life on the Island.</u>
We have noted in the Introduction the rapid increase in economic life here in Guam and the concomitant growth in the labor force. We are aware that Guam is critically short of labor and we are also aware that frequently the skills which are required by investors are not readily found on the Island. The Commission is concerned that the people of Guam participate fully in this economic growth; not solely for economic gain or narrow chauvinistic interest, but because without that participation there will arise in Guam the bitter resentment and hostility toward the off-Islander which is now found in the Virgin Islands where a similar rapid development has taken place.
The State Department and Immigration and Naturalization Service management of immigration has been much too cavalier, unnecessarily permitting the importation of personnel without due concern for the effect on the permanent residents of Guam. Methods have been found in other areas, most notably in American Samoa, to permit the off-shore areas to have greater control over all people on its Island. It is essential that similar control be vested in the Government of Guam.
We are concerned both for ourselves and for the United States that our growth take place in a context of harmony and understanding. It is our belief that it cannot take

---

*We should note the congressional attitude expressed in 10 <u>U.S.C.</u> § 2671 which directs the secretary of defense to require all hunting, fishing, and trapping at any military installation to be in accordance with the fish and game laws of the state or territory.

place in this fashion unless the people of Guam are given greater control over this area.[38]

The immigration question has, of course, been raised most vividly by the decision at the State Department level to use Guam rather than the Philippines as a major stepping-off point for Vietnam refugees. This has been a matter of some bitterness in the Guam Legislature, although the governor of Guam and the delegate have not expressed opposition.

Guam's International Presence

It was only during the 1970s that Guam became concerned about its international status. With respect to other territories the United Nations has been a sounding board for independence; but since this has not been an active movement in Guam, Guam's relations with the United Nations have been much less frequent and geography also has added to the tenuousness of the tie.

Guam has been interested in joining regional Pacific institutions which may be of value to it. Thus, the Legislative Status Commission concluded:

<u>Participation in regional Pacific institutions such as ECAFE and the Asian Development Bank would be desirable both economically and politically to Guam.</u>

The Commission has raised this particular point—although it has let others of equal, perhaps even greater, significance go unmentioned—because it raises graphically the status issue. Although in our view it would be of importance to the people of Guam both in terms of their sense of identity and because of the economic benefits to be given participation in regional Pacific institutions, the United States government has resisted this. We fear the needs of the people of Guam have been balanced against uncertain, and we would suggest inappropriate, foreign policy considerations of the United States. Instead of the United States government appearing—as indeed it must and should appear—to seek out and generously promote opportunities so that its most valuable possession—its citizens—can benefit from participation in the world community, the people of Guam have seen almost the contrary be the case. We have examined both the Constitutional and international legal issues that would be involved in Guam's participation in the regional Pacific institutions mentioned above. We can see no reason in law or policy why Guam is not permitted to participate.

Other States, frequently with less autonomy than even Guam has at present, such as the British Solomon Islands, Fiji, or Tonga, have actively participated in the organizations above. Although the people of Micronesia, who are not United States citizens, have gained the full endorsement by the State Department for their participation in these institutions, no such endorsement has as yet been forthcoming for Guam. We can only conclude that in some fashion Guam's present status as an unincorporated territory of the United States weighs to its significant detriment and permits various Federal agencies unfamiliar with Guam to take a less sympathetic attitude on matters of great concern to the people of Guam.[39]

It is interesting to note that the United States has been much more forthcoming in permitting involvement by Micronesia and the Marianas in foreign overseas activities without according similar status to Guam. Partly because of Guamanian reaction, the State Department issued a somewhat belated invitation to Guam to the Law of the Sea Conference in order to permit it to participate as part of the U.S. delegation without separate status.

The State Department has resisted Guam in its approaches to become a member of the Asian Development Bank or ESCAP.

The Role of the Federal Judiciary

The judicial power is vested both in the District Court of Guam and in the courts established by the law of Guam. The Guam District Court is presided over by a federal judge appointed by the president but with tenure of eight years instead of life tenure as is the case of the federal judges in the states. In addition, the Guam Federal District Court is given exclusive jurisdiction in Guam over territorial income tax prosecutions although the Guam government may prosecute a refund action outside of Guam in any appropriate Federal District Court. Appeals from the Guamanian court are to the Ninth District Court of Appeals.

The role of the jurisdiction of the Federal District Court and the local courts of the territory has become an issue in the Virgin Islands and an attempt is being made to initiate a study of the question.[40] Recently Guam took action to limit federal court power. The District Court had a special appellate jurisdiction over the local courts but this was changed by the Guam Legislature acting under its organic act authority.* The local and appellate court authority is particularly important since the U.S. Supreme Court has never taken a case from Guam.

Economic Aspects of the Relationship

Taxation

Guam is treated specially for federal income tax purposes under the organic act. All customs duties, taxes, and other federally imposed fees (other than employment and social security related taxes) are paid directly into the Guam treasury. The administration of these and other collections is carried out by the executive authority in Guam. This is similar to the Puerto Rican situation.

What is not similar is the preemption of the Guam local taxing mechanism. The organic act expressly converts the federal income tax into a "Guam territorial income tax" and "except where it is manifestly otherwise required," Guam and Guam authorities are substituted for the United States and the secretary of the treasury in the Federal Internal Revenue Code. Thus, Guam (and the same is true for the Virgin Islands) does not have the flexibility or the local taxing power that Puerto Rico has.

Permanent residents of Guam satisfy their income tax obligations under the U.S. Internal Revenue Code by paying their tax into the Guam treasury on income derived from all sources both within and outside Guam.†

Tariffs and Trade

Guam is outside the customs area of the United States. Therefore, Guam benefits from provision of General Headnote 3(a) of the Tariff Schedules of the United States, which exempts from duty articles which are grown, produced, or manufactured in the insular possessions

---

*Under Section 22(a) of the organic act, the District Court of Guam "shall have such appellate jurisdiction as the legislature may determine." Public Law 12-85 of the Twelfth Guam Legislature (16 January 1974) vests this appellate jurisdiction in a Supreme Court of Guam instead of the District Court.

†Two recent cases have dealt with the rights of nonresident U.S. citizens: Manning v. Blaz, 479 F.2d 333 (9th Cir. 1973), cert. den. 38 L.Ed. 755 (7 January 1974); Flores v. Guam (9th Cir. 1971). Because of this recent legislation the issues raised in these cases may no longer be a problem.

of the United States, including Guam, and imported into the "customs territory of the United States," provided they do not contain foreign materials valued at more than 50 percent of the total value of the articles. Utilizing the exception to the imposition of tariffs set forth in Headnote 3(a), the Virgin Islands developed an important watch industry which imported the parts into the island and assembled them there.

In 1966 economic consultants appointed jointly by the Department of the Interior and Guam identified products that might be attractive to entrepreneurs utilizing the Headnote 3(a) provision concerning local assembly or processing of foreign ingredients. Processing of the high-priority items identified (watches, tuna canning, and textiles) was discouraged by the department. In the early 1950s Guam had embarked on a plan for importing Australian wool, processing it in Guam, and then shipping it in to the United States, but abandoned it under federal pressure.[41]

Recent legislation granting the president authority to prohibit or curtail the exportation from the United States, when in the national interest, of any articles, materials, or supplies is applicable to Guam.[42] The power of the president to limit agricultural imports under Section 624 does not, however, apply.[43] The president does have authority to enter into multilateral agreements with foreign governments to limit the export of agricultural commodities from such countries.[44] The agreements could cover Guam, but need not do so.

Shipping

The coastwise shipping laws are explicitly extended to Guam as an island territory of the United States. The Virgin Islands and American Samoa are, however, exempted from their applicability.[45] The term "coastwise laws" refers to those sections of the United States Code which prohibit the transportation of passengers and merchandise between any two points in the United States or its territories in any vessel other than one built in the United States, documented under the laws of the United States, and owned by United States citizens.[46]

The effect of these provisions is to prevent foreign vessels from transporting passengers and merchandise between Guam and any part of the United States. Foreign vessels sailing from San Francisco to the Far East cannot stop in Guam to unload passengers and cargo collected in any United States port. Similarly, foreign vessels on their way to the United States cannot pick up passengers or property in Guam. By limiting foreign vessels to foreign trade only, the amount of shipping available between Guam and other parts of the United States is seriously restricted. The unfairness is more pointed when it is recalled that Guam is considered outside the territorial limits of the United States for the purposes of customs and tariffs. The commission studying the applicability of federal law to Guam recognized the disadvantageous effects of these provisions and recommended that the precedents excluding the Virgin Islands and American Samoa be followed and Guam be excluded; but such action was not taken.[47]

Federal Assistance and Grant-in-Aid Programs

Guam receives federal assistance under a variety of programs. There is no consistent pattern for this assistance; in some cases Guam is treated like a state, in others it is afforded special treatment.

Important factors—cultural, geographical, and political—compound the problem in Guam with respect to federal funds. The distance between Guam and the mainland makes communication and the interchange of information tremendously difficult and expensive. While some states are located far from Washington, regional offices of the various federal departments and agencies are usually within reasonable proximity. This is not true in Guam.

Finally, the political status of Guam as an unincorporated territory contributes to the complexity of the federal aid situation. While it is doubtful that Congress would have the constitutional power to discriminate against a particular state in the application of federal grant programs, its plenary territorial clause powers authorizes such discriminations against territories. Congress has discriminated against Guam in the application of federal aid programs either by excluding Guam entirely or by limiting the amount of grants it is eligible to receive.

In a number of programs under which grants are made on the basis of formulas, Guam and the other outlying areas are statutorily excluded from the normal process of distribution, based on need, and are subject to a distinct allocation formula, a "set-aside." In essence, this separation formula works as follows: from the total amount appropriated for a particular program, a statutorily determined percentage, ordinarily 2 or 3 percent, is set aside for allocation among the outlying areas "according to their respective needs." (In addition to Guam, the term "outlying areas" usually encompasses Puerto Rico, American Samoa, Virgin Islands, Canal Zone, Trust Territory of the Pacific Islands and, in some cases, Indian children in schools operated by the Department of the Interior and overseas dependents in schools operated by the Department of Defense.)

The Nixon Administration proposed a movement away from categorical grant programs to one which provides a good deal more state and local flexibility: revenue sharing. Guam was not included under the general revenue-sharing program, the State and Local Fiscal Assistance Act of 1972.[48] It was included under the special revenue-sharing program, the Comprehensive Employment and Training Act (Manpower Training), which was passed in 1973, and in the other proposed special revenue-sharing bills.[49]

Also, the fact of not being a federated state has indirect implications with respect to federal aid. In the situation in which there is no automatic entitlement to a specified percentage of grant funds available under a particular program—as in the case of competitive (project) grants and federal development programs—the perceived political importance which an area has may be an important factor in its success or failure in securing funds from the federal government. In this regard, Guam, because of its great distance from the United States, coupled with its lack of presidential electors and voting representatives in Congress, is in a disadvantageous position.

Labor

The Fair Labor Standards Act (FLSA),[50] which sets minimum wages, fixes maximum hours, and prohibits the use of child labor, is fully applicable to Guam as a "territory" of the United States.[51] This is in marked contrast to the situation in Puerto Rico and the Virgin Islands, which are excepted by specially tailored provisions of the act.[52]

In 1956 an amendment was added to the act in order for American Samoa to fall under the special industry committees established under Section 205 for Puerto Rico and the Virgin Islands.[53] While such an amendment has not been passed for Guam, the Commission on Application of Federal Laws to Guam, when surveying federal legislation in 1951, did recommend that it would seem "soundest to consider this problem at such a time when effective enforcement . . . of the Fair Labor Standards Act is sought."[54]

NOTES

1. This early period is discussed in Paul Carano and Pedro Sanchez, A Complete History of Guam (Tokyo: Chas. E. Tuttle Co., 1964). See also Charles Beardsley, Guam: Past and Present (Tokyo: Chas. E. Tuttle Co., 1964).

2. For good historical reviews of the period 1898-1950, see William Tansill, Guam and Its Administration (Lib. of Cong. 1951); and Laura Thompson, Guam and Its People (Princeton: Princeton University Press, 1947). The latter was famous for its attack on military policies in Guam.

3. Treaty of Paris, ratified by the Senate on 6 February 1899, 30 Stat. 1754, Art. II.

4. Quoted in John P. Bloom, The American Territorial System (Athens, Ohio: Ohio University Press, 1969), p. 215.

5. 12 U.S.C. § 1842(d).

6. Downes v. Bidwell, 182 U.S. 243, 342, 345 (1901).

7. 25 Op. Att'y Gen. 292 (1904).

8. 25 Op. Att'y Gen. 59 (1903).
9. U.S. Sen., Hearings on S. 75th Cong., 1st Sess. (1936).
10. 6 F.R. 1015 (19 February 1942).
11. Civil Regulations with the Force and Effect of Law in Guam, ch. 21, para. 1, at 45 (G.P.O., 1947).
12. Barrett and Ferenz, Peacetime Martial Law in Guam, 48 Cal. L. Rev. 1, 3 (1960).
13. Letter from Naval Operations, serial no. 5235P21 (4 December 1950).
14. Guam Master Plan Prepared for the Territory of Guam by Greenleaf/Telesca-Ahn, 6-7 (June 1972).
15. Guam Master Plan Prepared for the Territory of Guam by Greenleaf/Telesca-Ahn (June 1972).
16. Barrett and Ferenz, Peacetime Martial Law in Guam.
17. U.S.C. §§ 2152.
18. Feliciano v. United States, 297 F. Supp. 1356 (D.P.R. 1969); aff'd. per curiam, 422 F.2d 943 (1st Cir. 1970); cert. den. 400 U.S. 823, which upheld the president's authority to create the Cuelebra Island Naval Defensive Sea Area.
19. Governor's Annual Report to the Secretary of the Navy (27 September 1915).
20. Robert K. Coote, Land-Use Conditions and Land Problems on Guam (Washington, D.C.: Office of the Secretary, Dept. of the Interior, 1951).
21. Annual Report of the Governor of Guam (1935) at 23.
22. Hearings Before the House Comm. on Naval Affairs on H.R. 6547 to Authorize the Secretary of the Navy to Acquire in Fee or Otherwise Certain Lands and Rights in Land on the Island of Guam, 79th Cong., 2d Sess., 29 May 1946.
23. Post-War Land Takings on Guam, Report of Special Comm. on Federal Problems, Eleventh Guam Legislature (September 1972).
24. Letter to the Hon. Sam Rayburn, 17 August 1945, reprinted in H. Rpt. No. 1136, 79th Cong., 1st Sess.
25. Act of 15 November 1945, ch. 483, 59 Stat. 582.
26. Hearings Before the House Comm. on Naval Affairs on S. 1139 for the Relief of the Residents of Guam through the Settlement of Meritorious Claims (18 October 1945).
27. Supplementary Rpt. of the War Claims Comm. With Respect to War Claims Arising out of World War II, 83rd Cong., 1st Sess., H. Doc. No. 67 (1953).
28. Hearings Before the Subcomm. on Territorial and Insular Affairs of the House Comm. on Interior and Insular Affairs, 92nd Cong., 2d Sess. 12 (1972).
29. Executive Order 10077.
30. Law passed 14 August 1964, Public Law 7-163, Seventh Guam Legislature.
31. Status of Guam, Report of the Twelfth Guam Legislature (1974), p. 19.

GUAM 131

32. Proposition No. 26-A, which would have amended Sections 1 and 3 of the organic act.
33. Proposition No. 62, which would have amended Section 9-A of the organic act.
34. Va. Const. art. IV, § 18; Alaska Const. art. IX, § 14; P. R. Const. art. III, § 22.
35. Status of Guam, p. 20.
36. Ibid., pp. 13-14.
37. Bordallo v. Camacho, 475 F.2d 712 (9th Cir. 1973).
38. Status of Guam, p. 15.
39. Status of Guam, pp. 16-17.
40. Marsh, An Examination of the Judicial System of the Virgin Islands, Judicature (June 1974).
41. Van Cleve, The Office of Territorial Affairs 90 (1974).
42. 50 App. U.S.C. § 2403(b)(1).
43. 7 U.S.C. § 610(f), § 624.
44. 7 U.S.C. § 1854.
45. 46 U.S.C. § 877; 48 U.S.C. § 1664.
46. 46 U.S.C. §§ 289, 883.
47. Resource Material Used in the Preparation of the Report of the Commission on Application of Federal Laws to Guam, printed for the use of the Committee on Interior and Insular Affairs (1952), at p. 221.
48. Act of 20 October 1972, P.L. 92-512, 86 Stat. 919.
49. For example, Sec. 101(g) of S. 1612 (92nd Cong., 1st Sess.), Rural Community Development Revenue Sharing Act of 1971.
50. Fair Labor Standards Act, 29 U.S.C. §§ 201 et seq.
51. 29 U.S.C. §§ 203(c), 213(f).
52. 29 U.S.C. §§ 205, 206, 208.
53. 8 August 1956, ch. 1035, Sec. 2, 70 Stat. 1118.
54. Resource Material Used in the Preparation of the Report of the Commission on Application of Federal Laws to Guam, pp. 170-71.

CHAPTER

6

THE COOK ISLANDS

Although the Cook Islands are small, they have been the pioneer in associated state thinking, especially influential in the Pacific but also important within the United Nations experience. Although there is now some discussion of independence for the islands, further status change was not envisioned in their relationship with New Zealand. Rather, what was envisioned was a continuing permanent association. It is this relationship which is examined at some length in this chapter.

The 15 islands which constitute the Cook Islands are spread out over 850,000 square miles of ocean, extending from nine degrees south of the equator to just above the Tropic of Capricorn. There are some islands which have almost no population. Manauae, for example, was listed in 1973 as having two male inhabitants, while Suwarrow had one.

While the Cook Islands cover a large area, the islands themselves comprise only 93 square miles. They are divided into two groups. The southern islands are sparsely populated and are basically coral atolls which can support almost no agricultural activity. The northern group, the more populous of the two, contains what arable land exists. Among the islands of this group is Rarotonga, the most heavily populated island, containing 60 percent (11,388) of the islands' total inhabitants (21,227). The sparseness of the Cook Island population is exacerbated by the constant exodus of Cook Islanders to New Zealand, where greater economic opportunities exist. In 1971 over 1,000 Cook Islanders—about 5 percent of the populace—left, most of them bound for New Zealand, to seek employment and to learn a trade.[1]

The Cook Islands are geographically isolated. The Cook Islands' first premier, Albert Henry, put it this way:

> It is many hundreds of miles to the East of Fiji, Tonga and Western Samoa; several hundreds of miles to the west of French Polynesia; thousands of miles to the south of the

Hawaiian Islands; and almost 2,000 miles northeast of
New Zealand. If this is not isolation, maybe you can tell
me what is.[2]

In addition, the islands are situated in the hurricane zone and not infrequently suffer extensive damage as a result of these storms. Thus, what crops are cultivated (primarily citrus fruit, pineapple, coconuts, coffee, yams, taro, and pepper) are in constant jeopardy from the elements.

Most Cook Islanders are ethnically related to the New Zealand Maoris, claiming a common heritage and ancestry and sharing with them a similar language.

HISTORICAL BACKGROUND

The historic relationship between the Cook Islands and New Zealand, before the institution of the present arrangement, can be divided into three periods: (1) the nineteenth century, when the Polynesian society of the Cook Islands came under the influence of British missionaries and eventually under the protectorate of the British government; (2) the period from 1901 to 1946, the first phase of New Zealand control, when there was little indigenous movement for self-government or economic self-determination; and (3) the period from 1946 to 1964, when the forces which propelled the Cook Islands into self-governing status came to the fore.

Pre-1900

In the centuries before the imposition of British rule upon the Cook Islands, island society was broken down into various clans with each clan having its own hierarchy, culture, and form of social organization. In most of the clans, ownership of land was communal. The British Christian missionaries began to come in the 1820s; and from 1835 to 1880, the period which historian of the Pacific Ernest Beaglehole referred to as the "height of the mission theocracy," the indigenous cultures and social organizations were suppressed.[3]

A British protectorate was established over the Cook Islands in 1888. The British government, through a resident agent appointed by the New Zealand government, supervised the political affairs of the islands, while a federal parliament with representatives from each one of the islands provided a semblance of local autonomy.

MAP 6

The Cook Islands

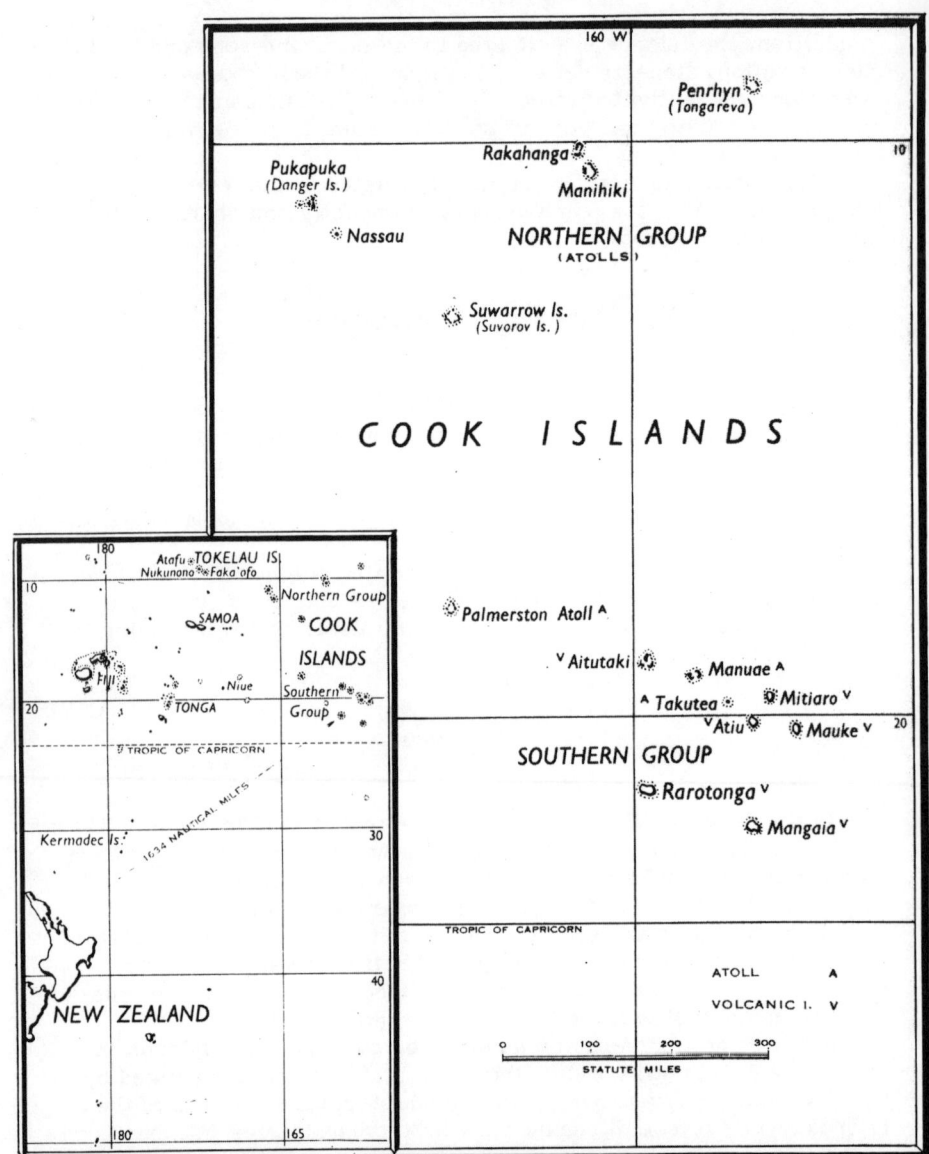

Source: T. F. Kennedy, A Descriptive Atlas of the Pacific Islands (New York: Praeger, 1969).

1901-1946

In 1901, under international political pressure, the British government, after obtaining certain guarantees, ceded the Cook Islands to New Zealand under the 1895 Colonial Boundaries Act.[4] The cession had very strong support in the New Zealand Parliament.

The years of New Zealand rule, up to the post-World War II era, were characterized by a continuous strengthening of control in Wellington. The 1915 Cook Island Act generally set out the framework of the constitutional arrangement under a New Zealand-appointed minister of island territories who supervised the appointed resident commissioner and resident agents.

The resident commissioner, stationed in Rarotonga, had complete control over public revenue and responsibility for the resident agents. While the island councils did not have their authority taken away from them, the resident commissioner automatically became ex officio president of Rarotonga Island Council. Although the Cook Island courts were to be continued, the Supreme and Appeals Courts of New Zealand were to be used for cases on appeal. The Cook Islands Federal Council was abolished and each one of the islands functioned under the direction of its island council and the resident agency which in turn was under the supervision of the secretary for the Cook Islands in New Zealand. The traditional sources of leadership and authority in the Cook Islands, the arikis (clan leaders), were left basically powerless. Local authority was almost completely dissolved.[5]

1946-1965

This basic constitutional arrangement continued with minor modification until the 1960s when, under pressure from the United Nations, the Cook Islands and New Zealand were propelled into discussing other forms of association. The process began following World War II when the Cook Islands' straitened economic circumstances led to the formation of the Cook Islands Progressive Association (CIPA) in 1945.

Along with the economic demands voiced by the CIPA (which functioned as a quasi-labor union on the wharves of Rarotonga) for higher wages and improvement of shipping facilities in the islands were a set of political and constitutional demands. These included the revival of the Federal Council of the Cook Islands, Cook Island representation in the New Zealand Parliament, and the election of island councilors, who until then had been appointed.

There was some support in New Zealand for these demands, especially among certain Maori groups (stirred by the common ancestry they shared with the Cook Islanders) and certain union forces, notably the Auckland Trades Council. Because of this support, the CIPA was able to achieve a modest amount of legislative success in New Zealand; and the 1947 Cook Islands Amendment Act provided for the Cook Islands Legislative Council which was to be a partly elected, central legislative body for the Cook Islands. Further, according to this 1946 legislation, the Island Councils would have a certain number of elected members, although the others continued to be appointed ex officio.

The new Legislative Council, composed of 10 members appointed by the various Island Councils and 11 official members, was to have powers limited to "making laws for the peace, order and good government of the Cook Islands and to imposing rates, tolls, fees, fines and taxes." The Legislative Council could not levy any kind of import or export tax nor did it have the ability to spend any of the islands' revenues. It met only a few weeks each year and there was no system by which members could be familiarized unofficially with work of the administrative departments or meet together between sessions. Further, the resident commissioner, who presided over the Legislative Council, was given veto powers.[6] This provided only a limited amount of internal self-government and the Cook Islanders pressed for further changes.

In 1954 protest demonstrations were organized in the islands against New Zealand taxes because of a lack of local participation in the imposition of taxes or control over how the tax funds were to be spent. This issue caused the New Zealand government to establish a commission to analyze the administrative relationship. The report, which was submitted to the New Zealand Parliament in 1955, not only called for increased health and educational services for the Cook Islands, but discussed the need for greater local responsibility in internal affairs by strengthening the powers of the Legislative Council, establishing standing committees, and curtailing the number of official members. It recommended giving the islands' Legislative Council greater financial discretion.

The report stressed that the commission was not responding to nationalist sentiment in the Cook Islands, of which there was very little, but was concerned with the "bewilderment on the part of a people which is not too sure where its future lies." It concluded that the New Zealand Parliament should recognize that the present relationship was not going to be a permanent one and that it should begin to think about modification.[7]

Further steps towards autonomy were taken when the Parliament of New Zealand passed the 1957 Cook Islands Amendment Act. That act changed the name of the Legislative Council to the Legislative Assembly and augmented its powers, giving it full control over all revenue to be collected in the Cook Islands. In 1962 the New Zealand cabinet gave the Cook Islands Legislative Assembly complete control for allocation of all financial resources, including those given by New Zealand. A separate and autonomous Cook Islands Public Service was created which was to operate separately from the New Zealand public service. After this legislation the first Cook Islands-wide election was held for the seats in the Legislative Assembly.[8]

The key step toward the present relationship took place in July 1962 when New Zealand's minister of island territories addressed the Cook Islands Legislative Assembly and requested a determination by the Cook Islanders of their future relationship with New Zealand. He presented to the Legislative Assembly four alternatives, any one of which he felt would be acceptable to New Zealand and would, he hoped, satisfy the United Nations. The first was independence; the second, annexation and integration into New Zealand; the third, the possibility of the Cook Islands joining at some point in the future an undefined Polynesian federation; and fourth, internal self-government, with continued association with New Zealand. The last would permit a continued high level of New Zealand economic support.

With only two assemblymen dissenting (favoring complete integration with New Zealand), the Cook Islands Assembly voted in favor of internal self-government with continued association with New Zealand. Over the course of the next two years the Cook Islands Legislative Assembly and the New Zealand Parliament worked out the details of the Cook Island Constitution Bill, which was passed by both the New Zealand Parliament and the Cook Islands Assembly in 1964.

The next stage in the process took place in April 1965 when the Cook Islanders went to the polls to elect a new Legislative Assembly. (The previous assembly had been dissolved so that the election of legislators could be considered a referendum on the constitution.) The election, in which over 95 percent of the islands' population voted, was not contested on a partisan basis, although the old CIPA was resurrected in the form of the Cook Islands Party with Albert Henry once again directing its activities. New Zealand invited United Nations observers to be present during the Cook Islands elections and to attest to the democratic procedures being used. At those elections, over 50 percent of the votes went to the Cook Islands Party. The new Legislative Assembly met for the first time in April 1965, and, after making two amendments, passed the new constitution.

THE COOK ISLANDS CONSTITUTION

The constitution of the Cook Islands provides for a British parliamentary, or Westminster, system of government. The constitution grants citizenship to the Cook Islanders—although they may not vote in New Zealand elections and have no representation in the New Zealand Parliament—and limits the applicability of New Zealand law to only those cases where the Cook Islands government requests and consents to it. Recently the New Zealand government has suggested that the fact of Cook Island citizenship may impose obligations and restrictions on activities by the Cook Islands government:

> For the reasons I have already indicated, the bond of citizenship does entail a degree of New Zealand involvement in Cook Islands affairs. This is reflected in the scale of New Zealand's response to your country's material needs; but it also creates an expectation that the Cook Islands will uphold, in their laws and policies a standard of values generally acceptable to New Zealanders.
> It seems to my Government that this is the heart of the matter. The special relationship between the Cook Islands and New Zealand is on both sides a voluntary arrangement which depends upon shared interests and shared sympathies. In particular, it calls for understanding on New Zealand's part of the Cook Islands' natural desire to lead a life of their own, and for equal understanding on the Cook Islands' part of New Zealand's determination to safeguard the values on which its citizenship is based.[9]

The most distinctive feature of the constitution is that it permits the Cook Islands to opt out of the agreement with New Zealand, totally or partially, by a two-thirds vote of the Legislative Assembly. This "escape clause" can serve to prevent any abuse of power on the part of New Zealand and can operate for the benefit of the Cook Islanders should they decide that they are interested in total independence rather than internal independence and self-governing status. It was this provision, Section 41 of the constitution, which was cited repeatedly in the UN discussion of the evolving status of the Cook Islands. For those members of the committee who were critical of the limited degree of power accorded the Cook Islands under the association, Section 41 was pointed to as the major mitigating factor.

POLITICAL RELATIONS

The High Commissioner

The constitution begins by stating that the head of state for the Cook Islands is the Queen of England and that her representative in the Cook Islands is the high commissioner. The person who exercises that position is also the representative of the New Zealand government in the islands, who is appointed by the governor-general of New Zealand. The high commissioner must act only on the advice of the premier of the Cook Islands, the cabinet of the Cook Islands, or the appropriate

Cook Islands minister. Not only must he solicit the advice of these Cook Islands functionaries, but if any of them gives advice to the high commissioner and he has not responded within 14 days of the offering of that advice, "the High Commissioner shall be deemed to have accepted" it.

The premier of the Cook Islands, in turn, has very little responsibility to the high commissioner. He must inform him about the affairs of the islands and tell him about proposals which are being considered by the Legislative Assembly. He must also ensure that the high commissioner receives copies of the agenda and minutes of the cabinet meetings.

The ceremonial nature of the high commissioner's position was emphasized by the New Zealand representative to the UN who informed the committee considering the status of the Cook Islands:

> The powers of the High Commissioner in the Cook Islands under the constitution would be similar to those of the Queen in New Zealand: in substantive matters, he would act on advice or in accordance with constitutional provisions, and in those few matters in which he had discretion his powers were formal rather than effective and were bound by convention.

House of Arikis

As already mentioned, the arikis were the traditional clan heads of the Cook Islands, and their role in the constitution was inserted at the behest of the Cook Island Party. The House of Arikis consists of up to 15 members to be appointed by the high commissioner. It is required to meet at least once every 12 months and to consider any matter which deals with the welfare of the Cook Islands and its residents and which has first been discussed by the Legislative Assembly. The House of Arikis itself has no initiating powers.

The Executive

The executive is divided into two bodies: the cabinet and the executive council. The cabinet is directly responsible to the Legislative Assembly and is made up of the premier and three to five other ministers.

The high commissioner and the cabinet make up the Executive Council. The high commissioner is given some discretion with respect to the decisions of the cabinet. If there is no dissent on the high commissioner's part, the cabinet decision goes into effect. However, if the high commissioner does not agree with the decision, the cabinet may be requested to reconsider. If it reconsiders and maintains its original decision, the decision takes effect anyhow. Thus, the high commissioner can delay temporarily the decision of the cabinet but he cannot block it entirely.[10]

The executive authority in the Cook Islands may "be exercised on behalf of Her Majesty by the High Commissioner," but the Legislative Assembly may at its own discretion confer executive power to "persons or authorities other than the High Commissioner."

The Legislature

The Legislative Assembly consists of 22 members elected by universal adult suffrage. (The voting age is 18, an issue that was slightly embarrassing to New Zealand, which sets the legal age at 21.) Assemblymen represent particular islands, with Rarotonga, the most populous of the islands, having nine representatives while other islands must share one single representative. In order to be qualified to vote in the Cook Islands and to hold a seat in the Legislative Assembly an individual must be a British subject and must have lived in the Cook Islands for three months. (In some cases the three months of residency need only have been at some point within the preceding twelve months.)

The leader of the Legislative Assembly is the Speaker who is elected by whatever manner the assembly decides (popularly by the Assembly) provided that if the Speaker is not an assemblyman he must be qualified to be one. The constitution provides for a bilingual parliamentary system with all bills, records, and reports being issued in both English and Maori ("as spoken in Rarotonga").

The Legislative Assembly has sole power and authority for making laws for "the peace, order, and good government of the Cook Islands" in addition to laws dealing with "extra-territorial operation." (This subclause is not further elaborated upon and may perhaps conflict with the agreement that New Zealand has retained responsibility for the Cook Islands in matters of defense and external affairs.) The only limitation upon the authority of the Legislative Assembly is the provision that the tax structure may not be altered without the recommendation of the high commissioner. This is true also for certain other financial matters.

As noted above, the Cook Islands may unilaterally alter the constitution even to the extent of unilaterally repealing it. In order to amend the constitution, a bill must receive the votes of at least two-thirds of the total membership of the Legislative Assembly. If the Legislative Assembly wishes to repeal any of the "entrenched clauses," which are those that define the nature of the Cook Islands-New Zealand partnership, it must have the support of two-thirds of the assembly and a vote of two-thirds of the qualified electorate in a plebiscite.

The Judiciary

The judiciary of the Cook Islands is somewhat less independent of New Zealand than the legislative or the executive. The constitution sets up two courts solely for the Cook Islands: the High Court of the Cook Islands and the Land Court of the Cook Islands. At the appellate level the constitution establishes the Land Appellate Court of the Cook Islands, composed of judges from the Land Court of the Cook Islands and the Maori Land Court of New Zealand. The presiding judge for the Land Appellate Court is the chief judge of the Land Court of the Cook Islands, and the chief judge of the Maori Land Court of New Zealand presides only when his colleague from the Cook Islands is absent.

Cases can be appealed from the High Court of the Cook Islands to the Supreme Court of New Zealand if the high court feels that there is a significant interpretive issue involved; or if the high court has sentenced an individual to death or to a jail sentence of more than six months; or if a substantial fine is involved.

Defense and Foreign Affairs

The New Zealand government has retained responsibility for the discharge of defense and external affairs for the Cook Islands. This provision has given rise to some question. The section states:

> Nothing in this Act or in the Constitution shall affect the responsibilities . . . of New Zealand for the external affairs and defense of the Cook Islands. Those responsibilities to be discharged after consultation with the Premier of the Cook Islands.[11]

The issue is whether the request and consent provision—the need for Cook Islands concurrence—applies in this area as it does elsewhere. The language, which limits the Cook Islands role to "consultation," and the specific distinct character of the provision suggest that it does not. Many in the New Zealand government feel otherwise, however. Although the issue is unresolved, and is likely to remain so, the recent Niue Constitution (which has in all other key aspects the same language as that of the Cook Islands) has a new Section 8 designed to make clear the bilateral relationship in the foreign affairs area:

6. External affairs and defense—Nothing in this Act or in the Constitution shall affect the responsibilities of Her Majesty the Queen in right of New Zealand for the external affairs and defense of Niue.

7. Economic and administrative assistance—It shall be a continuing responsibility of the Government of New Zealand to provide necessary economic and administrative assistance to Niue.

8. Co-operation between New Zealand and Niue—Effect shall be given to the provisions of sections 6 and 7 of this Act, and to any other aspect of the relationship between New Zealand and Niue which may from time to time call for positive co-operation between New Zealand and Niue, after consultation between the Prime Minister of New Zealand and the Premier of Niue, and in accordance with the policies of their respective Governments; and, if it appears desirable that any provision be made in the law of Niue to carry out these policies, that provision may be made in the manner prescribed in the Constitution, but not otherwise. [12]

Regardless of the resolution of this issue New Zealand has taken pains to operate very carefully in this area. Thus New Zealand's "sole control of air traffic rights into and out of the Cook Islands" is stipulated by the Civil Aviation Agreement passed by the Cook Islands Legislative Assembly in 1969. In general, however, New Zealand handles the limited foreign relations of the Cook Islands.

New Zealand has nevertheless sponsored a certain degree of Cook Island independence in the external affairs area. The islands are represented in international bodies by New Zealand, but have separate membership in the South Pacific Forum, South Pacific Bureau for Economic Cooperation, Asian Development Bank, Pacific Island Planters Association, South Pacific Conference, and the UN Economic Commission for Asia and the South Pacific.

Because of the recent discovery of manganese nodules in the seabeds around the Cook Islands, the islands were interested in the Law of the Sea Conference held in Caracas, Venezuela, in the summer of 1974. The Islands did attend but did not have a separate delegation. Albert Henry, Premier of the Islands, went as a member of the New Zealand delegation.

Control of Immigration Policy

Cook Islanders are New Zealand citizens and as such have full and direct emigration rights to New Zealand. This right has been a mixed blessing since the constant flow of Cook Islanders to New

Zealand has been a contributing force to the chronic economic problems of the Cook Islands.

Significantly, immigration to the Cook Islands is at the discretion of the minister of immigration of the Cook Islands and anyone landing in the islands must have authorization. Any person intending to settle in the islands must deposit with the minister of immigration's office a sum of money or a return ticket unless the individual has been guaranteed by a Cook Islander or a Cook Island firm. There does not seem to be any provision making immigration to the Cook Islands from New Zealand easier or more difficult than from any other country. In fact, there is very little movement from New Zealand to the Cook Islands.

Applicability of Federal Law

The New Zealand Parliament can legislate for the Cook Islands with permission of the Cook Islands government. Section 46 of the constitution provides:

> No Act, and no provision of the Act of the Parliament of New Zealand passed on or after Constitution Day shall extend or be deemed to extend to the Cook Islands as part of the law of the Cook Islands, unless . . . the Act . . . or provision has been requested and consented to by the government of the Cook Islands.

That request must come from the Cook Islands Legislative Assembly; or, if it is not in session, from the high commissioner acting in accordance with the advice of the cabinet.

Although Article 46 leaves the initiative for New Zealand legislation to the Cook Islands government, in practice the New Zealand Parliament legislates in a substantial number of areas at its own initiative. The provisions of Article 46 are then fulfilled by an annual New Zealand Laws Bill put before the Cook Islands Assembly for that body's approval.

TRANSITION TO INTERNAL SELF-GOVERNMENT

The constitution provides for the technical steps in the transfer of power and the transitional steps to be taken to facilitate the change in the status of the Cook Islands. The governor-general of New Zealand may request that the Cook Islands enact particular pieces of legislation, or he may enact, with the request and consent of the government of the Cook Islands, "regulations, not inconsistent with any provision of this Constitution, for the peace, order and good government of the Cook Islands."

The Public Service

The chief administrator of the Cook Islands Public Service is appointed by the high commissioner on the advice of the premier. He has responsibility for the appointment, employment terms, and termination of members of the Cook Islands Public Service.

New Zealand Audit of Public Revenues

All expenditures from the Cook Islands government account must be approved by the Legislative Assembly, which can pass appropriation acts that lapse at the end of the year for which they were passed. The Audit Office of the New Zealand government is, however, also the auditor of the Cook Islands government account and all other public funds and the funds of all of the departments of the government. At least once a year the Audit Office is required to submit to the Speaker of the Legislative Assembly an assessment of the government account.

ECONOMIC RELATIONS

Land Laws

All land in the Cook Islands[13] is owned by the Maoris, who may not sell, mortgage, or dispose of land. The notable exception is permission to mortgage land to a cooperative society or to the Housing Board for the purposes of securing a housing loan.

According to a 1970 law, landowners grouped together in a "body corporate" may lease land for a maximum of 60 years for commercial purposes. Under this law the owners of the land must be given shareholding rights of a minimum of 10 percent of the equity capital, in addition to the rental fees. Since the landowners must be Cook Islanders, this protects the Cook Islands from encroachment by outside—notably New Zealand—business interests.

Land may be sold or leased to the Crown for more than 60 years, but only for public purposes, or to a religious body for religious purposes. The minimum land rental is N.Z. £5 per acre.

Foreign Investment and Foreign Trade

The Cook Islands have control of all investment in the islands, including foreign investment. With respect to foreign trade, in practice a common market with New Zealand is in operation. Thus New Zealand customs duties operate in the islands, although there may be specific modifications because of the particular commercial needs of the islands. All New Zealand goods to the islands are exempt from duties; and, similarly, goods from the Cook Islands to New Zealand may enter free of duty. About 90 percent of the export produce from the Cook Islands is shipped to New Zealand.

Federal Financial Assistance

New Zealand has provided considerable financial assistance to the Cook Islands ranging from N.Z.£275,000 to N.Z.£500,000 in the decade prior to the adoption of the constitution. Following the adoption of the constitution, the New Zealand aid more than doubled. In 1973 it was estimated at $3.7 million, about two-thirds in grants and one-third in loans.

NOTES

1. New Zealand Official Yearbook: 1973, pp. 925-29.
2. Statement by Albert Henry at Law of the Sea Conference (29 July 1974), Press Release from New Zealand Embassy, p. 3.
3. Ernest Beaglehole, "Social and Political Changes in the Cook Islands," Pacific Affairs 21 (December 1948): 386-87.
4. Ibid., p. 389; W. S. Lowe and W. T. G. Airey, "New Zealand Dependencies and the Development of Autonomy," Pacific Affairs 17 (September 1945): 252.
5. S. D. Wilson, "The Record in the Cook Islands and More 1901-1945," in Angus Ross, ed., New Zealand's Record in the Pacific Islands in Twentieth Century (Auckland, New Zealand: Longman Paul Ltd., 1969), pp. 24-59.
6. Ernest Beaglehole, Changes in the Cook Islands, pp. 391-92.
7. S. D. Wilson, "Cook Island Development 1946-1965," in New Zealand's Record, pp. 74-88.
8. Ibid., pp. 87-88.
9. Excerpt from Exchange of Letters Between the Prime Minister of New Zealand and the Premier of the Cook Islands Concerning the

Nature of the Special Relationship Between the Cook Islands and New Zealand (4 May 1973; 9 May 1973).

10. Sec. 25, 1965 No. 2, An Act to Amend the Cook Islands Constitution (7 June 1965).

11. Sec. 5, 1964 No. 69, An Act to Make Provision for Self-Government by the People of the Cook Islands and to Provide a Constitution for Those Islands (17 November 1964).

12. Secs. 6, 7, and 8, No. 52-2, An Act to Make Provision for Self Government by the People of Niue, and to Provide a Constitution for Niue, as reported from the Island Affairs Committee (21 August 1974).

13. The effect of modernization on the native land tenure system is examined in R. G. Crocombe, Land Tenure in the Cook Islands (Melbourne: Oxford University Press, 1964).

CHAPTER

7

PAPUA NEW GUINEA

If the Cook Islands has a problem because of its small size, then Papua New Guinea may be in exactly the opposite position. It is large, but its sense of direction and nationalism is much less developed. Although independence was granted in 1975, the associated state relationship with Australia, developed as a transitional measure, was longer in duration than first envisioned. Many aspects of this relationship may be transferable both to other parts of the British Commonwealth and to territories of the United States.

Papua New Guinea is the name given to the eastern half of the island of New Guinea located just north of the Australian continent. The western half of the island, formerly under the control of the Netherlands, is now under the sovereignty of the government of Indonesia and is known as Irian Jaya. Papua New Guinea is the result of the political union of the Trust Territory of New Guinea and the Territory of Papua, which have both been under Australian supervision since after World War I, except during a brief Japanese invasion during World War II which suspended civil administration.

The Trust Territory of New Guinea encompassed the northeastern portion of the island, including the Bismarck Archipelago with its three main islands of New Britain, New Ireland, and Manus, and the two northernmost islands of the Solomon group, Bougainville and Buka. The Territory of Papua encompassed the southeastern portion of the island, the Trobriand and D'Entrecasteaux Islands, and the Louisiade Archipelago. The total land area of Papua and New Guinea is roughly 180,000 square miles and supports a population of approximately two and one-half million people. Of these, almost 700,000 live in Papua.

Situated wholly within the tropics, Papua New Guinea has a typically monsoonal climate. Topographically the entire area is incredibly rugged, with the main island dominated by a massive cordillera that extends across the full 1,500 miles of the island of New Guinea.

MAP 7

Papua New Guinea

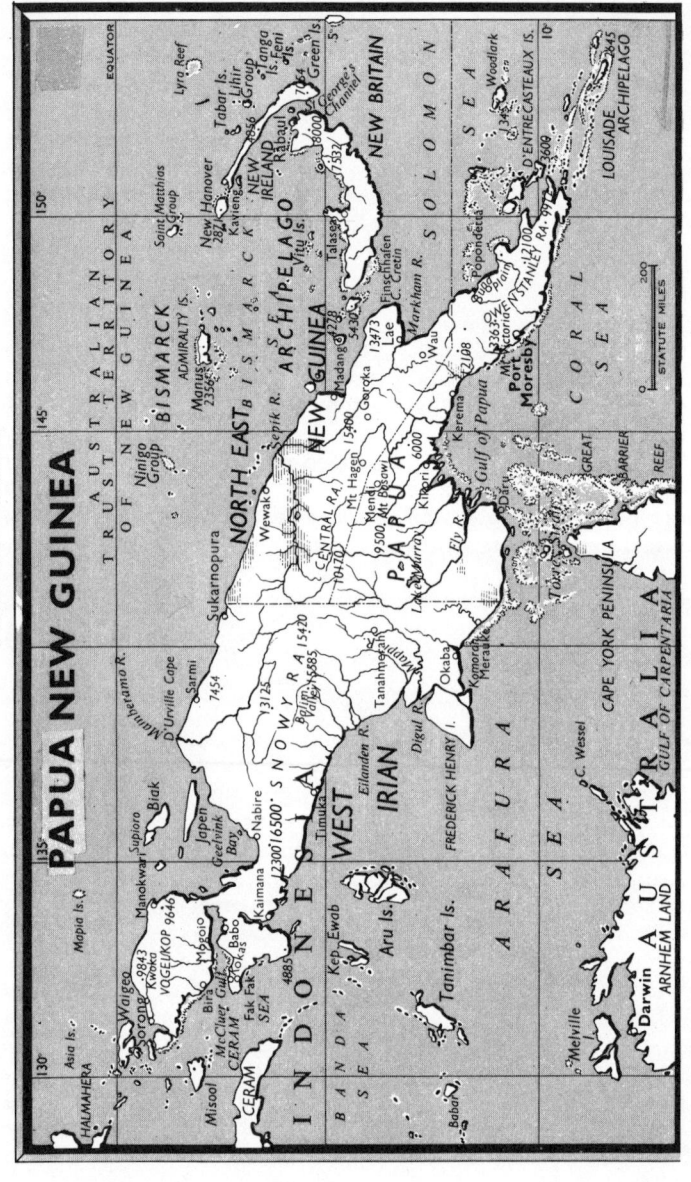

Source: T. F. Kennedy, A Descriptive Atlas of the Pacific Islands (New York: Praeger, 1969).

The rough topography and low density of population has resulted in great diversity and fragmentation of the people on the island.

Although the people generally are Melanesian, there are a wide variety of religious, tribal, and linguistic groups. It has been estimated that over 500 distinct languages are used within the country. The 100 most widely used languages embrace in aggregate more than a million speakers. The more widely used languages have over 50,000 speakers; among these are Chimbu with approximately 60,000 and the Enga dialects with approximately 100,000 speakers. Many of the remaining approximately 400 languages have very few speakers, from "a few dozen to a few hundred."[1] Pisin (Neo-Melanesian), which was spoken previously in German New Guinea, Motu from Papua, and English are the official languages used in the national legislature.

HISTORICAL BACKGROUND

Pre-1950

The island of New Guinea was first sighted by Portuguese and Spanish explorers in the early part of the sixteenth century. During the next two centuries other European navigators visited the coast but there were few settlements.

Not until the late 1800s, when trade in coconut oil became major and there was a minor gold rush to Port Moresby, did European contact with what is now Papua New Guinea become substantial. In 1884 Germany claimed formal possession of the northeast portion of the main island as German New Guinea, and Britain proclaimed the southern coast and the islands adjacent thereto as a possession in 1888, naming it British New Guinea. The Dutch laid claims to the western end of the island, agreeing with Great Britain to define their boundary as the 141st meridian of longitude.

After the enactment in 1900 of the Commonwealth of Australia Constitution Act which both granted internal self-government to Australia and set it on the road to independence,* King Edward VII transferred authority for British New Guinea to the Commonwealth of Australia.

---

*Sixteen years after the enactment of the Commonwealth of Australia Constitution Act, the foreign policy and defense of Australia, as in other commonwealth countries, was still controlled by the United Kingdom. As late as 1931 the power of Australia to legislate with extraterritorial effect was still questioned. Not until the enactment of Section 3 of the Statute of Westminster was the validity of extraterritorial legislation certain. (The Statute of Westminster, 22 Geo. V, c. 4, Sec. 3 [1931].)

When World War I broke out the United Kingdom requested Australia to occupy the German colony and, after a few brief skirmishes, by mid-1915 all German posts were occupied. After World War I, Australia received German New Guinea as a mandated trust territory under the League of Nations while continuing to hold Papua (British New Guinea) as a colony.

The different political status positions, combined with economic circumstances, resulted in somewhat different attitudes toward Australia (and toward foreigners in general) which are still present. Papua was smaller, and its inhabitants were poorer; Australian citizens had considerable control of their economic development. New Guinea was larger, wealthier, considerably more populous; its inhabitants were not Australian citizens, and were less concerned with local institutional control.

The first act combining the two territories occurred during World War II, when they were administered under a combined military command to combat the Japanese who had invaded and occupied positions on both Papua and New Guinea. With the surrender of the Japanese in 1945, civil administration was progressively restored and the joint administration was continued under the provisions of the Papua-New Guinea Provisional Administration Act of 1945-46.

The General Assembly of the United Nations approved the terms of the Trusteeship Agreement for the Territory of New Guinea, formulated by the government of Australia, on 13 December 1946; and thus the territory was brought under the UN trusteeship system. Article Five of this agreement allowed Australia to "bring the Territory into a customs, fiscal or administrative union or federation with other dependent territories," thus authorizing the joining of Papua to New Guinea.

This provision for unification had been questioned by various members of the Trusteeship Council who felt that the administrative union would inevitably lead to political unification, which would threaten the independence of the Trust Territory. The Australian government tended to pooh-pooh such notions without, on the other hand, precluding the possibility. It said it

> had no intention of compelling the virtually identical peoples of the two Territories to form a single state . . . it would regard it as equally inconsistent with its basic responsibilities under the Charter to deny to those peoples at some future date the right to choose such a solution.[2]

Most importantly, the trusteeship agreement permitted, as the mandate did not, a military buildup in New Guinea in accordance with perceived national security interests of Australia after the Japanese invasion in World War II. This was articulated most clearly by Australia's minister of external affairs, Herbert V. Evatt, during the debate on the ratification of the trusteeship agreement by Australia in 1949.

The mandate system did not hurt us except that it prevented
us from establishing defences in mandated territories.
Under the trusteeship system we are free to establish
defences in territories under our trusteeship. That, broadly,
answers the criticisms. . . .³

Australia ratified the trusteeship agreement and provided an administrative union for the government of the two territories by enacting the Papua and New Guinea Act of 1949.⁴ This law also initiated the Westminster parliamentary form in the territory and began the legal/constitutional evolution toward local autonomy and finally independence. It created a nine-man Executive Council, appointed by the Australian civil service, to advise and assist the administrator—parallelling the Australian constitutional provision with its Federal Executive Council to advise the governor-general. A Legislative Council was also established in Papua New Guinea, consciously beginning parliamentary government, although at this time there was no requirement that members of the Executive Council be chosen from the Legislative Council.

The first elected representation was initiated with 3 of the 38-member Legislative Council being elected by the territorial inhabitants. Three others were appointed "native" members; 3 were to represent the interests of Christian missions; and 3 were appointed without restriction. The remaining 16 members, a majority, were "official members," Australian government officials.

Uniform Development and Continued Australian Control

With political power, therefore, still resting within the Australian government, Sir Paul Hasluck, who served as minister for territories from 1951 to 1963, embarked on a policy which envisioned dependency by Papua New Guinea upon the Australian government for some time in the future; that is, uniformity of development in all parts of the territory and consequently decentralization of control and spreading of expenditures.⁵ "For some years to come, it is inevitable that Papua and New Guinea will be administered as a territory and that the administration will become increasingly centralised in Australia."⁶ It postponed any major decision about the ultimate destiny of the territory—full integration with Australia, independence, or some form of association. This growth was to be consistent with Australia's strategic military interests.

Our purpose in relation to these external territories will be
to ensure that they shall be administered and developed in
a way best calculated to protect the welfare of the native
inhabitants and, at the same time, to serve Australia's

security interests. Considerations of security interests clearly require that our efforts shall be directed towards establishing in these territories a population of a strength and quality that will enable us to build up in those areas a friendly, loyal and prosperous people who will be able in times of crisis to assist in the protection of their own interests and to provide, strength, not weakness, to the Australian nation, to which they must inevitably turn as their protector.[7]

Some increased measure of self-government was granted with the passage of the Papua and New Guinea Act of 1960[8] which reconstituted the Legislative Council. Of the now 37 members, only 14 were representative of the Australian government (generally officials close to the Papua New Guinea administration), less than a majority. Australia kept effective control for its program, however, since the governor-general appointed 10 other members on the advice of the administrator. Only 12 members were locally elected. Further, the Legislative Council Ordinance 1951 still excluded "natives" from the rolls of eligible voters.[9] There was a special provision to allow the indigenous inhabitants to choose 6 of these 12 elected members, with the other 6 being elected by nonnative, nonalien voters.[10]

The advisory Executive Council was replaced by the Administrator's Council and the six members, other than the administrator, were required to be members of the Legislative Council. But unlike the governor-general of Australia, who is required by custom and constitutional interpretation to follow the advice of the Federal Executive Council,[11] the 1960 act did not require the administrator to act in conformity with the advice of the Administrator's Council. This freed him somewhat from the conservative planter and missionary interest that dominated the council at that time. The Administrative Council members were appointed by the minister for territories on the nomination of the administrator.

Few matters even came to the attention of the Administrator's Council. Only when an ordinance passed by the Legislative Council directed consultation did the administrator operate within the broader group. If the administrator received advice from the council and acted contrary thereto, he was only required to file a statement of his reasons for such action with the Legislative Council.[12]

SHIFT IN AUSTRALIAN POSITION

In the early 1960s, with the emergence of a number of independent African nations (30 new states from 1960 to 1962), pressures mounted in the United Nations for self-government to be given to Papua New

PAPUA NEW GUINEA   153

Guinea. In December 1960 the General Assembly adopted a Declaration of the Granting of Independence to Colonial Countries and Peoples, the fifth paragraph of which read:

> Immediate steps shall be taken, in Trust and Non-Self Governing Territories and all other Territories which have not yet attained independence, to transfer all powers to the people of those territories, without any conditions or reservations, in accordance with their freely-expressed will and desire, without any distinction as to race, creed or colour, in order to enable them to enjoy complete independence and freedom.

When Ruanda-Urundi became independent in 1962, only Nauru and Micronesia—both much smaller than New Guinea—remained under the Trusteeship Council.

A major study by the International Bank for Reconstruction and Development focused on the need for economic development, and within the United Nations the Committee of 17—later the Committee of 24—became increasingly critical of the inadequate educational facilities and the absence of the local populace from responsible positions in the government and the economy.

The UN Visiting Mission in 1962, headed by Sir Hugh Foot, launched a comprehensive attack on Australia's policy of slow uniform development. This attack came on top of the apartheid discussion at the Prime Minister's Commonwealth Conference the year before. The discussion there had focused on South Africa but the potential applicability to Australia's immigration policy and activities in New Guinea bothered Prime Minister Menzies. Finally, the Dutch had been expelled from West New Guinea. Abrupt change had come to the island itself.

The result of all of the above factors was that the Australian government reversed itself and decided to move rapidly to grant independence to Papua New Guinea, although there had been no clear expression of local desire on either the timing or the determination of ultimate status.

The evolutionary pattern toward self-government followed that used generally throughout the British Commonwealth: increased power over local legislation and the development of an advisory council which would eventually be able to act as the cabinet under the Westminster form of government. The development began with the enactment of the Papua and New Guinea Act of 1963.[13]

A new 64-member House of Assembly replaced the smaller Legislative Council and, for the first time, a majority of the members were to be elected. The governor-general still appointed 10 members of the legislature and 10 additional places could not be filled by indigenous inhabitants, although they could vote for the election of the Europeans who would fill them.[14] The remaining 44 were all elected from a common electoral roll of indigenous and nonindigenous inhabitants of the territory. There were no suffrage requirements, but there developed subsequently a literacy requirement of an educational certificate showing completion of the ninth grade.[15]

Even this limited amount of legislative power in the local constituency was severely constrained by the Australian government. The administrator retained a veto over legislative acts and appropriation bills could only be introduced with his written consent. Every ordinance passed by the House was presented to the administrator for his assent. The administrator could either approve the ordinance, return it with recommended amendments, veto it without returning it with recommendations, or reserve it for the approval of the governor-general, who would follow the wishes of the Australian ministers. Further, the administrator was required to reserve for the governor-general any ordinance dealing with such matters as defense, the public service, treaties, or immigration.

Section 55 of the Papua and New Guinea Act 1960-63 provided that the Administrator shall reserve for the Governor-General's pleasure any ordinance that:

(a) relates to divorce;
(b) relates to the granting or disposal of lands of the Crown or of the Administration;
(c) whereby a grant of money or of an interest in land is made to the Administrator;
(d) may not, in the opinion of the Administrator, be fully in accordance with the treaty obligations of the Commonwealth or with the obligations of the Commonwealth under the Trusteeship Agreement;
(e) relates to naval, military, or air forces;
(f) relates to the sale of, or other disposition of or dealing with, land;
(g) relates to the employment of persons;
(h) relates to arms, ammunition, explosives, intoxicating liquor or opium;
(i) relates to immigration, emigration or deportation;
(j) relates to Public Service;
(ja) removes any matter or class of matters from the jurisdiction of the Supreme Court;
(jb) makes provision affecting the practice or procedure of the Supreme Court;
(jc) establishes, or provides for the establishment of, a court; or
(k) contains a provision having substantially the same effect as a provision in an ordinance, or in a part of an ordinance, to which the Governor-General has withheld his assent or which the Governor-General has disallowed.

PAPUA NEW GUINEA   155

In the executive branch the elected members of the legislature now constituted a majority of the Administrator's Council, but the council remained advisory only and the minister for territories had full control of appointment and removal of the ten members from the House.

DEVELOPMENT OF THE MINISTERIAL SYSTEM

The Legislative Council, in one of its last acts, passed the Parliamentary Under-Secretaries Ordinance Act of 1963 which allowed the administrator to appoint up to 15 elected members of the House as parliamentary under-secretaries, although the administrator retained full control over their dismissal and the definition of duties.[16] This marked a major step toward the full ministerial system in Papua New Guinea.

Taking the initiative, the House of Assembly in 1965 created a select committee to draft a set of constitutional proposals to serve as a guide for future constitutional development in the territory. Following the pattern already in practice, the committee recommended in its final report, issued in June 1967, that the advisory council to the administrator, renamed the Administrator's Executive Council (AEC), should be the principal instrument of the executive government in the territory, but that the administrator should retain the power to act contrary to the advice of the council. However, the recommendations concerning the appointment of ministers marked a significant advance toward the Westminster parliamentary form. Each minister would be a member of the AEC and would share responsibility with the official head of the department he was to administer.

The Australian government accepted the majority of the recommendations and enacted the Papua and New Guinea Act of 1968.[17] The House of Assembly was increased to 94 members, 10 of them still "official" appointees. Legislation could still be vetoed by the exclusive heads and the AEC would still only advise the administrator at his request or when directed by ordinances. Included as members of the AEC would be the administrator, three official members of the House of Assembly, and the seven ministerial members. The three official members were appointed and subject to the removal by the Australian minister for territories, but the procedure for appointment and removal of the seven ministerial members gave the legislature, for the first time, some degree of control over the executive branch. While the ministers were appointed and removed by the minister for territories, he could only appoint those members of the House nominated by the House with the concurrence of the administrator. Removal required the resolution of the House that the appointment should be terminated.

The functions and duties performed by each ministerial member in matters dealing with a specific department were to be in accordance with the arrangements and designations approved by the minister of territories. These designations and approved arrangements provided a flexible tool by which increased responsibility for self-government could be given to the local ministers without the need of formal amendment to the Papua and New Guinea Act.[18] The theoretical disadvantage, of course, was that the minister of territories retained ultimate control over the exercise of ministerial powers, but this was unimportant in the context in which the Australian government was eager to devolve control onto the Papua New Guinea authorities.* The initial determinations provided for joint exercise of responsibility by the ministerial members and the departmental heads of the executive departments to which they were assigned. In the event of a disagreement which could not be resolved by consultation and cooperation, the matter was to be referred to the administrator for his decision. The Australian government viewed this method as permitting the territorial representatives to become experienced in the operations of government.

In March 1970 the minister of territories vested responsibility for the day-to-day decisions in the ministerial members.[19] The ministerial member still was subject to the authority of the Australian Commonwealth through the administrator and could only work within the approved budget for his department. But ministerial members could submit legislative proposals to the AEC and present estimates of annual expenditures; and in a break from collective responsibility, a ministerial member who dissented from a decision taken on the advice of the AEC might have his dissent officially recorded. In the House of Assembly, the ministerial member was still to represent the administration and guide legislation approved by the AEC or the minister for external territories through proceedings in the House.

A further step forward came in August with a new determination,[20] approved arrangements,[21] and instructions from the governor-general to the administrator.[22] The grants of authority were still quite modest. Generally speaking, the AEC or the ministerial members were to have authority for decisions involving primary, secondary, and technical education, public health, tourism, cooperatives, business advisory services, the mails and telegraphs, local taxation and price control, coastal shipping, civil defense, prisons, registration and leasing of customary land, land use, and urban development. All other matters continued under Australia's final authority. Specifically, Australia would retain final authority over (1) international relations, defense, and security; (2) civil aviation; (3) banking and currency; (4) public works costing more than $200,000 financed by Australia; (5) higher

---

*In 1951 the designation of the minister for external territories was changed to "minister for territories" and in 1968 it reverted to the original title.

education; (6) external trade and tariffs; (7) immigration; (8) the judicial system; (9) determination of wages and conditions of employment; (10) offshore fisheries; (11) petroleum and mining exploration; (12) telecommunications; (13) public utilities and land development.[23] The administrator was instructed to follow the advice given by the AEC on all matters within the responsibility of the ministerial members and assistant ministerial members.

With the increased responsibility given to the territorial executives, modifications were called for in the adoption of the territorial budget and fiscal policy. The ministerial members would formulate their proposals for expenditures and the AEC would be the final authority in drafting the territorial budget proposal. Negotiations would then take place between the Australian government and the territory. Recurring and minor expenditures were to be jointly financed by taxes collected by the House of Assembly and the negotiated lump-sum payment, called a "grant-in-aid," from Australia. Once the amount of this annual payment was agreed upon, the allocation between the territorial departments would be subject to the modification and control of the AEC. For large development projects, the budget would include a development grant financed by Australia and supervised by Australian authorities.

Veto power over legislation from the House of Assembly remained vested in the administrator and the governor-general. Although the authority existed, very few bills had been vetoed over the preceding few years and no ordinance had been refused assent by the administrator. The administrator did return one bill to the House with his recommendations in 1965 and reserved 203 bills for the assent of the governor-general between 1964 and 1970. The governor-general refused assent on only two and returned another five to the House with recommendations.

The AEC was not yet receiving much success. Even after the approved arrangements in August 1970 the AEC meetings remained relatively few and, for the most part, perfunctory.

Transfer of responsibility to the territorial ministers had been carried out unilaterally—without formal consultation with local authorities—by the Australian government. Expatriate planters and some highlander groups objected to the speed of transfer. The Papua New Guinea House of Assembly in September resolved that any future transfers of power or constitutional changes would be unacceptable until such changes were agreed to by a majority of its members.[24]

MOVEMENT TOWARD INTERNAL SELF-GOVERNMENT

The House of Assembly's Select Committee on Constitutional Development issued its report to the House of Assembly in 1971 amidst accusations that the committee had been unduly pressured by the Australian government. The committee took an ambivalent attitude toward self-government. The majority concluded that internal self-government should come no sooner than 1976-80. What exactly self-government would include was uncertain although the chairman of the Select Committee, P. Arek, expressed the view in November 1970 that self-government would mean that the ministers of the House of Assembly would determine the <u>internal</u> affairs of government, an arrangement much like Australia's position with the United Kingdom and within the Commonwealth in the early 1900s. Australia would remain responsible for the territory's defense and external affairs and there would be joint control with respect to the police, internal security, the judiciary, trade, banking, and civil aviation.

Those opposed to early self-government, particularly from the western and southern highlands, felt that there was much need for economic, social, and educational development before self-government would be viable.[25] The crucial question was the amount of aid or assistance Australia would provide after self-government had been bestowed. They argued that Australia was promoting separation to save the cost of extensive development of the territory.

Both Australia and Papua New Guinea agreed that target dates for self-government would not be formally set and that the time for independence would be considered when internal self-government was reached. As late as September 1972 the chief minister of Papua New Guinea, M. Somare, spoke of not rushing the decision for self-government, although the majority National Coalition Government initially targeted 1 December 1973.

The Australian Parliament implemented the Select Committee's proposals by enacting the Papua New Guinea Act of 1971.[26] The act also validated the National Identity Ordinance, passed by the House of Assembly, which had changed the name of the territory to Papua New Guinea and adopted a national emblem and a national flag. The act increased the size of the House of Assembly to 100 elected members (82 at large, 18 from regional districts, and 4 official members). In a statement made in May 1972, the minister for external territories explained that the official members of the House would play a reduced role and would not vote on any matters for which the territorial ministers were finally responsible.[27] The administrator and the governor-general retained the right to veto any ordinances passed by the House. On the executive side, the act moved toward the creation of the office of prime minister by directing the ministers to appoint one of their number to the new post of deputy chairman who was to be chairman of the AEC.

The Australian minister for external territories still determined the designations, functions, and scope of responsibilities of the ministers as heads of the executive departments. But there was a change in operating style. The minister of territories promised that the Australian government would seek the views of the AEC "on all important policy matters" and would "continue to give increasing weight to its views and advice."[28] When he made minor additions to the approved arrangements in April 1972, he did request approval by the House of Assembly. The program envisioned the Papua New Guinea cabinet becoming involved in the full range of governmental activities.

INTERNAL SELF-GOVERNMENT

In late April 1973, with the appointment of the National Coalition Government in Papua New Guinea, the date for full internal self-government was fixed at 1 December 1973.

The minister for external territories approved new arrangements outlining the responsibilities of the 17 ministerial positions, including that of the chief minister.[29] Unlike the 1970 arrangements, which were made unilaterally by Australia, these were the result of extensive consultation between the Australian government and Papua New Guinea, with even the local minority opposition party being included in the discussions.

Earlier projections envisioned full independence within 12 to 18 months after achievement of self-government. Chief Minister Somare often mentioned his goal of independence by 1 December 1974. On 8 June 1974, however, the People's Progress Party announced that it would break with the governing coalition and not support the December 1974 date. This aided the position taken by the opposition that independence be made the issue for the elections to the 1976 House of Assembly, since a referendum on the date was highly unlikely. Chief Minister Somare continued his opposition to any referendum on independence; and Australia, too, indicated that it would look to the House of Assembly on this score. Independence was in fact obtained in September 1975 without a referendum, and, interestingly enough, the United Nations has accepted this.[30]

The form of the constitution was subject to much debate.[31] Chief Minister Somare wished the document to be fairly short, leaving less important principles and more detailed proposals to ordinary legislation. The majority of the Constitutional Planning Committee, however, wished to incorporate into the constitution the fundamental national goals towards which the people and their leaders are working. The proposed National Goals and Directive Principles are extensive,[32] broader and more comprehensive than the Eight Point Improvement Plan which was unanimously adopted by the House of Assembly in 1973. The "Eight Aims" are:

A rapid increase in the proportion of the economy under the control of Papua New Guinean individuals and groups, and

in the proportion of personal and property income that goes
to Papua New Guinea;

More equal distribution of economic benefits, including
movement toward equalisation of incomes among people and
toward equalisation of services among different areas of
the country;

Decentralisation of economic activity, planning and
government spending, with emphasis on agricultural
development, village industry, better internal trade, and
more spending channelled to local and area bodies;

An emphasis on small-scale artisan, service and
business activity, relying where possible on typically
Papua New Guinean forms of economic activity;

A more self-reliant economy, less dependent for its
needs on imported goods and services and better able to
meet the needs of its people through local production;

An increasing capacity for meeting government spending
needs from locally raised revenue;

A rapid increase in the active and equal participation
of women in all forms of economic and social activity; and

Government control and involvement in those sectors
of the economy where control is necessary to achieve the
desired kind of development.33

Generally speaking, the proposed national goals would be to prevent exploitation of the indigenous population and maximize benefits for citizens of Papua New Guinea by promoting self-reliance and full integration into the economy by Papua New Guineans. Chief Minister Somare objects to incorporating these goals into unchangeable constitutional principles; however, it appears likely that whether or not it remains within the body of the constitution, control of foreign investment will be the subject of substantial legislation.

Other key constitutional issues of continuing concern include the institutional structure of the new government, such as the retention of the basic parliamentary form of government and the abolition of the artificial heads of state, and the relationship and powers of district or local government to the new central political institution.

We shall discuss the relations of Papua New Guinea with Australia prior to independence when it acquired local self-government (local control over all internal matters) and a growing, but still subservient, participation in matters of defense and foreign relations, in addition to Papua New Guinea's controls to be exercised with independence.34

POLITICAL RELATIONS AND STRUCTURE

The Executive

The new arrangements divided the executive functions of government in Papua New Guinea into three categories: (1) those for which the territorial ministers would have final responsibility; (2) those in which the territorial ministers would have final responsibility for day-to-day decisions, but final broad policy would be determined by the Australian government; and (3) those that would be the sole responsibility of the Australian government.

Australian government control remains extensive, although increased consultation between the Papua New Guinea and the Australian governments on all policy-making matters made these distinctions less firm in practice. The administrator was renamed high commissioner with responsibility for determining the respective designations for all the ministerial offices other than chief minister. (The act renamed the deputy minister the chief minister to be more in accord with normal parliamentary nomenclature and to avoid the suggestion of subservience.)

Section 13 of the act states that "the Government shall be administered by the High Commissioner of Papua New Guinea." He remains a member of the Executive Council (renamed from the Administrator's Executive Council) and remains the official head of state. The assent of the high commissioner is still formally required for all legislation. In practice, this veto has not been exercised in the past few years; but it, along with the need for continued Australian international support and technical and monetary aid, has moderated any attempts at radical legislation.

Local authorities have gained control over the civil service.[35] This had long been an issue in Papua New Guinea-Australia relations; in fact, it was not until June of 1968 that Australia told the UN Trusteeship Council that it would stop recruiting civil servants from overseas "except in very exceptional circumstances."[36]

All executive power would be vested in a National Executive Council composed of all ministers (approximately 15-27) who are also members of the National Parliament. Decisions of the council would be made collectively by no less than one-third of the ministers. In order to enforce this concept of collective responsibility, new procedures would be adopted for meetings of the council. The National Parliament would elect the prime minister by means of an ordinary resolution when it meets after a general election. The prime minister would then choose the other ministers from within the parliament and allocate portfolios among them. He would retain the power to remove any minister and reshuffle the portfolios. While this ensures that the ministry is reasonably cohesive by vesting formal control in the prime minister, in actual practice the extent to which the prime minister has a free hand in choosing or changing the ministry would depend on prevailing political circumstances.

The National Parliament would retain the power to remove any individual minister on grounds of (1) inability to perform his duties "arising from infirmity of body and mind" and (2) "misbehavior." The National Parliament would also retain the ability to remove the National Executive Council and elect a new prime minister. This would be achieved by the adaptation of the "constructive vote of no confidence." In order to ensure greater stability in government, however, this motion could not be made during the first six months the prime minister was in office. Any such motion would have to be signed by one-tenth of the members of Parliament, contain the name of the proposed successor to the prime minister, and be passed by an absolute majority of the Parliament. If the motion were successful, the prime minister would be removed and the Speaker would appoint the named successor.

It should be noted that Papua New Guinea did not institute the practice of subject matter committees which is being used in various Westminster systems. Such a practice generally strengthens the parliament and weakens the cabinet.

Some have criticized Australia's imposition of a parliamentary form of government in Papua New Guinea. Critics claim it is not appropriate for the problems and capabilities of the country. The parliamentary system requires a firm coalition or majority party the members of which are unified upon all the major issues facing the government. The lack of cohesiveness resulting from linguistic and educational differences makes the Westminster system difficult to administer. In addition, it requires a loyal opposition; it is a two-party system. The typical history of new states has been the development of a strong one party rule to unify the country and this may be the desideratum here.[37]

There are, in fact, strong regional and separatist movements in the country. The strongest secessionist movement comes from the Bouganville district comprised of the major close-lying islands of Bouganville and Buka, in addition to two Melanesian islands (Nissan and the Carterets) and three more distant Polynesian groups (the Fead, Tasman, and Mortlocks). Bouganville Island itself is only six miles from the British Solomons. Bouganville was once part of this group and the people are closer to the Solomons—by interest and culture (there is considerable intermarrying) besides geography—than to the large islands of Papua New Guinea. Combining this with the racial difference (Bouganvilleans are considerably darker of skin), the relative economic strength in Bouganville as a result of the copper mines, and the distinctive Catholic presence on the island results in a formidable separatist element.

There are lesser separatist strains as well. Papuans, who are not Australian citizens as are New Guineans, have received less economic support from the Australian government, which has invested its funds in areas yielding the highest return following the policy recommendation of the World Bank Report of 1964. Its stronger, more outspoken nationalistic politicians, such as Josephine Abaijah, have gained strong electoral support. Nevertheless, the Australian government has uniformly refused to encourage this development and much of the strong nationalistic sentiment appears designed to gain increased recognition within the larger entity than to separate completely.

The other group which has been vigorously asserting its interests is the Tolais of East New Britain, the most educated and wealthy group in New Guinea, which asked the Selection Committee on Constitutional Development for

> an independent government for the Gazelle Peninsula. The patron requested your Committee to record in this Report that the Association and its followers would break away from the Territory of Papua and New Guinea if its wishes were not satisfied.[38]

This interplay of local political forces will have to be handled by permitting a good deal of regional control, but it is another force shaping the future Papua New Guinea-Australian relationship and one which the Westminster system will have to manage.[39]

Scrutiny of Officials' Actions

Citing the political corruption rampant around the world, and Watergate in particular, the committee suggests various institutional methods to assure that the government will be responsive to the best interests of the citizens of Papua New Guinea. (The First Guam Constitutional Convention, 1969-70, proposed these same types of provisions; for example, suggested amendments to the organic act would have directed the Legislature to require financial disclosure by all elected officials of the government of Guam and also would have created the independent office of ombudsman.)

Leadership Code

The committee looks to the development of a code of conduct for all elected officeholders, senior public officials, officials of registered political parties, and members of provincial governments to assure that these leaders do not use their position in ways that "threaten these goals, for example, by accumulating personal wealth, by collaborating with foreign or national businessmen, by accepting bribes." The most restrictive provisions of the leadership code will be with respect to transactions with foreign controlled enterprises, including the "giant multi-national corporations."

Ombudsman Commission

An independent Ombudsman Commission would be established to receive complaints by people who feel aggrieved by the government bureaucracy. While there is a tendency in some developing countries to see the role of the ombudsman as a substitute for the court system, the committee believes it should have more of a supervisory and investigatory role. The ombudsman would receive complaints, investigate the alleged unfair conduct, and recommend to the administrative authority ways to correct the situation.

The Legislature

To signify a break with the past, with independence the current House of Assembly would be renamed the National Parliament. However, the unicameral character would be retained to avoid unneeded expense and increase efficiency. All members would be chosen by district elections and there would be no official or appointed member, nor "regional" or "special" electorates. All members would be subject to the same literacy, age, citizenship, and residency requirements. The committee proposes that members be required to be able to speak, read, and write either Pidgin, Hiri Motu, or English. The proposed age prerequisite is 23, with the additional condition of two years of continuous residence in an electorate immediately prior to candidacy or five years' continuous residence in the electorate during some time in the past. The Constitutional Planning Committee suggests an odd number (in order to break deadlocks) of around 100 members.

The National Parliament will have all the sovereign powers of government to make laws for the "peace, progress and welfare of Papua New Guinea." It will also have input as to whether or not the country should enter into treaties or international agreements. Under normal circumstances, all treaties and agreements would be tabled in the parliament and referred to the appropriate committee for consideration and report; and no commitment could be accepted by the government until it had been before the parliament eight to twelve days. In urgent circumstances, this requirement could be waived if the prime minister and the speaker jointly certified that the matter was too urgent for the normal procedure to be complied with.

Most legislation will be introduced by the majority coalition or the government of the day. The constitution should, however, include protection of the right of any member to introduce bills, move motions, and present petitions for the consideration of parliament. Once legislation has passed the parliament, it is not subject to veto by the ministers. The executive may recommit a bill to parliament for reconsideration, but it can do so only once.

The parliament will have ultimate control over the raising and and expenditure of government funds. The day-to-day management of the national economy must, however, be in the hands of the executive. All taxes, rates, duties, or other impositions should be set by law, and all these moneys will be paid into a consolidated fund unless the national parliament approves the setting aside of certain funds for special purposes. The national parliament needs to have the power to examine the budget presented by the executive as a whole, and to reject it in whole or in part. Parliament should have the power to cut particular items of expenditure or particular taxes proposed by the executive. But, the ultimate task of management, of raising, allocating, reallocating, and then spending funds, remains an executive responsibility.

Ordinarily under the Westminster system the parliament may be prematurely dissolved at almost any time. The committee suggested a fixed term of four years with an early dissolution allowed in two cases: (1) if, during the fourth year of its term, the Executive Council is defeated specifically in a vote of no confidence or on an issue which the prime minister has declared to be one of confidence; or (2) if at any time the parliament resolves to dissolve itself.

The Judiciary

Until 1965 the justice system in Papau New Guinea remained as it was from early colonial times. Under Australian rule, local courts in New Guinea and Papau continued to operate quite informally but with a jurisdiction limited to natives. In 1965 the courts for native affairs were abolished and district courts were established with jurisdiction over all races. The new law, however, although it tried to accommodate to local problems (there was a concomitant recognition of native customs in Native Custom Recognition Ordinance of 1963), imposed a formality of procedures and a distance between the people and the settlement of disputes which was not there to the same degree before.[40] Appeals from the local courts are to the High Court of Australia.

Under independence, the existing court structure is retained but a new Supreme Court would be the final court of appeal for Papau New Guinea, eliminating the practice of appeals to the High Court of Australia. The Supreme Court would consist of three judges of the National Court; any judge who heard a case in the National Court would be ineligible to sit on the Supreme Court to hear an appeal against an earlier verdict of his own. The National Court would have the broad power to dispense justice throughout the country and its jurisdiction would be determined by ordinary legislation. Judges would be appointed for renewable terms of 10 years. However, it is suggested that during the first 10 years after the constitution comes into force, judges should be appointed for trial 3-year periods, after which they would be renewed to a 10-year term.

Amendment to the Constitution

The new constitution will be relatively easy to amend, requiring only the approval of the National Parliament. A purposeful delay is built into the process and more than ordinary majorities are required. Thus, amending bills have to be distributed to all members of parliament at least one month prior to their presentation and a period of at least three months must elapse between the making of the first substantive speech by the mover of the bill and the continuation of debate or the taking of a vote on the bill. Generally, a two-thirds majority of the total membership in parliament is necessary for adoption of any amendment although varying proportions are required, depending on the importance of the issue. Thus, a three-quarters majority is necessary for changes in citizenship, the right to a fair trial, political decentralization through provincial government, and alterations of the parliament's lawmaking powers. Other provisions, relating to the number of members of parliament, procedures of the National Executive Council, and procedures of the public service, would require only a three-fifths vote. Certain other issues, such as the financing of political parties and election campaigns, would require only an absolute majority of the parliament.

Defense and Foreign Affairs

Australia retains full control over defense and foreign affairs. Although the range of legislation over which the approval of the governor-general is necessary has been substantially reduced, [41] bills dealing with the matters of defense and foreign relations still require his approval. [42]

Negotiations have continued with Australia, New Zealand, and Britain on national defense arrangements and Australia has agreed to help pay for a defense of 3,500 men and light air support. New Zealand has already furnished two military instructors to the territory and has agreed to aid Papua New Guinea in the amount of $1.5 million over the next three years.

Since self-government, West Germany, Britain, and Indonesia have opened consulate offices in the territory and similar arrangements are being worked out with the United States, New Zealand, Japan, and Fiji. Australia will continue, even under independence, to provide staff assistance and physical prerequisites when asked in order to help Papua New Guinea representation abroad.

Australia, however, gave increased weight to the wishes of the territorial government in these areas, even prior to independence. Thus, Papua New Guinea was represented at the first talks of the Australia-Japan Ministerial Committee in 1972 and before that became an associate member of the Economic and Social Commission for Asia and Pacific, the Asian Development Bank, the World Health Organization, and the South Pacific Forum. As a transitional step toward independence, the government of Papua New Guinea created the office of minister of defense and foreign relations.[43]

Applicability of Federal Law

On the same date as the final revisions to the Papua New Guinea Act were made, the Australian Parliament authorized the governor-general to make regulations determining what act or parts of acts by the parliament would have effect or cease to have effect in Papua New Guinea.[44] Australia retained full control over land occupied by the Australian government, banking and monetary affairs, and internal security. It maintained broad policy supervision over mineral and oil development, tariffs, immigration, higher education, telecommunications, and public works. Thus, although the structure of local self-government had been put in place, the retained powers of the Australian government during the transitional period were very great and intruded considerably upon the local autonomy.

Citizenship

As a reaction to foreign economic domination, the constitution of the independent country of Papua New Guinea provides that citizens will have certain rights that will be theirs alone. "Up until now, it has been foreigners, most of who happen to be of different racial groups from us Papua New Guineans, who have taken the overwhelming bulk of these benefits of this country's wealth."[45] Recent statistics given in Table 2 show the continuation of expatriate control.[46]

TABLE 2

Ownership of Papua New Guinea's Resources

Nationality of Owners	1960/61	1965/66	1969/70
Indigenous	37.5	36.0	32.0
Nonindigenous	62.5	64.0	68.0
Total	100.0	100.0	100.0
%m	79.2	154.7	300.6

Any person born in Papua New Guinea before adoption of the suggested citizenship provisions ("C-Day") shall automatically qualify if he is not a "real" citizen of a foreign country and has at least two indigenous grandparents. Those born outside Papua New Guinea but with two indigenous grandparents could qualify by proper registration and renunciation of any other citizenship, as could persons born within Papua New Guinea of a citizen parent after "C-Day." Any indigenous grandparent is defined as a grandparent all of whose own grandparents were born in Papua New Guinea, Irian Jaya, the British Solomon Islands, or the Torres Strait Islands. Citizens of foreign countries who wish to become naturalized Papua New Guinean citizens would have to wait eight years after "C-Day."

The proposed eight-year residency requirement before naturalized citizenship could be granted has already stirred controversy and the People's Progress Party has suggested one of a short duration. This uncertainty has caused many expatriates to leave Papua New Guinea and has increased the demand for skilled workers. While Papua New Guinea wants its citizens to hold the positions of high responsibility with good pay, it lacks the number of skilled workers and entrepreneurs needed for an immediate takeover. Because of this, Chief Minister Somare has offered to guarantee employment for three years and a continuation of the Australian standard of living to key foreign public servants thinking of leaving the country.

The major effect of the citizenship provisions is upon control of land. The Commission of Inquiry Into Land Matters has recommended that all land be converted into government leaseholds,[47] and in late August 1974 the House of Assembly passed legislation granting to the Papua New Guinea government the power to take land from foreign owners. During debate, Chief Minister Somare said that the government would pay fair compensation to plantation owners for any land taken over.

Under the commission's plan, the government would lease the land for a period of 40 to 60 years. Unlike citizens, noncitizens would have no automatic right of renewal. The government would also have the power to insist on development of any undeveloped land. The ultimate goal is to prevent foreign investors from controlling urban areas and exploiting national workers on privately held plantations. Noncitizens who involve citizens in substantial ownership and management of the business on the land would be granted a longer leasehold interest.

In some areas, such as oil and gas development, Papua New Guinea recognizes that it will need to allow substantial foreign investment in order to obtain technical assistance and needed capital. In areas of transportation and agriculture, where foreign technicians are not so vital, foreign investment would be discouraged.

Papua New Guinea has already shown open displeasure with the relationship worked out by the Australian government for Papua New Guinea's return on the operation of the highly successful Bougainville Copper Company. Despite a firm stand taken by the company's management, Papua New Guinea was able to renegotiate the contract.

Employment would also be restricted. Foreigners would be allowed to enter and work in Papua New Guinea only under limited conditions. Noncitizens would not be eligible for election to public office, but those who are currently holding elected office could serve out their terms. Critics who have seen in these provisions an unfortunate racism have been answered by the Constitutional Planning Committee:

> "Our primary responsibility is to the future, and in particular to the future of the majority of this country's inhabitants, the indigenous people of Papua New Guinea. Their interest must be safeguarded above all."[48]

This view is in accord with the United Nations Development Program—sponsered Overseas Development Group (University of East Anglia):

> Maximisation of the growth of Papua New Guinea's domestic product has not, of itself, been set as a long term objective. In that sense it may be said that we believe that the emphasis of the next plan should be on localisation/indigenisation, rather than on growth.[49]

ECONOMIC RELATIONS

Currency and Banking

Papua New Guinea has made plans for its own currency to be introduced, although at present it is part of the common currency area with Australia. At present, therefore, it is subject to Australia's exchange control policies and its currency is backed by the Australian reserves.

Papua New Guinea no longer operates under Australian banking legislation, however, and has its own central bank, the Bank of Papua New Guinea.

Federal Financial Assistance

Financial support has been the principal issue surrounding the negotiations between the two governments. Prime Minister E. Gough Whitlam has pledged $500 million (Australian currency) to Papua New Guinea to be spread over the first three years of independence.[50] This is a substantial increase over the $80 million a year provided previously by Australia, but the House of Assembly had urged one billion dollars for the first three years.[51] In August 1974, Chief Minister Somare stated that, because of inflation, the $500 million figure would not be nearly enough. Australia has given an undertaking with respect to guaranteeing Papua New Guinea borrowing which may be of substantial assistance.

In February 1974 the president of the World Bank, Robert McNamara, visited Papua New Guinea and pledged the continual support of his organization which has loaned Papua New Guinea $70 million over the last five years. Britain broke with its established procedure and announced its offer of technical assistance even before self-government was reached.

NOTES

1. Wurm, "The Papuan Linguistic Situation," in <u>Current Trends in Linguistics,</u> ed. T. A. Sebeak (The Hague: Mounton, 1971).
2. U.N. Trusteeship Council, <u>Official Records,</u> 24th Session, 1018th Meeting, 1959, para. 7.
3. <u>Debates</u> CCIV (5 October, 1949), 988-89.
4. Papua and New Guinea Act 1949 (No. 9 of 1949) (25 March 1949).
5. P. Hasluck, "Present Tasks and Policies," in <u>New Guinea and Australia,</u> ed. Wilkes (1958), at 76, quoted in <u>Brookfield, Colonialism Development and Independence</u> (1972), at 99.
6. Hasluck, speaking in 1952; quoted by R.S. Parker, "The Growth of Territory Administration," in <u>New Guinea on the Threshold,</u> ed. E. K. Fisk, (Canberra: 1966), p. 165.
7. <u>Debates</u> CCVIII (1 June 1950), 3637.
8. Papua and New Guinea Act (No. 2) 1960 (No. 47 of 1960), 17 October 1960.
9. Legislative Council Ordinance 1951 (No. 28 of 1951), Sec. 8(1).

PAPUA NEW GUINEA 171

10. Papua and New Guinea Act (No. 2) 1960 (No. 47 of 1960), 17 October 1960.
11. The Commonwealth of Australia Constitution Act, 63 and 64 Vict., c. 12, Sec. 64 (1900).
12. Administrator's Council Ordinance 1960 (No. 43 of 1960).
13. No. 27 of 1963 (30 May 1963). The broad power in the Australian Government to legislate with respect to its territories is found in its constitution, Sec. 122. Some discussion and comparison of this section with the U.S. territorial clause discussed earlier is found in Pitti Lane, The Australian System with United States Analogues (Sydney: Australian Law Book Co., 1972), pp. 731-62.
14. The Electoral (Special Electorates) Ordinance of 1963 (No. 43 of 1963).
15. The Electoral (Open Electorates) Ordinance of 1963 (No. 42 of 1963).
16. No. 44 of 1963.
17. No. 25 of 1968 (27 May 1968).
18. Arrangements approved by the minister for external territories, C. E. Barnes (7 June 1968).
19. Arrangements approved by the minister for external territories, C. E. Barnes (4 March 1970).
20. Determination made by the minister for external territories, C. E. Barnes (21 August 1970).
21. Arrangements approved by the minister for external territories, C. E. Barnes (21 August 1970).
22. Instructions from the Governor-General to the Administrator (20 August 1970).
23. Statement in the Trusteeship Council of the United Nations by the Special Representative of Australia, Mr. Pearsall, United Nations Trusteeship Council Provisional Verbatim Record of the Thirteen Hundred and Eight-first Meeting (7 June 1971), Document No. T/PV, 1391, at 6.
24. Amendment by Mr. Dutton to a motion by Mr. Pena Ou, House of Assembly Debates, Second House, 11th meeting, 1st sess., vol. II., No. 11, 3372-8 (22 September 1970).
25. Final Report from the Select Committee on Constitutional Development, presented to the House of Assembly 4 March 1971, House of Assembly Debates, Second House, 13th meeting, 3rd sess., vol. II, No. 13, Appendix G, Sec. 9.
26. Papua New Guinea Act (No. 2) 1971 (No. 123 of 1971) 13 December 1971.
27. Address by the Minister for External Territories, Mr. A. S. Peacock, to the Australian Universities Liberal Federation, Sydney (18 May 1972).
28. Ibid.
29. Arrangements approved by the minister for external territories, W. L. Morrison, 30 April 1973. Determination made by the minister for external territories, W. L. Morrison, 30 April 1973.

30. Gen. Assembly Res. 3109 (XXVIII), 12 December 1973.

31. Some interesting commentary from an Australian professor who was a consultant to the Papua New Guinea Legislature is found in Davidson, From Dependency to Independency in 8 J. of Pacific History 158 (1973). Some of the basic material is found in Bayne and Colebatch, Constitutional Development in Papua New Guinea, 1968-1973 in New Guinea Research Bulletin 51 (1973).

32. Draft Narrative of the Constitutional Planning Committee Report 1974 (hereinafter cited as Draft Report), Chapter 2, "National Goals and Directive Principles," Schedule—Foreign Investment Code, between pages 2/5 and 3/1. This schedule lists 23 provisions which foreign investment in Papua New Guinea would be required to meet if it wishes to be welcomed in the emerging country.

33. Draft Report, at 2/2.

34. Papua New Guinea Act (No. 2) 1973 (No. 120 of 1973), 30 October 1973, Sec. 5.

35. Papua New Guinea Act 1973 (No. 69 of 1973), 18 June 1973.

36. N. Oram, "Administration, Development & Public Order," in Alternative Strategies for Papua New Guinea, ed. A. Clunies Ross and J. Langmore (London: Oxford University Press, 1973), p. 53 (hereinafter Alternative Strategies).

37. Waddell, "Constitutions and the Political Culture," in Alternative Strategies, p. 94.

38. Territory of Papua and New Guinea House of Assembly: Final Report from the Select Comm. on Constitutional Development (Port Moresby, March 1971), p. 3.

39. The separatist movements are discussed in Griffin, "Movements for Separatism and Secession," in Alternative Strategies.

40. N. Oram, "Administration, Development and Public Order," in Alternative Strategies, p. 35.

41. See Section 55 of the Papua and New Guinea Act 1940-63.

42. Ibid. Since external affairs are interpreted broadly under Australian law this reserve power is quite great. Const. S. 51 (xxix) The Australian Federal System (1972) p. 132-54.

43. Papua New Guinea Act 1972 (No. 74 of 1972), 5 September 1972. The international issues facing an independent Papua New Guinea are explored in J. D. B. Miller, "Papua New Guinea in World Politics," 27 Australian Outlook 191 (August 1973).

44. No. 121 of 1973 (30 October 1973), relating to acts that have effect in Papua New Guinea.

45. Draft Report, at 4/1.

46. The issue of indigenous versus expatriot economic holdings is a major one. The figures are provided in R. J. May, "Economic Relations Between Australia and an Independent Papua New Guinea" (University Public Lecture, Canberra [4 April 1973]).

47. "New Guinea Plan to Wipe Out Freeholds," Pacific Islands Monthly 45, no. 1 (January 1974): 9.

48. Draft Report, at 4/1.
49. United Nations, A Report on Development Strategies for Papua New Guinea (1973).
50. Statement made 1 March 1974.
51. 8 March 1974.

CHAPTER 8

WEST INDIES ASSOCIATED STATES

The West Indies Associated States did not break new ground in constitutional theory; but did in constitutional practice. For it is here that the termination option has been exercised by the lesser sovereign and it is here, too, that the full power of the reserve clause has been exercised by the larger state.

Much of the academic discussion has revolved around the relationship of the Associated States to one another rather than to Great Britain. We shall discuss this almost not at all but will, for the reasons noted above, focus on the relationship of the Associated States with the former colonial power.

LEEWARD ISLANDS

There are two associated states in the former British Leeward Islands, governing five inhabited islands. The administration of St. Kitts-Nevis-Anguilla includes the three islands of St. Kitts (with a land area of 68 square miles and a population of approximately 38,500), Nevis (with 50 square miles and approximately 12,500 people), and Anguilla (with 34 square miles and 6,500 people). The relationship of Anguilla to the state is unsettled. The other associated state, Antigua, includes the inhabited islands of Antigua (with 108 square miles and 58,000 people) and Barbuda (with 62 square miles and about 1,000 inhabitants). It also includes the large uninhabited and isolated rock, Redonda. (There is a third administration, outside our concern here, that of Montserrat, a small island of 38 square miles and about 13,500 people.)

The nearest neighbor to the south is the large French island of Guadeloupe, which is about 40 miles from Antigua. Between St. Kitts and Anguilla lie the Dutch islands of St. Eustatius, Saba, and St. Martin (this latter divided between French and Dutch administration).

WEST INDIES ASSOCIATED STATES 175

The islands are small and there is considerable communication among the fishermen and small traders. The Dutch islands are mainly English-speaking and many people from Anguilla travel to and from work in the Dutch islands.

Anguilla

Anguilla is a long, thin, low-lying island. Since the rainfall is less than 40 inches a year and the soil is poor and shallow, the main occupation of the inhabitants has been seafaring and fishing. Most of the people, including the larger property owners, are of African or mixed origin (unlike those of St. Kitts where most of the larger property owners are white).

Individualism is strong in Anguilla, giving rise to a lack of sympathy with those on St. Kitts who are preoccupied with trade union and labor matters, the heritage of the latter island's estate economy. Politically, Anguillans support the People's Progressive Party, opposed to the ruling Labour Party of St. Kitts-Nevis-Anguilla headed by Premier Bradshaw, and blame rule from St. Kitts for the deplorable state of their public utilities.

St. Kitts

St. Kitts' estate economy, wholly geared to sugar, has a most concentrated pattern of property ownership. Thirty-five estates grow almost all the sugar cane on the island.

For many decades St. Kitts, the oldest settlement in the West Indies, was also the wealthiest of the Leeward and Windward Islands. But its dependence on sugar has not served it well and in 1958 with its economy stagnating after several years of critical budgetary difficulties, St. Kitts accepted a recurrent grant-in-aid from the United Kingdom which it is still receiving on a large scale.

The only crop that has been of any economic importance in recent years, besides sugar, is sea island cotton, which is grown on a number of estates on St. Kitts (and by peasants on Nevis), generally on lands too dry or poor to support sugar cane.

Nevis

Nevis is only three miles from St. Kitts. It once had rich volcanic soils, but the past exploitation of these lands has caused severe soil

MAP 8

Leeward Islands

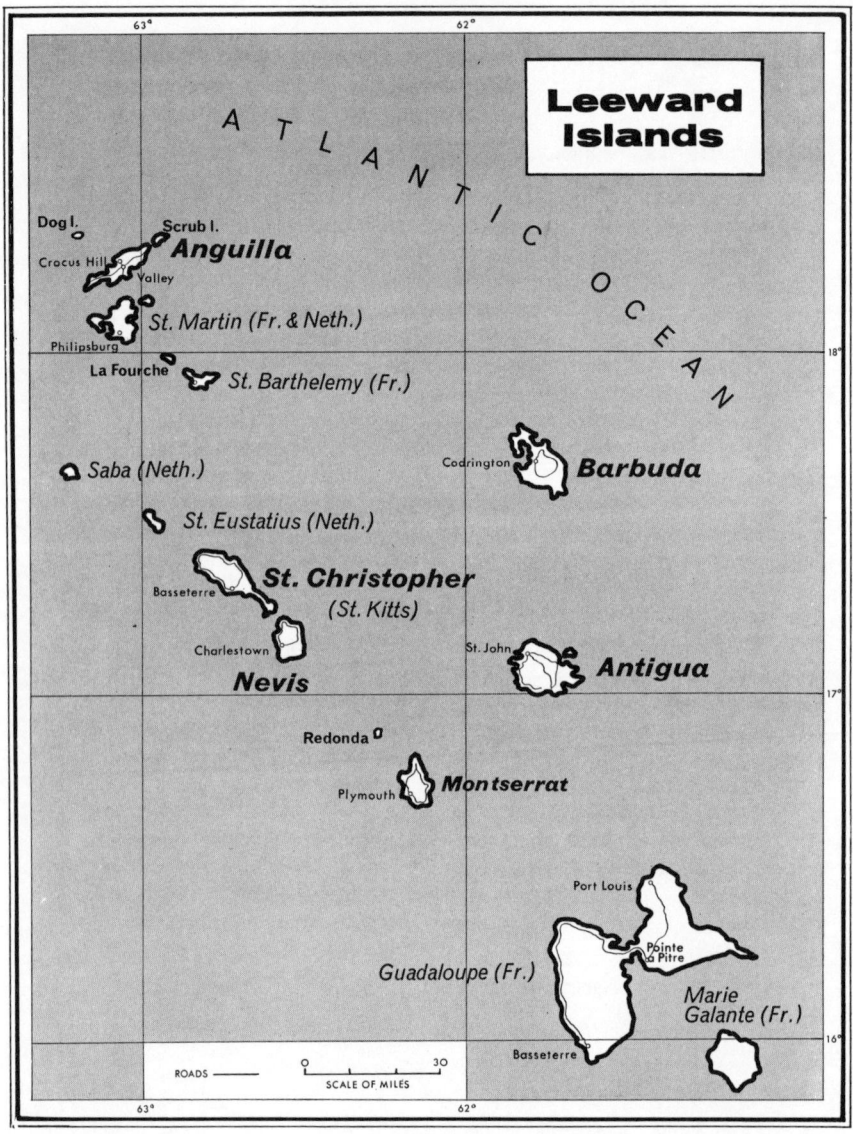

Source: West Indies and Caribbean Year Book—Caribook Ltd., Toronto, Canada.

erosion. Nevertheless, even today agriculture continues to be the primary source of employment. The decline in agricultural output, coupled with heavy population pressures due to high birthrates and diminishing emigration outlets (exacerbated by the British West Indies Act of 1962 curbing access to Britain), has resulted in serious poverty.

Antigua

Antigua is one of the most easterly of the Leeward Islands. Because of its comparatively low elevation, the island is considerably drier than its neighbors. Until very recently, Antigua's poverty was among the worst in the West Indies. Income from sugar was uncertain and, at the best of times, poor compared, for example, with that of St. Kitts. In the semi-arid conditions, a good food crop economy never developed.

Since the mid-1960s, however, Antigua, with some of the best beaches in the Caribbean set in exceptionally fine coastal landscapes, has emerged as one of the largest tourist centers in the Caribbean. The low rainfall, which is such a disadvantage to agriculture, has proved of great benefit to tourism. Antigua also has considerable historical interest, particularly in the field of naval history, contributing to the tourist promotion program. Antigua has benefited sufficiently from tourism to forgo resumption of British budgetary assistance, dropped in 1962, and today has the highest GNP per capita of any associated state (even though the figure is quite low by world standards).

WINDWARD ISLANDS

In the former British Windward Islands, the three states in association with Britain—Dominica, St. Lucia, and St. Vincent—are joined by two former British dependencies which are now sovereign nations—Barbados and Grenada. From 3 March 1967 until 7 February 1974 Grenada was also a state in association with Britain. These islands all lie in the southern section of the Lesser Antilles and are all larger in area and population than any of the Leeward Islands.

The Windwards are all mountainous and volcanic. They have a strong common economic bond in the overwhelming importance of the banana industry. The economies are geared to the needs of a single buyer, Geest Industries, a British-based firm of Dutch origin that is now the largest banana importer into the United Kingdom.

Despite the close similarities in geography and economics, the islands are more culturally heterogeneous than the Leewards. Dominica and St. Lucia retain a Creole language of French origin as their

MAP 9

Windward Islands

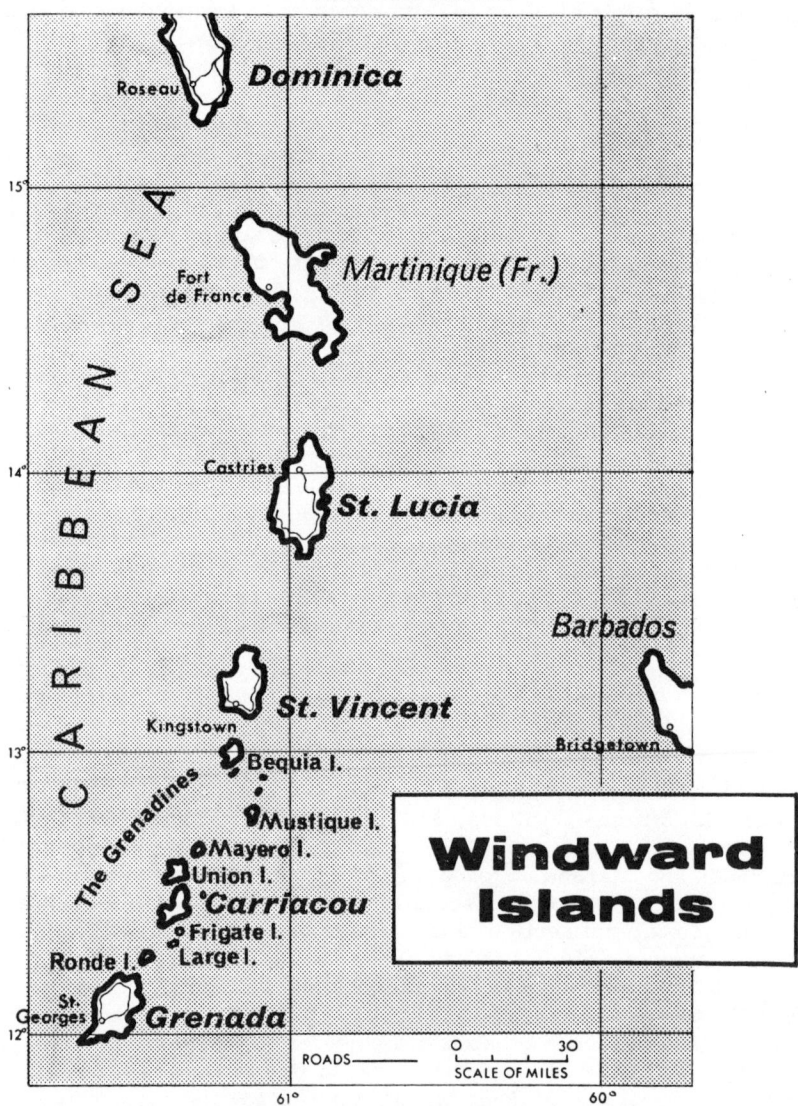

Source: West Indies and Caribbean Year Book—Caribook Ltd., Toronto, Canada.

native tongue and Roman Catholicism as the predominant religion. St. Vincent is mainly non-Catholic and, perhaps because of strong ties with Barbados, shows a great deal of English influence. St. Vincent and Dominica both have sizable numbers of the surviving original American Indian inhabitants as well.

Partly because the islands were continually fought over by the English and the French, they have no history of common government. Control over the islands changed many times—four times for Dominica, nine times for St. Lucia, four times for St. Vincent, and five times for Grenada.

Although large estates have existed in the Windwards, the islands, with the possible exception of St. Vincent, could not at any time have been classified as estate economies. The European interest was military rather than economic. In fact, the Windwards provided virgin lands on which escaped slaves and other small settlers sought refuge from the estate system, giving birth to a strong peasant tradition. Government in the past has been weaker and less effective than in the Leewards and standards in education and social services are low.

Dominica

Larger than any other island in either the Leewards or the Windwards, but with a population of only 70,000, Dominica is the only island in the Lesser Antilles that can be considered underpopulated. The population is, however, distributed very unevenly, with the coastal towns and villages overcrowded and lacking open spaces while virgin forest still covers the greater part of the island's land area.

Emigration was heavy during the period 1955-61; but high unemployment, coupled with shortages of important skills, remains a major problem. The island's economy, typical of the Windwards, is based mainly on agriculture, with the export sector dominated by bananas. The recent depression in the banana industry has had a severe effect on the trade balance but the effect on the economy as a whole has been largely ameliorated by financial assistance from abroad. Nevertheless, Dominica has the second lowest GNP per capita in the lesser Antilles.

St. Lucia

St. Lucia has a population of 100,000, about half of which is concentrated in the capital, Castries. In the past the island was considered one of the poorest in the West Indies, with a serious lack of key social services (medical and educational standards were particularly low). The island is more dependent on bananas for export earnings than any other island in the Lesser Antilles, with approximately 80 percent of the value of the island's exports derived from that product. The banana boom of the late 1960s helped the island financially, while at the same time the island became increasingly dependent on the United Kingdom in order to market the fruit.

Most recently, rapid economic growth has taken place in the interrelated activities of tourism and construction, so by the mid-1970s tourism had become the principal source of income for the island and the GNP per capita was the second highest of the Associated States.

St. Vincent

In the past St. Vincent, with a population of approximately 100,000, had one of the wealthier and better organized agricultural economies. It has become heavily dependent upon the banana industry as a result of a series of diasters that struck its other agricultural industries (cotton ginning, coconut milling, the arrowroot industry, and sugar production).

The high population growth is straining the key social services (health, education, and housing), while at the same time the gross domestic product dropped; so as of the mid-1970s the island had the lowest average per-capita income in the eastern Caribbean.[1]

HISTORICAL BACKGROUND: 1624-1945

The first British colony established in the Leeward and Windward Isalnds was St. Christopher (St. Kitts), founded in 1624. From this base, English colonization spread to other islands in the Leewards (Nevis, Antigua, and Montserrat) and the British Virgin Islands (Barbados, Jamaica, and the Bahamas), as well as to the coast of Central America. British domination spread with the capture of Trinidad from Spain in 1797. The Windwards (Dominica, St. Lucia, St. Vincent, and Grenada) were taken from France at various times in the eighteenth and early nineteenth centuries.

Population in the newly founded English colonies, especially Barbados and the Leewards, increased rapidly during the first few decades of colonization. By 1640 there were nearly 30,000 white settlers on Barbados and 20,000 on St. Christopher and Nevis, making these the most densely populated territories in the Caribbean at the time. The early settlers relied principally upon agriculture, with privateering and the cutting of logwood providing supplemental income. Landholdings were small, tobacco being the leading export crop, followed by indigo, cotton, and ginger.

The introduction of sugar in the late seventeenth and early eighteenth centuries revolutionized life on the islands. The pattern of land tenure changed rapidly from small holdings to large estates. Successful sugar planters squeezed out the tobacco farmers, who left the islands. The resultant increased demands for labor led to importation of large numbers of Negro slaves. Consequently, the composition of the population changed from predominantly European to predominantly African. As sugar planting expanded, the lowland forests were rapidly cut down, making way for the cane fields which became the chief feature of the agricultural landscape. Large planter estates with their villagelike slave quarters replaced the dispersed homesteads of the small tobacco farmers.

But the sugar economy rested on fragile bases which were destroyed in the late eighteenth and early nineteenth centuries. American independence, the growing industrialization of England, the shifting of British imperial interests from the Caribbean to the Indian Ocean, and the increasing clamor for abolition of the slave trade and for the emancipation of slaves doomed the sugar plantation.

The independence of the North American colonies destroyed the old colonial scheme on which the sugar territories of the West Indies depended. With independence, North America became a foreign area subject to the restrictive provisions of the British Navigation Laws, and, therefore, difficult for West Indies planters to reach.

In 1807, England abolished the slave trade and in 1834 emancipated the slaves in British territories. In 1845 foreign sugar was admitted into the British market on a par with colonial sugar. The British sugar market collapsed and the West Indian Island economies collapsed with it. Other crops, such as bananas, were cultivated, but the long-term economic decline of the islands had begun.

In the Windwards, where the history of the plantation was shorter and the dependence on sugar much less pronounced, the changes brought about by emancipation and the decline of the colonial system had a less disruptive effect. In the Leewards, there was little unoccupied land available and the freed Negro had to stay on the plantation if he wished to stay on the island.[2]

THE POSTWAR PERIOD: 1945-1967

Since World War II Great Britain has attempted to formulate a political and economic relationship with its former colonies in the Caribbean which would permit it to disengage and, at the same time, meet its obligations to the islands and to the Caribbean area.[3] It focused initially on a federation within the West Indies which as a whole would have a certain status relationship to Great Britain. This attempt failed partly because of the great distances among the islands, the disparities in size among the federation's members, the lack of careful planning for its promotion and growth, and the fact that it was imposed from without.[4]

Following the dissolution of the Federation of the West Indies in 1962 and subsequent negotiations about the status of the individual Caribbean territories, England proposed a new constitutional status for the six territories. Under the proposals as subsequently developed in 1967 (in the case of Antigua, Dominica, Grenada, St. Kitts-Nevis-Anguilla, and St. Lucia) and in 1969 (in the case of St. Vincent), each territory became a "State in association with the United Kingdom" with control of its internal affairs and with the right to amend its own constitution, including the power to terminate this association with the United Kingdom and eventually to declare itself independent. The government of the United Kingdom retained powers relating to the external affairs and defense of the territories. In July 1974, Grenada opted for independence and is no longer an associated state.

Other alternatives had originally been put forward. Integration along the lines of Northern Ireland was suggested, but was rejected for a number of reasons. Integration would have meant that all the Leewards and Windwards combined would have sent only one member to Westminster—assuming the same proportional representation as that applying to Northern Ireland. This representation would not have been sufficient to safeguard the islands' singular positions and very special economic problems. But in the end, the most important factor thwarting this plan was economic. The benefits of the welfare state and the higher educational standards which would have followed such an integration might have been attractive to the islands, but the extra burden that would have fallen on Great Britain made the plan unacceptable on that score to the British.

The adoption of a relationship similar to that between New Zealand and the Cook Islands was suggested. At the end of 1965, the Colonial Office prepared a White Paper presenting its first constitutional proposals for Antigua, St. Kitts-Nevis-Anguilla, Dominica, St. Lucia, St. Vincent, and Grenada.[5] The proposals as originally put forward in this document fell far short of the degree of independence enjoyed by the Cook Islands. Under these proposals Great Britain's "powers will extend to the making of any provision (including provision relating to the field of internal government) which appear to . . . Her Majesty . . . necessary to prevent circumstances arising or continuing in the territory that may prejudice the discharge of Britain's responsibilities." The references to preventive action and interference with internal government were eliminated in the final act.

Further, under the 1965 proposal, a regional superior court was to have been established with strong powers to investigate complaints or departures from the provisions of unit constitutions. The president of the court was to be appointed by the Lord Chancellor of England. Most importantly, there was to be a British government representative in the region (distinct from Her Majesty's representative) who would have powers to initiate proceedings in the court. The court would have the right to issue "to any person or authority any orders or directions which it considers necessary to ensure that the constitution is complied with and to enforce these orders and directions."[6] Legal opinion in the West Indies was alarmed at the proposal that a court, as part of the judicial structure of the proposed states, should have political powers of this nature and that actions could be initiated from outside the area.

THE SITUATION SINCE 1967

Great Britain substantially modified its 1965 proposal as a result of the cool West Indian response to it.[7] These later modifications were accepted and became the nucleus for the constitutional relationship between Great Britain and each associated State.[8] In general, they followed the Cook Islands precedent (the parallel was specifically noted by the United Kingdom representative in the United Nations debate), with territorial autonomy over internal affairs and continued metropole control over military and foreign affairs.

Political Relations: The Constitution

The constitutions which came into force in February and March of 1967 for Antigua, Dominica, Grenada, St. Kitts-Nevis-Anguilla, and St. Lucia, and in October 1969 for St. Vincent, are virtual copies of one another. Each establishes a parliamentary form of government under which the legislature and cabinet, headed by a chief minister or premier, run the government. Under the constitutions, the people of the associated state remain British citizens unless the associated state establishes separate citizenship. The constitution provides for the a basic government structure of governor, cabinet, and legislature.

The governor is appointed by the Queen and fulfills a largely ceremonial function. He is required to act in accordance with the advice of the cabinet or of a minister acting under the general authority of the cabinet. In accordance with Westminster practice, the cabinet is collectively responsible to the legislature. It consists of the premier, the attorney-general (ex officio), and other ministers.

The appointment, dismissal, and disciplinary control of public officers is vested in the local Public Service Commission and the Police Service Commission.

The legislature, which in each state except Antigua consists of one House of Assembly, may make laws for the "peace, order and good government" of the territory, subject to the assent of the governor. The

House of Assembly, with a membership of about ten, consists of both elected and nominated members. Two nominated members are appointed on the advice of the premier and one on the advice of the leader of the opposition (or, if there is no leader of the opposition, by the governor at his discretion).

Nominated members are entitled to vote except on motions of no confidence and on bills for the alteration of the constitution. The House elects a Speaker, who, if he is not already a member, becomes one by virtue of his office.

The elected members of the House of Assembly are elected under universal adult suffrage in single-member constituencies, of which there are at least one in Anguilla, at least two in Nevis, and at least seven in St. Kitts.

A person is qualified for election or nomination to the House if he is a British Commonwealth citizen, has attained the age of 21 years, and was born and is domiciled in the territory, or is domiciled and has been resident in the territory for 3 years. A person is qualified to vote if he has attained the age of 21 years and has such qualifications regarding residence and domicile as may be prescribed by the legislature.

Antigua has established another legislative chamber—a Senate—composed of ten appointed senators. All are appointed by the governor, but seven appointments must be made in accordance with the advice of the premier. On the whole, the House is the more powerful body, particularly in regard to money bills.

General Applicability of Federal Law

The former British government authority to reserve or disallow bills passed by the territorial legislature ended with the adoption of the constitution. Although the territorial legislature can, by a two-thirds vote, alter the constitution, it may not do so with respect to the "basic clauses" (the bill of rights). Except for acts affecting responsibilities which the British government keeps (external affairs, defense, and citizenship), no acts passed by the British Parliament are applicable to the territories unless they have the consent of the legislature of the associated state. Britain may "alter that constitution or any part of that constitution" of an associated state so long as the state requests such a change by a simple resolution of its legislature. Furthermore, Britain may, upon similar request, "federate or otherwise unite two or more associated states with each other . . . (or with) other territories which are not associated states," or "divide an associated state into two or more separate territories," or "transfer part of the territory of an associated state to another territory."[9] English common law remains the law of the territory.

As a result of the modifications of the 1965 proposals, the West Indies Associated States Supreme Court is a superior court of record with the usual powers and duties to protect and interpret the constitution. It consists of a Court of Appeals, comprising the chief justice as president and two justices of appeal, and a High Court of Justice, comprising the chief justice appointed by the Queen and six puisne judges appointed by the Judicial and Legal Services Commission. Unlike the 1965 proposals, there is no mention of any special relationship between the Supreme Court and a British government representative to the court. Generally, the provisions of the court are materially the same as judicial provisions in the constitutions of independent British Commonwealth countries. Thus, appeal from the Supreme Court lies with the British Privy Council. The British Privy Council is designated as the Court of Appeals from the Superior Court's rulings.

Foreign Affairs and Defense

Although the islands were to be in effect internally self-governing, foreign affairs and defense were to remain the responsibility of the United Kingdom; and it was stated that "for the discharge of this responsibility, the British Government will have the necessary executive powers in the territory."[10] The British Parliamentary Act authorizing the establishment of associated states for the islands is the West Indies Act of 16 February 1967, which provides in Section 2:

> The United Kingdom shall have no responsibility for the government of any associated state except in respect of (a) any matter which in the opinion of . . . the United Kingdom is a matter relating to defence (whether of an associated state or of the United Kingdom or of any other territory for whose government Her Majesty's Government in the United Kingdom are wholly or party responsible) or to external affairs; (b) any matter relating to nationality or citizenship; and (c) any matter relating to the Succession to the Throne or the Royal Style and Titles.

The United Kingdom agreed to delegate executive authority to the governments with respect to membership in international organizations, negotiation of trade agreements, and agreements for government-to-government technical assistance. Conflict soon arose, however, since the Chief Minister of St. Kitts-Nevis-Anguilla refused to accept that the United Kingdom should have sole authority to negotiate agreements relating to civil aviation.[11] Control over communications is most important to the islands.

In the matter of the executive powers that could be exercised by the British government in pursuance of its defense responsibility, the right of the Antigua government to be consulted is more clearly laid out; but it appears to fall short of the degree of independence in the Cook Islands' constitution, which declares that powers are to be used only after consultation between the prime minister of New Zealand and the premier of the Cook Islands.[12]

It has usually been hoped and expected that the issue of retained authority would not arise so that the full extent of this power would be left unclear; but the question did in fact arise immediately due to the instability of the situation with respect to St. Kitts-Nevis-Anguilla. Although the situation is freakish, it is worth examining in detail to see the inherent powers which the metropole holds in reserve.

Since early in the nineteenth century, Anguilla has sought a separate relationship in order not to be dominated by St. Kitts.[13]

In 1825 Great Britain decided to form two distinct governments in the Leeward chain, consolidating the administration of St. Kitts-Nevis-Anguilla and the British Virgin Islands. Since a British magistrate nearly always resided in Anguilla, interisland jealousy and competition were manageable. Over time, however, St. Kitts used its position as the largest island and headquarters for the government to obtain various infrastructure benefits denied Anguilla, such as paved roads, electricity and water systems, telephones, and direct communication with the Caribbean and abroad. Further, secondary education for Anguillans has to be completed on St. Kitts where Anguillans faced considerable discrimination.

The colonial reforms of the late 1930s, following the Moyne Commission which investigated the mass riots on St. Kitts in 1935 occasioned by sugar workers' demands for higher wages and improved working conditions, actually exacerbated relations between St. Kitts and her smaller sister islands.[14] The result of the Moyne Report was that St. Kitts got a degree of self-government in 1937 at Anguilla's expense. Britain decided that three of the delegates to the Legislative Council (which served the three islands) should for the first time be subject to election. (Previously all eleven members of the Council had been nominated by Britain and a majority of the council had been European.) The first three elected councilmen were Kittitian merchants hardly concerned with the problems of small farmers on Anguilla and Nevis. With universal adult suffrage and election of all council members in 1952, mass politics—favoring the islands' only organized mass movement, the Trade and Labour Union of Robert L. Bradshaw on St. Kitts—further differentiated the interests of the three islands.

Quinquennial elections from 1952 to 1967 on the three islands demonstrated Anguilla's antipathy to the St. Kitts relationship. In each election, Anguilla returned nominal independents despite pressures and threats from Bradshaw's party. This heightened mutual bitterness. Bradshaw opposed almost all programs for improvements on the smaller island, preferring to aid his particular constituents, St. Kitts' sugar workers. Not surprisingly, Anguillans came to regard their island as a "colony of St. Kitts," preferring the more benign (more distant) colonialism of Britain to clear political subjugation by St. Kitts.

By January 1967, Anguillans, previously apathetic or ignorant of the political changes about to transpire under "associated statehood," became conscious of and hostile to the proposed political arrangement. The St. Kitts-Nevis-Anguilla constitution did not appear unduly prejudicial toward Anguilla.* Electoral districts in the all-powerful House of Assembly (a council patterned, naturally, on the House of Commons) were drawn to represent blocs of some 5,500 resident citizens. Thus, under the 1967 constitution, 38,500 Kittitians are represented by seven assemblymen, 12,500 Nevisians by two, and Anguilla by only one. What concerned the Anguillians was the power vested in the House of Assembly and its premier. The House retained authority to legislate on nearly all issues pertaining to any or all three islands and the probability of Kittitian bloc voting meant that Anguilla was unlikely to obtain the measure of self-government it was seeking.

A last bid to prevent the new state from coming into being was made in February 1967, when Peter Adams (an Anguillian leader) and Dr. William Herbert (leader of the St. Kitts-based People's Action Movement) flew to London to appeal in vain for a delay until the problems of local government were settled. They also protested that the associated state constitution made no provision for Anguilla to secede unilaterally if it so desired.

Statehood was declared on 27 February 1967, but events of the next months proved its fragility. On 31 May Anguilla sent four representatives to request legal separation from the central government. In a plebiscite held in July 1967 more than 98 percent of the Anguillan voters favored secession; and Anguilla then proceeded to adopt one of the world's briefest constitutions (13 provisions) and formally declared itself independent, although unilateral declaration of independence was not recognized by either the central government in St. Kitts or by Great Britain.

St. Kitts retaliated by discontinuing salaries of Anguillan civil servants, including teachers and nurses. Mail carrying remittances from relatives abroad was seized in Basseterre, and Anguillians' savings deposited in the Kittitian branch of the National Mid-Atlantic Bank were frozen. The Basseterre government threatened the Esso Company—

---

*In order to explain the Constitution to Kittitians, Nevisians, and Anguillians, the resident tutor of the University of the West Indies delivered eight radio lectures later compiled in a pamphlet, Victor C. Josse, The Anatomy of the Constitution (St. Kitts: Government Printery, 1967). The focus is upon comparing St. Kitts-Nevis-Anguilla constitutional provisions with the organic law of Great Britain.

Anguilla's only source of fuel—with reprisals if it continued to serve the smaller island.

The British position was that associated status had been granted to the three islands as a unit, and was revocable only on request of St. Kitts-Nevis-Anguilla. As far as Britain was concerned, Anguilla's secession was an internal matter to be dealt with by that central government in St. Kitts; and the unilateral declaration of independence was considered an illegal act. Britain assisted in St. Kitts' policy of economic pressure on the small island by terminating grants and aid to Anguilla.

Finally, in December 1967, Anguilla's council was persuaded to accept an "interim" settlement with Britain. Under this plan, which was signed by Lord Shepherd late in January the following year, Anguilla was granted temporary separation from St. Kitts. The fact, however, that the interim status was granted for "one year, more or less" caused considerable anxiety. In agreeing to the status, the British stipulated that it would not affect legal relationships between Anguilla and St. Kitts.

As the end of the interim period approached, Ronald Webster, the popular leader of the Anguillans, tried to create a more permanent—if unilaterally declared—status. An eight-page constitution for the Republic of Anguilla was drafted and presented to a referendum of all adult citizens in February. This document created a bicameral legislature, one chamber elected from six districts, the other chosen in an at-large election. Fairly broad guarantees of worship, speech, habeas corpus, and judicial remedies were provided. Under the constitution, a president and vice-president elected in a "national" election would serve four-year terms. Several controversial features of the constitution included separation of church and state (interpreted by some as disestablishing the Anglican Church on the island) and restrictions placed on the government's competition with private businesses. The constitution was approved by a vote of 1,739 to 4.

On 31 December, with unanimous approval of the council, Webster addressed a conciliatory letter to London. In it, the Anguillans reiterated their preferences for continuing the "interim" status. After considerable delay, William Whitlock, parliamentary undersecretary for foreign and commonwealth affairs, flew to Anguilla and proposed dissolution of the Republic and selection of a British commissioner. To make the plan more palatable, vague proposals for further development assistance, appointment of a permanent magistrate by Britain, establishment of a land registry office, and a general amnesty for the past 21 months' political activities were promised; but the Anguillans were adamant.

Then, to everyone's shock and consternation, the British used force and invaded Anguilla before dawn on 19 March 1969. They encountered no resistance, partly because Anguilla's government had expected nothing more than a show of force. In Parliament, the British government pointed to Section 7(2) of the West Indies Act referring to external relations control by England and furthermore noted that the United Kingdom had acted with the full concurrence of the government of the associated state.

Negotiations resulted in the enactment of the Anguilla Act of 1971, with the agreement of the Anguillans, whereby the United Kingdom reassumed direct responsibility for the administration of the island pending a final test of the wishes of the Anguillans in regard to their future status.

The Anguilla (Administration) Order, 1971, which was made on the basis of this act on 29 July and came into effect on 4 August 1971, provides for the appointment of a commissioner by the Queen and for the establishment of a Council for Anguilla. The commissioner is directly responsible to the United Kingdom government and is empowered to make such ordinances, after consultation with the council, as he considers necessary to secure and maintain peace, order, and good government in the island. The majority of the Anguilla Council is elected, with a minority appointed by the commissioner.

The first elections under the ordinance took place on 24 July 1972, and Webster's party, the PPP, won six of the seven seats in the new Anguilla Council. He announced that the council would soon resume negotiations with the United Kingdom for an "absolute and final separation" from the territory of St. Kitt-Nevis-Anguilla. There the matter rested with a plebiscite on Anguilla's future status expected within a year.

On November 17, 1975, the negotiations were concluded with the announcement that a new order in council would be submitted replacing the present Anguilla Administrative Order. Under this legislation Anguilla will obtain its own constitution effective in early 1976. The new constitution establishes parliamentary government with continued express and implicit power reserved to the commissioner. A ministerial system, with a chief minister who will be the elected member commanding the support of a majority of the elected members of the legislative assembly, is to be established. Two other ministers will be appointed on the advice of the chief minister from among the elected members of the legislative assembly. The legislative assembly will have seven elected members, three officials (chief secretary, attorney general, and financial secretary), and two members nominated by or after consultation with the chief minister. The executive council will consist of the chief minister, the two other ministers, and two official members—the attorney general and the financial secretary. The three elected ministers will be directly responsible for all matters of government business except for the subjects explicitly reserved to the commissioner; namely, defense, external affairs, internal security (including the police) and the public service. Except for finance, which will be allocated to the financial secretary, the commissioner will act in accordance with the advice of the executive council on all matters except those explicitly reserved to him, subject to general provisions enabling him, with the approval of the secretary of state in Britain, to act otherwise in cases where the British government's ultimate responsibility for public order, public faith or good government and for necessary financial control may so require. The constitution leaves it open for Anguilla to rejoin the West Indies Associated States Supreme Court, but provides for the present High Court and Court of Appeal to continue in the meantime.

The significance of the British action from a legal point of view is the possibility of internal intrusion of the most serious kind under the "external affairs" power of the metropole. It is interesting to note that the United Nations was not unduly critical of the United Kingdom's action since, as we shall discuss in greater detail in Chapter 9, there is great concern that the colonial territories may be fragmented. Nevis has already indicated that it wishes to obtain the same status relationship with Great Britain that Anguilla eventually obtains.

International Presence

Although Great Britain, as noted above, handles foreign affairs for the Associated States, there is considerable delegation of responsibility in some areas as well as consultation in others. Because of England's long-term desire to have the states federated with one another, there is considerable freedom of action and movement among the Associated States in the Caribbean.

The situation is worth considering with respect to other sections of the world, such as Europe. Although there was considerable consultation on the matter when Great Britain joined the Common Market, the Associated States in the Caribbean were referred to "as the territories dependent on the United Kingdom" which "will be associated with the enlarged community in accordance with the provisions of Part IV of the EEC treaty."[15]

ECONOMIC ASPECTS OF THE RELATIONSHIP

Tariffs and Trade

The British have long had a Commonwealth preference operative with respect to British exports to the region and also important to the Associated States with respect to their sale of products to England.

This latter has been particularly important with respect to the marketing of sugar, bananas, and citrus. For example, under the

WEST INDIES ASSOCIATED STATES 191

Commonwealth sugar agreement, Britain has since 1953 provided long-term guarantees, both price and market, for the overwhelming bulk of the Associated States' sugar exports. The sugar agreement, in addition to the other Commonwealth preferences, was a key issue at the time of the accession of Great Britain to the European Economic Community. Under Section 55 of the accession treaty, it was agreed that the Commonwealth sugar agreement would continue to operate until 31 December 1974. After that,

> "the community would have as its firm purpose the safeguarding of the countries whose economy depended to a considerable extent on the export of primary products, and in particular sugar. . .in the framework of the relations to be established between them and the community.

This latter language applied to Barbados, Guiana, Jamaica, Trinidad, and Tabago. In the case of the Associated States, Great Britain would continue to negotiate for them and would continue the preference.

Federal Financial Assistance

Great Britain has provided substantial bilateral aid to the Associated States, primarily in the form of development grants. In addition, budgetary assistance has been provided to Dominica, St. Kitts-Nevis-Anguilla, and St. Vincent. Receipt of such aid seems less a function of status relationship than of economic position within the Commonwealth. Antigua no longer receives budgetary support, but it is also true that all islands which have declared independence from Great Britain have also lost budgetary support. These latter have continued to receive considerable bilateral aid.

TERMINATION

The British followed the Cook Islands precedent and permitted the associated state to terminate the relationship unilaterally. The procedure for this termination was spelled out clearly and was not very simple. The territory could terminate the relationship only by a two-thirds vote in its legislature, coupled with a two-thirds majority of those voting in a referendum. In order to assist any Caribbean federations, no referendum was required if it was proposed to terminate the arrangement in favor of association with some other Commonwealth country in the Caribbean. In the case of Britain, no procedures were laid down since it was not thought the British would take advantage of the provision. But in the course of the discussions, Britain agreed that a period of notice would be given if it decided to terminate the association.

Although these "option-out" provisions are modelled after those for the Cook Islands the provision for a referendum as well is unique to the West Indies and made termination that much more difficult. Nevertheless, the West Indies Associated States experience has given us the only example to date of their operation. Prior to the Grenada election of 28 February 1972, E. M. Gairy, the leader of the Grenada United Labor Party, indicated that if his party won he would seek independence for Grenada. Status then became a key issue in the two-party election and Gairy's party won overwhelmingly, capturing 13 of the 15 elected seats. When presented with Premier Gairy's demand, the British took the position that independence would not be withheld if requested by the people of Grenada in accordance with the referendum requirement. Premier Gairy contended that such a referendum was unnecessary given his party's overwhelming victory. The negotiations became strained, with the United Kingdom standing by the referendum provision and generally desiring the Associated States to operate as a unit to the greatest possible extent.

Despite organized protest against independence in Grenada, Premier Gairy was able to force the issue. He pressed the British to terminate the relationship since the procedure there was more flexible. Finally the British gave in and terminated the association at their own initiative by an order-in-council of the British Parliament. Grenada thereby became independent on 7 February 1974.

NOTES

1. The economic problems of the islands are partly due to history and location but also to size. The best review of the issue is William G. Demas, The Economics of Development in Small Countries with Special Reference to the Caribbean (Toronto: McGill University Press, 1965). The prime minister of St. Vincent has poignantly described the issue in "The Exquisite Isle" (speech delivered before the San Francisco Chamber of Commerce in 1972). The politics of small size have been explored in Patricia Blair, The Ministate Dilemma (New York: Carnegie Endowment for International Peace, 1968).

2. The standard history is Eric Williams, From Columbus to Castro: The History of the Caribbean 1492-1969 (New York: Harper & Row, 1970). See also Mitchell, Europe in the Caribbean (New York: 1973).

3. The modern period is related within a broad social and cultural background in Gordon Lewis, The Growth of the Modern West Indies (New York: Monthly Review Press, 1967).

4. The federation has had no end of mourners and historians. A brief review is found in Harold Mitchell, Caribbean Patterns, (Edinburgh: 2d. ed., John Wiley & Sons, 1972), pp. 121-35; the issues of integration are explored fully in Robert Cassweller, The Caribbean Community (New York: Praeger Publishers, 1972); and the economic issues in Havelock Brewster and Clive Thomas, The Dynamics of West Indian Economic Integration (Institute of Social and Economic Research, Jamaica: University of the West Indies, 1967).

5. Constitutional Proposals for Antigua, St. Kitts-Nevis-Anguilla, Dominica, St. Lucia, St. Vincent, and Grenada, Cmnd. 2865 (London: H.H.S.O., 1965). (Hereinafter Constitutional Proposals.)

6. Constitutional Proposals, paragraphs 17 and 18.

7. Report of the Antigua Constitutional Conference, Cmnd. 2962 (London: H.M.S.O., 1966).

8. A recent book focusing on the islands being discussed here is Carleen O'Loughlan, Economics and Political Change in the Leeward and Windward Islands (New Haven: Yale University Press, 1968). Its focus is primarily economic.

9. West Indies Act [of 16 February] 1967, §§ 5(a), 9, and 19.

10. Constitutional Proposals, paragraphs 17 and 18.

11. Report of the Constitutional Conference of St. Kitts-Nevis-Anguilla, Cmnd. 3031 (London: H.M.S.O., 1966).

12. Cook Islands Constitution, New Zealand General Assembly Papers, No. 69 of 1964; see also An Act to Amend the Cook Islands Constitution, No. 2 of 1965.

13. The history is given in detail in William Brisk, The Dilemma of a Ministate: Anguilla (Columbia, University of Southern California, 1969).

14. J. H. Parry and P. M. Sherlock, A Short History of the West Indies, 2d. ed., (New York: St. Martin's Press, 1966), pp. 283-84.

15. Commission of the European Community, The Enlarged Community: Outcome of the Negotiations with the African States (Brussels, 22 January 1972).

CHAPTER

9

THE UNITED NATIONS AND DECOLONIZATION

There has been one noteworthy omission in our discussion, and that is the United Nations; specifically, its Committee on Decolonization or Committee of 24 (officially known as the "Special Committee on the Situation with regard to the Implementation of the Declaration on the granting of Independence to Colonial Countries and People"). Before summing up, it is appropriate to look to the UN standards and relate these association relationships to them.

ARTICLE 73: NON-SELF-GOVERNING TERRITORIES

The United Nations' involvement in the decolonization process is based on Article 73 of the UN Charter, which requires colonial powers administering non-self-governing territories to report "statistical and other information of a technical nature relating to economic, social and educational conditions in the territories" and "to promote . . . the well-being of the inhabitants . . . and to develop self-government." Nowhere in the charter is there a definition of self-government, nor is there any specific indication concerning those nations and territories to which the article was meant to apply. Nonetheless, seven UN members—Australia, Belgium, France, the Netherlands, New Zealand, the United Kingdom, and the United States—voluntarily declared that they were administering 74 non-self-governing territories and, pursuant to 73(e), began transmitting the required information.

In the United Nations there were many discussions and several General Assembly resolutions concerning the extent of the coverage of Article 73, but it was impossible to arrive at a consensus concerning the meaning of self-government. Some members expressed their concern that by 1952 reports were no longer being submitted on 15 of the 74 territories on the original list, since these had, the administering nations said, achieved the "full measure" of self-government required by the charter.[1]

The concern that administering nations would ignore requirements of Article 73 by self-serving statements as to the self-governing status of their territories caused the General Assembly to establish in 1949 (over the objections of the administering nations) an Ad Hoc Committee on Information which, in 1952, gave rise to a series of recommendations and a list of factors to be considered in connection with the requirement of self-government. The factors were divided into three categories: (1) those indicative of the attainment of independence, (2) those indicative of the attainment of other systems of self-government, and (3) those showing free association of a territory with all or any part of its metropole or other country. In the third category were (a) general factors (political advancement, opinion of the population, geographic considerations, ethnic and cultural considerations), (b) legal or constitutional nature of the association, (c) considerations with respect to status of the territory (legislative representation, citizenship of territory's inhabitants, eligibility of officials from the territory to public offices of the central authority), and (d) internal constitutional conditions (universal suffrage and free, periodic elections characterized by an absence of undue influence; scope of territorial legislative rights of the inhabitants; method of choosing local officials). The weight to be given to the inclusion or omission of any one of these was not stated.

THE EVENTS OF 1953

During the General Assembly's eigth session, two important, closely related items were on the agenda: (1) the criteria to be used to measure self-government (the factor problem) and (2) cessation of further information under Article 73(e) on the Netherland Antilles, Surinam, and Puerto Rico.

The Committee on Factors had again made recommendations, changing in a number of particulars the list of factors adopted the year before.[2] The new set of recommended factors now required any association of territory to be on an equal basis with the metropole or other country as an integral part of that country or in any other manner. Most importantly, the recommendations of the committee—which, together with the new list of factors, were later adopted by the General Assembly—asserted, among other things

"the competence of the General Assembly to consider the principles that should guide the United Nations and the

Member States in the implementation of obligations arising from Chapter XI of the Charter and to make recommendations in connection with them."3

This competence of the General Assembly was one of the issues which split the United Nations membership. On one side, the United States, other administering states, and a very small group of other nations asserted that only the administering nations were competent to determine when a non-self-governing territory had acquired the "full measure of self-government." They argued that if they had been competent to determine in the first place which territories should be put on the list as non-self-governing, they were also competent to determine when that condition had ceased.* When in their judgment that event had come about, they were no longer obliged to send reports and the General Assembly was only to "take note" of the cessation. Some also argued that the determination of the status of the territories lay with the respective national parliaments or legislatures, and that for the United Nations to hold that what the legislature had determined was not correct would be unauthorized intervention in the internal affairs of the nation and a violation of its sovereignty.

Going one step further, some members indicated that the administering state might stop sending the reports even before the "full measure of self-government" was reached. The argument went thus: Article 73(e) spoke only of information relating to economic, social, and educational conditions in the territories. Since the achievement of self-government usually came about in steps or gradations, there might come a time when a territory controlled its economic, social, and educational institutions, even if politically it had not yet reached full self-government. Therefore, when that time arrived, it was no longer practical or even possible for the administering state to send in its reports as to those conditions, since it would not normally be receiving this type of information from the territory. †

The nonadministering members, on the contrary, alleged that the administering states had entered into a bilateral obligation from which they could not free themselves unilaterally. They indicated that the

---

*Both Portugal and Spain, when they joined the United Nations in 1955, declared their territories an integral part of the state and, therefore, not subject to the reporting requirement. The United Nations, on its own authority, put their territories on the list requiring reports, and acted similarly in the case of Southern Rhodesia in 1962.

† Cf. the 1952 General Assembly resolution which stated "for a Territory to be deemed self-governing in economic, social or educational affairs, it is essential that its people shall have attained a full measure of self-government." This was reaffirmed in the 1953 recommendations.

transmissions could not cease until conditions set by the article had
been satisfied, and that the administering states could not make the
determination themselves. They held that the assembly was competent
to examine each case to determine whether or not the "full measure of
self-government" had been attained by the territory and whether, therefore, the obligation to remit information continued or had ceased. (Some
members suggested that this type of interpretation of the charter should
not be done by resolution, but that an opinion should be requested from
the International Court.)

As to the degree of self-government required, many states indicated
that it was wrong to look just at subsection (e), which spoke only of
economic, social, and educational issues and not of "political" ones.
They argued that the whole of Article 73 must be considered, in addition to other documents such as the Declaration of Human Rights, which
stated that all should strive for the political advancement of all peoples.
In no case should the reports cease when the territory had not yet acquired political as well as economic, social, and educational self-
government, for sovereignty was indivisible. Some argued further that
there could be no true self-government without independence; others
that any association was suspect; and others that association with the
administering state based upon the territory's self-government was impossible unless it had been preceded by independence.*

The issue at this point was not academic. In the case of the Netherlands territories, which continued under their latest arrangement in
association with Holland, the Ad Hoc Committee on Information had not
reached a decision and had decided to refer the matter to the General
Assembly without recommendation. Mr. Schurmann, the Netherlands
representative, stated that the political and constitutional structure
of neither territory was final. Talks were shortly to be resumed to settle the final and complete terms of cooperation between the various
parts of the kingdom in such matters as national defense and foreign
policy. In matters of economic, social, and educational conditions,
however, the territories were fully autonomous. His position was that,
whether or not the territories had achieved a full measure of self-government, for constitutional reasons resulting from their interim status the
transmission of information under Article 73(e) could not continue, since

---

*The resolution recommended by the Ad Hoc Committee on Factors
considered that "the manner in which Territories referred to in Chapter
XI of the Charter can become fully self-governing is primarily through
the attainment of independence, although it is recognized that self-
government can also be achieved by association with another State or
group of States if this is done freely and on the basis of absolute equality." See Resolution 742 (VIII).

this would diminish the autonomy which the Netherlands Antilles and Surinam enjoyed. Other portions of Article 73, he admitted, might still be applicable to the territories.

After some debate, a draft resolution, later adopted by the General Assembly, was prepared in the Fourth Committee.[4] In this report the progress made by the territories toward self-government was noted with satisfaction, but it was stated that the new status of the territories could only be appraised after the negotiations had led to a final result and had been embodied in constitutional provisions. The government of the Netherlands was invited to communicate the result of the negotiations and was requested to transmit regularly the information specified in Article 73(e) until the General Assembly should take a decision that the remission should be discontinued.

Nevertheless, no additional information under Article 73 was remitted by the Netherlands. In a communication dated 13 March 1955 the Netherlands sent certain documents, including the charter of the Kingdom of the Netherlands of which the Antilles and Surinam now formed a permanent part.[5] The General Assembly, without any other alternative, engaged in a face-saving device and on 15 December 1955 approved a resolution, inter alia, (1) taking note of the documentation and (2) expressing the opinion that, without prejudice to the previous position, cessation of transmission under Article 73(e) was now appropriate.[6]

The Puerto Rican case was considered by the Fourth Committee after the case of the Netherlands territories. The United States, not admitting the power of the committee or the General Assembly to review the matter, had submitted for the information of the United Nations only the fact of the establishment of the commonwealth and the statement that in the United States' view the territory was no longer non-self-governing. The Ad Hoc Committee had unanimously adopted, with three abstentions, a resolution in favor of cessation of transmission of information on Puerto Rico as a result of the establishment of the commonwealth.[7]

Before entering into a consideration of the matter, the Fourth Committee considered a request for an oral hearing submitted by the president of the Independence Party of Puerto Rico. The United States delegate strongly opposed this request, arguing that it would be undesirable for the United Nations to afford minority political parties a platform from which to plead their cause against elected governments.

> On behalf of the Governments of both the United States and Puerto Rico, my delegation wishes to express its strong opposition to the granting of an oral hearing to the Puerto Rican Independence Party, which cannot win an election in Puerto Rico and is therefore asking you to come to its rescue. Members of the Committee will recall that in the full documentation which my Government transmitted to the United Nations in compliance with General Assembly resolution 222 (III), we have set forth in careful detail the series of

elections, referenda, and other democratic steps by which
the people of Puerto Rico have achieved a full measure of
self-government through a compact entered into by mutual
consent between Puerto Rico and the United States.

In the numerous democratic elections by which the
people of Puerto Rico have determined their destiny, they
have repeatedly and decisively rejected the views of the
Puerto Rican Independence Party. The Independence Party
is certainly not unique among defeated parties throughout
the world in being dissatisfied because it lost an election.
We cannot believe, however, that the United Nations is
going to take a step which would help this party's efforts
to undo the result of Puerto Rico's elections. One of the
great principles and strengths of the United Nations is its
constant efforts to promote the self-determination of all
peoples, and we are confident that the Fourth Committee
does not wish to undermine this principle, even if only
by implication, by challenging in any way the action of the
people of Puerto Rico in determining for themselves their
own political future. They would strongly resent, and
quite properly so, the granting of an oral hearing to the
Independence Party.[8]

It was also argued, among other things, that the charter granted no right of petition to the inhabitants of the non-self-governing territories (as opposed to those of the Trust Territories), and that there was no difference between a petition and an oral hearing.

The Indian delegation led the argument against the United States position:

Mrs. Menon (India) said she would vote in favour of the
request. Notwithstanding all the arguments and information placed before the Committee by the United States delegation, the Committee should not hastily take a decision
on so momentous a question as the cessation of the transmission of information concerning Puerto Rico. The fact
that there were parties in the island which opposed the
United States proposal made it desirable that the Committee should have further information from the people themselves. India would continue to regard Puerto Rico as a
Non-Self-Governing Territory until the General Assembly
had decided that it had attained a full measure of self-
government.[9]

The committee decided by a roll-call vote of 25 to 19, with 11 absten-
tions, to deny the request. (In favor: Afghanistan, Argentina, Bolivia,
Burma, Byelorussian SSR, Czechoslovakia, Egypt, Guatemala, India,
Indonesia, Iraq, Lebanon, Mexico, Poland, Saudi Arabia, Syria,

Ukranian SSR, Yugoslavia. Against: Australia, Belgium, Brazil, Canada, Chile, Colombia, Cuba, Denmark, Dominican Republic, Ecuador, France, Greece, Israel, the Netherlands, New Zealand, Nicaragua, Norway, Panama, Peru, the Philippines, Sweden, Turkey, Union of South Africa, the United Kingdom, the United States of America. Abstaining: China, Costa Rica, El Salvador, Haiti, Honduras, Iran, Liberia, Pakistan, Thailand, Uruguay, Venezuela).[10] A similar request was made by the Nationalist Party of Puerto Rico and it, too, was denied.[11]

The debate on the substantive issue and the self-governing status of the Commonwealth of Puerto Rico was quite extensive. Since the criteria for a self-governing territory were unclear, by emphasizing certain factors in the association and not others the delegates were able to support a variety of conclusions. Most delegates who felt that Puerto Rico was self-governing emphasized the referendum, the free choice given Puerto Rico to enter into this type of association,[12] and the mutuality principle of the compact.[13] Others—the British Commonwealth countries and other administering powers—refused to review the judgment of the United States but urged that the General Assembly "note" the decision of the United States no longer to report under 73(e) with respect to Puerto Rico.[14] Some of these delegates also limited their decision to the economic, social, and educational criteria mentioned in 73(e) and on these criteria concurred in the United States position.[15]

The delegates voting in favor of continued reporting noted the limited choice afforded in the referendum on Public Law 600 and the powers retained by the United States over Puerto Rican affairs. Many delegations were concerned by the absence of the possibility of independence as an alternative in the referendum submitted to the Puerto Rican people.[16] This omission was accented since one of the additional factors brought forward by the Committee on Factors earlier in the session had been the right of secession.[17]

Other delegates analyzed the relationship and felt that the United States' control over foreign affairs and defense,[18] the absence of a compact,[19] the economic dependence of Puerto Rico,[20] and the lack of a vote by the resident commissioner in the United States Congress (which could pass laws substantially affecting Puerto Rico)[21] meant that Puerto Rico was non-self-governing. It is interesting to note that only the Indonesian and Czechoslovakian delegates analyzed the relationship extensively in terms of the factors which had just been approved by the Fourth Committee.

At the request of the delegates of Guatemala, a vote was taken by roll call in the Fourth Committee on the operative paragraph permitting the cessation of information to the United Nations. The vote was very close but the United States won: 24 in favor, 17 against, and 17 abstentions. (In favor: Bolivia, Brazil, Chile, China, Colombia, Costa Rica, Cuba, Dominican Republic, Ecuador, Ethiopia, France, Iceland, Iran, Israel, Luxembourg, Nicaragua, Norway, Panama, Paraguay, Peru, Thailand, Turkey, the United States of America, Uruguay. Against: Burma, Byelorussian SSR, Czechoslovakia, Guatemala, Honduras, India,

Indonesia, Iraq, Mexico, the Netherlands, New Zealand, Poland, Ukrainian SSR, Union of South Africa, the United Kingdom, Yugoslavia. Abstaining: Afghanistan, Argentina, Australia, Canada, Denmark, Egypt, El Salvador, Greece, Haiti, Lebanon, Liberia, Pakistan, Philippines, Saudi Africa, Sweden, Syria, Venezuela.)

During the last few years Puerto Rican independence partisans have come to the United Nations to argue the invalidity of the Commonwealth as a self-governing territory. The Committee of 24 has been receptive and has reported the testimony to the General Assembly, where the matter has died. No authorization has come forth to examine or reopen the 1953 UN vote.

THE SPECIAL COMMITTEE OF 24

On 14 December 1960, the General Assembly adopted Resolution 1514(XV) in which it proclaimed independence as the preferred goal. The resolution declared:

> the necessity of bringing to a speedy and unconditional end colonialism in all its forms and manifestations . . .
> All peoples have the right to self-determination; by virtue of that right they freely determine their political status and freely pursue their economic, social and cultural development . . .
> Immediate steps shall be taken, in trust and non-self-governing territories or all other territories which have not yet attained independence, to transfer all powers to the peoples of those territories, without any conditions or reservations, in accordance with their freely expressed will and desire, without any distinction as to race, creed or color, in order to enable them to enjoy complete independence and freedom.

The General Assembly also expressed the conviction that the continued existence of colonialism prevented the development of international economic cooperation, impeded the social, cultural, and economic development of dependent peoples, and militated against the United Nations' ideal of universal peace. (The resolution had the approval of 90 of the 99 member nations. Abstaining were: Australia, Belgium, Dominican Republic, France, Portugal, Spain, Union of South Africa, United Kingdom, and the United States.)[22]

In November 1961, in its sixteenth session, the General Assembly established a 17-member special committee to examine the application of the 1960 declaration and to make recommendations on the progress and extent of its application. The original members were: Australia, Cambodia, Ethiopia, India, Italy, Madagascar, Mali, Poland, Syria,

Tanganyika, (now part of the United Republic of Tanzania), Tunisia, USSR, the United Kingdom, the United States of America, Uruguay, Venezuela, and Yugoslavia. In the General Assembly's seventeenth session (1962) seven new members were added,—Bulgaria, Chile, Denmark, Iran, Iraq, Ivory Coast, and Sierra Leone—giving rise to its present total membership and shortened sobriquet of the "Committee of 24." In the 1963 session, the General Assembly dissolved the Committee on Information and transferred its functions to the Special Committee, which—apart from the Trusteeship Council—is now the only UN body under the General Assembly related to dependent territories.

Resolution 1514 was important because of its strong stand in favor of independence; but perhaps of greater import over the long run was Resolution 1541, adopted that same year by the UN General Assembly. This had annexed to it a set of principles to guide members in determining whether Article 73(e) had been fulfilled. This set of principles permitted a non-self-governing territory to reach a full measure of self-government short of independence, by free association with an independent state. Association was defined as follows:

Principle VII
(a) Free association should be the result of a free and voluntary choice by the peoples of the territory concerned expressed through informed and democratic processes. It should be one which respects the individuality and the cultural characteristics of the territory and its peoples, and retains for the peoples of the territory which is associated with an independent State the freedom to modify the status of that territory through the expression of their will by democratic means and through constitutional processes.
(b) The associated territory should have the right to determine its internal constitution without outside interference, in accordance with due constitutional processes and the freely expressed wishes of the people. This does not preclude consultations as appropriate or necessary under the terms of the free association agreed upon.

Principle VII contains five elements: (1) the need for free choice by the electorate, (2) the need for awareness of the issues, (3) the need for universal suffrage ("democratic process"), (4) no outside interference in the constitutional process, and (5) the right to subsequently select an alternate status.

Although these conditions were carefully selected, the committee was suspicious of this association concept and the administering territories under whose aegis it might come about. It had expressed a preference to observe at first hand in all cases the key events leading to the cessation of reporting. This was true a fortiori in the case where the termination of reporting was to be coupled with continued association.

The Cook Islands association with New Zealand has become the precedent-setting case. On 9 February 1965, New Zealand responded favorably to the committee's desires for first hand knowledge of the situation and invited the UN to send an observer team to the Cook Islands elections and the subsequent parliamentary proceedings. Pursuant to a General Assembly resolution, a Sudanese jurist, Omar A. H. Adeel, was commissioned to perform this task.

The Cook Islands election as noted earlier, was not directly upon the free association issue. Rather, the electorate chose a parliament who had campaigned for this status and subsequently adopted a constitution drafted by constitutional experts in New Zealand. Adeel's report was favorable to the free, informed, democratic (94 percent participation) character of the elections. He said that "the people of the Cook Islands were not interested in full independence." He also was convinced that in accepting the constitution, the members of the Cook Islands Legislative Assembly were not pressured by New Zealand.

In addition, the prime minister of the Cook Islands, Albert Henry, noted the constitutional provision permitting unilateral revision of the constitutional status by a two-thirds vote.

Despite Adeel's report and the fact that there was little real controversy in the Cook Islands over the acceptance of the provisions of the constitution (the only discussion being over the residency requirements and the decision to include the two amendments), there was considerable controversy in the United Nations over the form of the acceptance of the constitution and the amount of influence exerted by New Zealand in the initial phases of drafting the legislation.

The discussion in the United Nations was fairly positive towards the decision taken by the New Zealand and Cook Island governments, but there was some question raised as to how well informed the Cook Islanders had been about the nature of the constitution and about exactly what was being offered to them. For example, the representative of Mali noted that although New Zealand had invited UN representatives to watch the voting process, the Cook Islanders had not been given the opportunity to vote directly on the constitution. Rather, they voted only for candidates to the assembly who in turn approved the constitution. The Bulgarian delegation noted that the constitution had been drawn up by the colonial power and that the acceptance of the document by the Cook Islanders was not an adequate act of self-determination. The most vigorous criticism of the New Zealand activities came from the Soviet Union, who emphasized the fact that New Zealand had played a large role in drafting the legislation and deciding who might run for office. According to the Soviet delegation, "the whole machinery had been subordinate to the colonial power and not separate from it. The role of the UN representative had been merely to supervise the

the elections within the framework of the legislation drafted and implemented by the colonial power itself." There were, however, others present at the UN session who commended the smoothness of the transition of power to the Cook Islands and the openness of New Zealand in allowing UN observers to be present at the election.

But in the last analysis, it was the choice that was bothersome: the selection of a status other than independence with a UN observer giving sanction to the proceeding. Despite Resolution 1541, the Committee of 24 could not accept that and finally agreed that Adeel's report was to be treated only as a rapporteur's observations, not binding on the United Nations. It passed the issue to the Assembly in a carefully worded resolution which avoided the issue of self-determination and self-government, noted New Zealand's cooperation, and looked forward to future assistance to the Cook Islands. The committee's resolution merely "took note" of the situation. It accepted the reports and statements of the New Zealand and Cook Island officials and expressed the "hope that the General Assembly will recommend that the United Nations, in co-operation with the specialized agencies, endeavor to contribute in every way possible to the development and strengthening of the economy of the Cook Islands."

The General Assembly went further, however, endorsing the Cook Islands achievement.

> 4. [The General Assembly] <u>notes</u> that the Constitution of the Cook Islands came into force on 4 August 1965, from which date the people of the Cook Islands have had control of their internal affairs and of their future;
> 5. <u>Considers</u> that since the Cook Islands have attained full internal self-government, the transmission of information in respect of the Cook Islands under Article 73e of the Charter of the United Nations is no longer necessary;
> 6. <u>Reaffirms</u> the responsibility of the United Nations, under General Assembly resolution 1514 (XV), to assist the people of the Cook Islands in the eventual achievement of full independence, if they so wish, at a future date."[23]

The key substantive facts were, as noted, that the military and foreign affairs powers were in the hands of New Zealand and the independence option had not been directly offered. Yet the arrangement was approved. The standing option to unilaterally declare independence, and the request by New Zealand for a UN observer to report on what had happened, had become crucial.

The implementation of Principle VII, setting forth free association, has been erratic; but it appears that the United Nations has been influenced by two principles. The first of these is the willingness of the former metropole to permit UN observers to assure that the vote is indeed in accordance with "the freely expressed wishes of the people."

The United States, perhaps distrustful of the composition of the Committee of 24 and regarding itself as something of a sitting duck, has refused to permit any UN presence in either the Puerto Rican plebiscite or in any self-governing territory. UN observers were in the Marianas for their plebiscite because the rules of the Trust Territory were clearer in requiring a UN role.

The other principle focuses upon the associated territory's power to determine its internal constitution without restriction. This involves subtle questions of the applicability of federal law and questions of the power to amend the constitution. We have discussed this at considerable length; and as we have shown in the Puerto Rican case, the general applicability of federal law and the restrictions on the power to amend the constitution—which Congress insisted upon—places Puerto Rico in a dubious free association by UN standards.

The United Nations has recognized that foreign affairs and military security may be vested in the hands of a larger power. But as we have shown, this may be a substantial intrusion upon the local affairs of the former territory. This takes note of political reality. Major intrusions upon the local constitution are possible as long as there are rather free-ranging possibilities in the area of foreign affairs. This is especially true if there is no consultation role with respect to military activity and lack of full participation in the federal legislature.

Finally, the United Nations has been very much influenced by the Cook Islands experience. There, in recognition of the imbalance in the relationship between the associated territory and the formal colonizing power, the provision was developed, as discussed above, for a continuing unilateral option "out" so that if the bargaining gets too one-sided the associated territory may declare its independence. Appropriately, the United Nations has been impressed by this possibility. It is consistent with the position of the Committee of 24 that independence—the preferred position of the committee in the decolonization process—be offered at the time of the plebiscite for free association. Its constant availability assures that the continuing association is indeed voluntary. The refusal of the U.S. negotiators to consider the "Cook Islands" option was the specific cause for the breakdown of the Micronesia negotiations with the United States. It has also been a reason for the criticism of the Marianas plebiscite.

The legal and moral attack within the United Nations and from various groups in the United States on the Marianas plebiscite and the islands' decision thereby to join the United States involves two questions: (1) Was it consistent with the Trust Agreement to permit the Marianas to separate from the rest of Micronesia and choose a permanent association with the United States (the fragmentation question)? (2) Were the alternatives presented to the people of the Marianas too limited (the independence question)? In my view the answer to the first is no, and the answer to the second is yes.

The danger of fragmentation has been ever-present in the decolonization process and the Committee of 24 has been concerned with the division of territories in order to obtain continued colonial control. There are always some people who have vested interest in the status quo or who can be made to have such an interest by economic force. This is, of course, what happened in the case of the Marianas. To forestall that, the committee's famous Declaration on Colonialism of 1960 (Res. 1514), quoted above, said: "Any attempt aimed at the partial or total disruption of the national unity and the territorial integrity of a country is incompatible with the purposes and principles of the Charter of the United Nations." But the emphasis on the colonial territorial boundaries can lead to inequitable results for minority groups, especially when there is really no "national unity or territorial integrity."

Micronesia, as we have noted, is not contiguous. Its 115,000 inhabitants are spread out over 100 inhabited islands covering 3,000 miles. The ethnic character of the territory is also divisive. The 12,500 inhabitants of the Marianas are (as noted) generally Chamorron; and therefore, related to the people of Guam rather than the rest of Micronesia. (There are also about 4,000 migrants from the Caroline Islands in the Marianas, however, which complicates matters.) In any event, national unity is a consummation devoutly to be wished but hardly likely of achievement. There is no more reason for Saipan (the largest island in the Marianas) to be coupled with Truk and Ponape than for Saipan to be joined as part of Hawaii. The Marianas' concern, expressed continuously from the mid-1960s onward, is that as less populated islands they would be overwhelmed by the rest of Micronesia. Since the formulation of the Congress of Micronesia in 1965, territorial tax legislation has been passed over the objection of the Marianas, so the fear has a substantive basis.

In addition, the Marianas saw Guam's relative prosperity and attributed it to its association with the United States. (This led to their request in 1969 for integration with Guam, which the Guamanians turned down.) The Micronesian insistence on the unilateral right to terminate any association with the United States was a position not shared by the Marianas. They did not conceive this eventuality in any event.

It is true that the United Nations understands these arguments and has been unsympathetic. The 1973 UN mission, like every mission since 1961, was against any separate covenant with the Marianas:

> The United Nations has consistently opposed in principle the fragmentation of dependent Territories on tribal or regional lines. This is exemplified by the case of Namibia. On all other Trust Territories it has recommended that the Administering Authority should emphasize the unity of the country to overcome racial or regional cleavages. In the two instances when Trust Territories were divided, this was done only after a territorial referendum had taken place. . . .

No purely ethnic argument can be seriously advanced in support of separation. Of course, the Chamorros are not identical with the inhabitants of the Marshall Islands; nor are the latter the same as the residents of Yap or Ponape. Acceptance of the Marianas Islands argument would mean acceptance of the fragmentation of the territory.

It also would be naive to say that the United States did not encourage this separatist tendency. For example, the movement of the U.S. headquarters for the District of Saipan was directed not only at maintaining an association with Micronesia as a whole but also at assuring a relationship with the Marianas District. But even if the United States encouraged the separatist movement, it is also true that this separatist force had a deeply felt local origin. It seems to me there is no sufficient national unity or territorial integrity to prohibit the "peoples" of the Marianas from expressing and having their sought-after status relationship.

On the other hand, the U.S. position would look considerably better if the alternatives offered to the people of the Marianas and Micronesia were those put forth in Article VI of the trusteeship agreement and insisted on in that article. It was clear from the first that the United States has been reluctant to grant independence to all or any part of the territory. Its refusal even to negotiate this possibility with Micronesia has made this painfully obvious. But this U.S. position is contrary to the language and clear intent of the UN trust.

The original draft of the trusteeship agreement put forward by the United States envisioned the possibility of never offering independence to the territory. It indicated that the administering authority (United States) would have full powers over the territory "as an integral part of the United States," (Article III); and (in Article VI) the administering authority was to "foster the development of such political institutions as are suited to the Trust Territory and shall promote the development of the inhabitants of the Trust Territory toward self-government . . . and shall develop their participation in _local_ government."

This was the form in which the United States put the draft forward. The intent to keep the Trust Territory was clear. But the underlined words were struck when the Security Council finally voted the trusteeship agreement; and just to make doubly sure that the independence option was available, the Security Council went further and added the following underlined words in the key phrase quoted above in Article VI:

and shall promote the development of the inhabitants of the Trust Territory toward self-government <u>or independence as may be appropriate to the particular circumstances of the Trust Territory and its peoples and the freely elected expressed wishes of the peoples concerned</u>. (emphasis added)

The United States, in accepting the trust, continued to fight the problem. The U.S. representative said:

> the United States feels that it must record its opposition, not to the principle of independence, to which no people could be more consecrated than the people of the United States, but to the thought that it could possibly be achieved within any foreseeable future in this case.

As late as 1973 the United States was taking the same line but now because of military strategic considerations. The U.S. representative said to the Micronesian delegation in refusing to discuss the independence option:

> I should say again, however, that the circumstances which led to the Trust Territory's designation as a strategic trust will continue to exist whatever your future status might be. I cannot imagine, for instance, that my Government would agree to termination of the trusteeship on terms which would in any way threaten the stability in the area and which in the opinion of the United States endanger international peace and security.

But the report of the UN Visiting Mission in 1973 reiterated the importance of permitting this option:

> In our opinion, it is implicit in the Charter and in the Trusteeship System that the goal is eventual independence unless agreement is reached on some other status acceptable to the people of the Territories concerned through an act of self-determination. Micronesia is no exception to this rule. That being so, if one of the parties concerned wishes to discuss the question of independence as one possible option, the other should be prepared to join in such a discussion. What either party sees as the conditions which should or might apply in an independence situation would naturally emerge from these discussions. There should be no insistence by one on getting an explanation of how the other party sees those conditions, before agreeing in principle to discuss the option.

One can say that the form of the plebiscite question in the case of the Marianas is academic since there is no indication the Marianas would have chosen independence. But it is not an academic issue. The issue is the precedent for the rest of Micronesia and an indication of whether the independence option will ever be offered at all. The record is hardly a source of comfort.

Plebiscites are almost always rigged in the way the question is stated. The Marianas question was no worse in this regard than most. It offered the choice of an affirmative vote on the covenant or a negative vote which left unclear how the status issue would be resolved. The ballot said (in English, Chamorro, and Carolinian):

> I vote against commonwealth in political union with the United States as set forth in the covenant, recognizing that if commonwealth is rejected, the North Marianas Islands will remain as a district of the trust territory with the right to participate with the other districts in the determination of an alternate future political status.

Limiting the choice in this way follows almost standard procedure; but it is not defensible to do this when the legal background so clearly requires something more.

The covenant was overwhelmingly approved by public referendum. Of 5,005 votes cast (95 percent of the registered voters), there were 3,945 favorable votes (78 percent) and 1,060 voted no (22 percent). The vote was, interestingly enough, observed by a UN mission which attested to its democratic procedure.

Since the backing off of the Marianas has been so criticized by the United Nations, it is probable that the United States will not officially bring its actions before that body for its approval until the Micronesian negotiations have been completed and perhaps until the events contemplated there and in the Marianas are to take place. This may delay any UN official action until sometime in the 1980s.

But the other major Trust Territory, Papua New Guinea—albeit nonstrategic—has received UN review. What problem there was was resolved from the UN point of view by the decision to grant independence to Papua New Guinea. The grant of internal autonomy was regarded by many in the United Nations as a formal transfer of authority only.[24] But since there has been a decision recognized by Australia to grant independence and to permit UN visiting missions on a continuing basis, the situation has brought forth generally commendatory words, with questions relating to the nature of the continuing powers by Australia in defense and foreign affairs (which we have discussed above) and the Papua New Guinea attitude toward foreign investment. In this latter area the Soviet delegate has been particularly sharp, provoking an equally sharp retort by Mr. Kiki of the Papua New Guinea delegation at the 1974 Trusteeship Council discussions.

The General Assembly, in its resolution of 1 December 1973 commenting favorably on Papua New Guinea's acquisition of formal self-government, cited the "imperative need to ensure the national unity of Papua New Guinea"; and, interestingly enough, sanctioned the parliament—"duly elected"—to decide the issue of independence, rather than requiring a direct plebiscite.[25]

The British Associated States of the Caribbean have had a more difficult row to hoe in the United Nations. This led to Great Britain's withdrawal in January 1971—together with the United States—from the Special Committee of 24. The U.S. withdrawal was precipitated by the program of action worked out by the Special Committee of 24 on the tenth anniversary of Resolution 1514, the Declaration on the Granting of Independence to Colonial Countries and Peoples. It endorsed armed struggle and suggested that UN member states were required to support this violence: "Member states shall render all necessary moral and material assistance to the peoples of colonial territories in their struggle to attain freedom and independence."[26] The resolution, on top of a deteriorating working relationship, brought an understandable response by the United States.

But the British situation was different. The United Kingdom had advised the Fourth Committee in connection with the constitutions of the Associated States.

> The new status of the Associated States thus differed from the relationship between a colonial Territory and the metropolitan Power in three important ways: they had full and unqualified powers in their own internal affairs; the United Kingdom Government and Parliament had surrendered all their powers and responsibilities in relation to them except in narrow, carefully defined and mutually agreed spheres; and each Associated State was free to proceed to independence or any other status and thereby sever its association with the United Kingdom without the latter's approval. It was clear, therefore, that the Associated States had a full measure of self-government and that the responsibilities of the United Kingdom Government under Chapter XI of the Charter had been fully discharged and that it would no longer transmit information concerning them.[27]

The United Kingdom's position that the territories were now self-governing and that therefore reporting was not required was reiterated before the General Assembly,[28] which considered that Great Britain should continue to transmit information.[29] The General Assembly may have been influenced by the substantive relationship, but it appears to have been affected more by the general prejudice against association relationships and the refusal of the United Kingdom to allow UN visiting missions in the area.[30]

We have discussed the British intervention in Anguilla and indicated that the legal power for that action rested on British control over external relations. But that invasion once again raised the issue of fragmentation, or the degree of responsiveness in the United Nations to self-determination movements within larger entities.[31] In this area, the United Nations has been consistent. It is in favor of self-determination when the issue is a colony's right to break away from the metropole; but

THE UN AND DECOLONIZATION   211

it is against self-determination within the larger entity. In the United Nations' eyes, self-determination can never justify secessionist movements regardless of their foundation. U Thant, when he was secretary general, explained it as follows in connection with the Biafra-Nigeria conflict:

> So, as far as the question of secession of a particular section of a Member State is concerned, the United Nations attitude is unequivocable. As an international organization, the United Nations has never accepted and does not accept and I do not believe it will ever accept the principle of secession of a part of its Member State.[32]

Anguilla's efforts were in UN perspective secessionist efforts which were dangerous in their implications for many other states and, therefore, Great Britain's intervention was acceptable.

NOTES

1. See pronouncement of Mr. Djerdja (Yugoslavia), 4th Committee, United Nations General Assembly, Official Records, 8th Sess. (1953), at 36.
2. Agenda Item 33, Annexes, General Assembly Official Documents, 8th Sess. (1953), at 5 et seq.
3. Resolution 742 (VIII).
4. Resolution 747 (VIII).
5. Summary of Information Transmitted During 1955 by the Netherlands Government, ST/TRI/SER.A/12, 1957.
6. Resolution 945(X).
7. Fourth Committee, 8th Sess., at 98.
8. <u>United States Department of State Bulletin</u>, Vol. XXIX, No. 746 (12 October 1953) at 499.
9. Mrs. Menon, Fourth Committee, 8th Session, at 29-30.
10. Item 32, Annexes, 8th Sess., at 11.
11. Ibid.
12. Remarks of the Cuban delegate, ibid., at 220; Remarks of the Panama delegate, ibid., at 241; Remarks of the Canadian delegate, ibid., at 242; Remarks of the Brazilian delegate, ibid., at 245-47; Remarks of the Peruvian delegate, ibid., at 248; Remarks of the Iranian delegate, ibid., at 249; Remarks of the Costa Rican delegate, ibid., at 251; Remarks of the Haitian delegate, ibid., at 254; Remarks of the Bolivian delegate, ibid., at 259; Remarks of the Venezuelan delegation, ibid., at 261; Remarks of the Chinese delegates, ibid., at 261; Remarks of the Israeli delegates, ibid., at 252.

13. Remarks of the Panama delegate, ibid., at 241; Remarks of the Brazilian delegate, ibid., at 245-47; Remarks of the delegate from Ecuador, ibid., at 227-31.

14. Remarks of the Belgian delegate, ibid., at 254; Remarks of the delegate from the Netherlands, ibid., at 259; Remarks of the New Zealand delegate, ibid., at 260; Remarks of the delegate from the United Kingdom, ibid., at 261.

15. Remarks of the Canadian delegate, ibid., at 242; Remarks of the Costa Rican delegate, ibid., at 259; Remarks of the Swedish delegate, ibid., at 259.

16. Remarks of the Yugoslav delegate, ibid., at 236-37; Remarks of the Egyptian delegate, ibid., at 258; Remarks of the Lebanese delegate, ibid., at 261; Remarks of the Indonesian delegate, ibid., at 240.

17. Remarks of the Polish delegate, ibid., at 242; Remarks of the Canadian delegate, ibid., at 242.

18. Remarks of the delegate of the Ukraine, ibid., at 233-34; Remarks of the Indian delegate, ibid., at 235-36; Remarks of the Burmese delegate, ibid., at 237; Remarks of the Honduran delegate, ibid., at 239; Remarks of the Argentine delegate, ibid., at 251.

19. Remarks of the Yugoslav delegate, ibid., at 236-37; Remarks of the Czechoslovakian delegate, ibid., at 237-38; Remarks of the Honduran delegate, ibid., at 239; Remarks of the Indonesian delegate, ibid., at 240; Remarks of the Iraqi delegate, ibid., at 257.

20. Remarks of the Egyptian delegate, ibid., at 258.

21. Remarks of the Mexican delegate, ibid., at 222-24; Remarks of the delegate of the Ukraine, ibid., at 233-34; Remarks of the Indian delegate, ibid., at 253; Remarks of the Indonesian delegate, ibid., at 240.

22. United Nations Review 8:1 (January 1961), at 8.

23. UN General Assembly, Resolution 2064 (XX) (16 December 1965).

24. For example, remarks of Mr. Garrique-Guyamand, France, UN Doc. T/PV.1432 (17 October 1974), p. 18.

25. General Assembly Resolution 3109 (XXVIII), 12 December 1973.

26. General Assembly Resolution 2621 (XXV), 12 October 1970.

27. Remarks of Mr. Luard (U.K.), General Assembly, 22nd Sess., Fourth Committee A/C.4/SR. 1752.

28. Remarks of Mr. Lee Williams, A/C.4/SR.1867 (10 December 1969).

29. General Assembly Resolution 270 (XXV), (14 December 1970).

30. UN Doc. A/AC.109/PV.761 (1 September 1970).

31. See Rupert Emerson, Self-Determination in 65 Am. J. Int'l. Law 459 (1971).

32. U.N. Monthly Chronicle 36 (February 1970).

CHAPTER

10

CONCLUSION

We have explored the specific interrelationships of various federal systems in relation to the associated state relationships.

The UN Decolonization Committee, although formally permitting associated relationships as the end product of the decolonization process, has in practice resisted the associated state alternative despite its increasing use by various territories.[1]

United States academics have come at the problem differently. They have focused upon the ministate and have been concerned how that state would play a role in the international community.[2] There has been discussion of the development of a special UN office to handle problems of these states. These proposals envision a special dependency status for these areas.

The thrust behind this book's analysis of the associated state development is to come at the issue in terms of the states' own goals and to assure that the bargaining is not so one-sided as to make attainment of dignity for the small state unattainable. There is a belief here that the concepts of dependence and independence are not clear-cut. They are part of a continuum. The degree of dependence and independence can only be determined after examination of the specifics of each case.

This, of course, is what we have tried to do. The association relationship is developing to accommodate to the needs of many less powerful areas. It is important, it seems to me, that the international community and the metropole see in these relationships a positive means of political and economic development worthy of support, worrying less about the title of the area and more about its powers under the relationship.

NOTES

1. In addition to Resolution 1541 (XV) of 1960 cited earlier, see the 1970 Declaration of the Committee on Friendly Relations.

MAP 10

Oceania

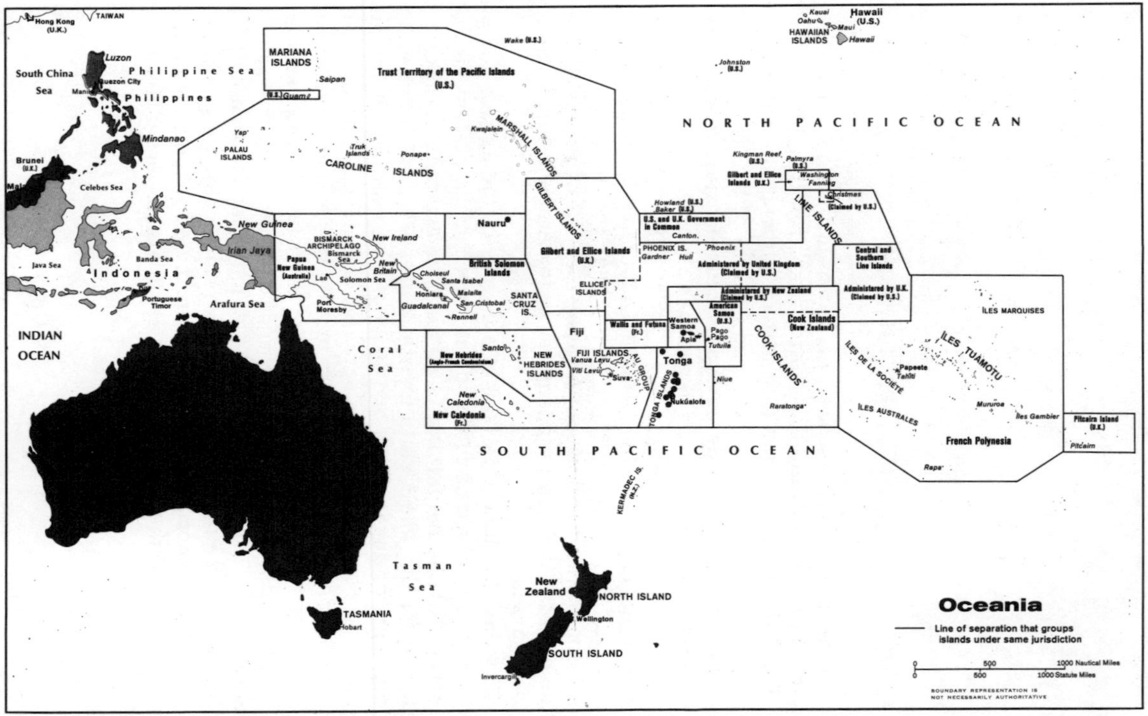

Source: U.S. Department of State

2. For example, Roger Fisher, "The Participation of Microstates in International Affairs," 1968 Proceedings, Amer. Soc. Int'l. Law 166 (Washington, D.C., 1968). The problem has also been studied by the United Nations. See UN/TAR, Status Problems of Very Small States and Territories (1968).

INDEX

Abaijah, Josephine, 163
Adams, Peter, 187
Albizu Campos, Pedro, 44-45
American Samoa, 2, 10, 85, 105; Fair Labor Standards Act (FLSA), 60-62, 94, 129; shipping, 127
Anguilla, 6, 176, 185-86, 187-90; Act of 1971, 189; Administration Order of 1971, 189; Constitution of, 189; Constitution of Anguilla-St. Kitts-Nevis, 187; Council, 189; relationship with UN, 210-11
Antigua, 177, 191
Asian Development Bank, 7, 142, 167
associated states, concept of, 5, 9, 10, 205
Australia: Commonwealth of Australia Act, 149; defense, 166-67; foreign affairs, 166-67; High Court, 165; relationship with Papua New Guinea, 2, 6, 149-55, 161, 162 [toward self-government, 157-59]

Bahamas, 180, 191
Barbados, 180
Barbuda, 176
Bonifacio, Andre, 17
Bradley, Willis, 109
Bradshaw, Robert, 186
British Solomon Islands, 147, 168
British Virgin Islands, 180, 186

Caribbean Development Bank, 7
Caroline Islands, 69
cases: Bordallo v. Camacho, 122; Balzac v. Porto Rico, 43; Calero-Toledo v. Pearson Yacht Leasing Co., 51, 52; In the Matter of Tapia, 43; insular cases, 40; Muratti v. Foote, 43; Rodriguez Cintron v. Richardson, 63
Committee on Public Lands, 116
commonwealth, concept of, 4, 6, 10, 20, 21-24, 67, 91-92, 190-91, 198
Cook Islands, 2, 3, 6, 9, 132-45; Amendment Act, 136; associated state, 132; Auckland Trades Council, 136; Civil Aviation Agreement, 142; Colonial Boundaries Act, 135; Constitution, 90, 137-38, 140, 143, 204; Cook Island Act, 135; Cook Island Federal Council, 135; Cook Island Party, 137; Cook Islands Progressive Association, 135; federal law, applicability of, 143; government, 138-41, 156; High Court, 141; House of Arikis, 139; immigration, 141-43; judiciary, 141; Land Appellate Court, 141; Land Court, 141; Legislative Assembly, 139, 140-41, 142-43; Legislative Council, 136-37; public service, 136-37; Rarotonga Island Council, 135; relationship with New Zealand, 133-37, 144, 145, 203-04; relationship with United Nations, 132; termination of agreement, 12
Culebra, 35, 56

Davis, George, 39
Denfield, Louis E., 71
Dominica, 179, 182, 191
Dominican Republic, 7

England (see, Great Britain)

Evatt, Herbert V., 150

Fair Labor Standards Act (FLSA), 46, 60-62, 94, 129
federal law, general applicability of, 11-12; in relationship to Cook Islands, 11-12, 143; in relationship to Guam, 11, 120, 128-29; in relationship to Marianas, 11, 120, 128-29; in relationship to Papua New Guinea, 11, 12, 167; in relationship to Puerto Rico, 43-44, 55-56; in relationship to United States, 11-12; in relationship to Virgin Islands, 11; in relationship to West Indies Associated States, 11-12, 183
Ferre, Luis, 54
Fiji, 167
Foraker Act, 18, 39, 42, 59, 60

Gairy, E. M., 192
Germany, 149
Great Britain, 6, 10; British Parliamentary Act, 185; relationship with West Indies Associated States, 180-83; termination of agreement with West Indies Associated States, 191-92, 198
Grenada, 179, 182, 192
Guam, 2, 5, 6, 7, 9, 10, 69, 71, 105-29; commonwealth, 105, 118; constitution, 118-19; Elective Governor Act, 117; federal law, 120, 128-29; government, 96, 111, 116, 117, 118, 121-22; Guam organic act, 72, 96, 112, 116-17, 119, 125-26; Law of the Sea Conference, 124-25; Political Status Commission, 118-22; relationship with Marianas, 91, 206; relationship with Spain, 124; relationship with United States, 108-12; Sella Bay Agreement, 122

Hawaii, 105
Hasluck, Sir Paul, 151
Henry, Albert, 137, 142, 203
Hensel, H. Struve, 115
Herbert, William, 187

Iglesias, Santiago, 45
Indonesia, 147, 166
International Bank for Reconstruction and Development (IBRD), 153
Ireland (Northern), 182
Irian Jaya, 147, 168

Jamaica, 180, 191
Japan, 167

Koror, 80

League of Nations, 70, 150
Leary, Richard P., 109
Luis de Sanvitores, Diego, 108

Manauae, 132
Mariana, 2, 6, 7, 9, 10, 12, 69, 71-72, 78, 80, 81, 90-101; commonwealth of, 91-92, 93, 97; government, 95-97; immigration, 96-97; Political Status Commission, 98; relationship with United States, 91-101; relationship with United Nations, 205-09
Marshall Islands, 69
McNamara, Robert, 170
McNutt, Paul, 27, 28
Mexico, 15
Micronesia, 2, 6, 7, 9, 10, 12, 69-70, 71, 72, 75, 80-81, 83-84; Congress, 72-73, 74, 78, 80-81, 82, 91; Council of Micronesia, 73, 77; free association, 80-82, 83; immigration, 10, 86; Independence coalition, 91; Joint Committee on Future Status, 77-78, 80, 83, 91; Law of the Sea Conference, 83; organic acts,

INDEX

72; relationship with United States, 71-76, 91, 207, 208 [compact of Micronesia, 83-90]; Treaty of Toresillas, 69
Miles, Nelson, 39
military, in Guam, 114-16; in Marianas, 98-100; in Micronesia, 77-79; in Philippines, 23-24, 31; in Puerto Rico, 56-57
Mona, 35
Munoz Marin, Luis, 44, 45, 46, 53
Munoz Rivera, Luis, 43, 50

Netherlands, territories of, 176, 197-98
Nevis, 175-76
New Zealand, Colonial Boundaries Act, 135; Laws Bill, 143; Maori Land Court, 141; Parliament, 136, 137, 143; relationship with Cook Islands, 2, 3, 6, 132, 133-37, 141-42, 144, 145, 203-04 [applicability of New Zealand law, 137-38, 143]; Supreme Court, 141

Pagan, Bolivar, 45
Palau, 69, 74, 80
Papua New Guinea, 2, 6, 9, 75, 147-70; Act of 1949, 150-51; Act of 1960, 152; Act of 1963, 153; Act of 1968, 155; Act of 1971, 158; Administrator's Executive Council (AEC), 155, 159; constitution, 157-58, 159-60, 164-66; federal law, 167; legislature, 164-66; National Identity Ordinance, 158; Ombudsman Commission, 164; Parliamentary Under-Secretaries Ordinance of 1963, 155; People's Progress Party, 159, 168; relationship to Australia, 149-54; Trusteeship Agreement, 150, 209; Trusteeship Council, 150, 153
Pedreira, Antonio, 44

Philippine Commonwealth, Act of 1940, 30; Assembly, 18; Commission, 18; constitution of, 22, 25; Filipinos, 15-17, 24; Independence Acts, 15, 21, 22, 23-24, 25, 26; Joint Preparatory Committee on Philippine Affairs, 24-25; Jones-Constigan Act, 25; Jones Law, 18; legislature, 18, 21, 25, 31; Marua Law, 17; Military Bases Agreement, 31; organic act for the Philippines, 18, 42, 44, 46; relationship with Spain, 15-17 [Cavite Mutiny, 17]; relationship with United States, 18-21; Supreme Court of, 19; Tariff Act of 1909, 20; Tariff Act of 1913, 21; Treaty of Paris, 17
Pinero, Jesus T., 46
Ponape, 69
Puerto Rico, 1, 3, 6, 7, 9, 10, 12, 35-63; Ad Hoc Advisory Group, 53, 54, 58, 59, 63; Charter of Autonomy, 38; Commission on Status of Puerto Rico, 52, 53; Commonwealth, 47-54; Constitution, 47-50; Elective Governor Act, 46; Fair Labor Standards Act, 46; Federal party, 39; Federal Relations Act, 47, 49-50, 59; Foraker Act, 18-39, 42, 59, 60; Free Associated State, 54-63; government, 37, 38, 47, 60; Independence party, 50, 53, 198-99; Joint-Dominican Republic-Puerto Rico Economic Commission, 58; Jones Act, 42-44; Massacre of Ponce, 45; Nationalist party, 44; Popular Democratic party, 46, 52, 54; Public Law 600, 47-50; relationship with Spain, 38-39; relationship with United Nations, 57-58, 198-200; relationship with

[Puerto Rico] United States, 39-47 [Compact with United States, 54-55]; Spanish Liberal party, 38; Statehood Republican party, 50, 53; Supreme Court, 42, 58; United Statehooders, 53; Universal Military Training and Service Act, 56

Quezon, Manuel, 25, 27

Roosevelt, Franklin, 45-46, 112
Root, Elihu, 39
Rota, 69, 72, 74

Saba, 174
St. Eustatius, 174
St. Kitts, 175-77, 180, 186; Constitution, St. Kitts-Anguilla-Nevis, 187
St. Lucia, 177-79, 182
St. Martin, 174
St. Vincent, 177-80, 182, 191
Saipan, 69, 72, 74, 76, 80
Sears, Mason, 49
Sherman, Forrest P., 114
Somare, M., 158, 159, 168
Spain, relationship with Guam, 107-08; relationship with Philippines, 15-17; relationship with Puerto Rico, 38-39 [Charter of Autonomy, 38]; relationship with West Indies, 180; Spanish Liberal party, 38
South Pacific Bureau for Economic Cooperation, 142
South Pacific Conference, 142
South Pacific Forum, 142, 167
Spanish-American War, 17, 39, 69, 108
State Local Fiscal Assistance Act of 1972, 62
Suwarrow, 132

Tinian, 69, 72
Torres Strait Islands, 168
Treaty of Paris, 17, 39, 41, 108

Trinidad, 180, 191
Truk, 69
Truman, Harry, 116
Trust Territory of the Pacific Islands, 2, 67, 86-87, 90; Agreement, 207-08; Compact, 83-90; UN Trusteeship Council, 161, 207
Tugwell, Rexford, 45
Tutuila, 110
Tydings Bill, 28-30

United Nations, 2, 7, 8, 57-58, 70, 71, 77, 194-211; Ad Hoc Committee on Information, 195, 197, 198; Charter, 48, 194, 206; Declaration of the Granting of Independence to Colonial Countries and Peoples, 153, 206; Economic Social Council on Asia and Pacific, 7, 142; General Assembly, 48-49, 70-71, 194-98; Special Committee on the Situation with Regard to the Implementation of the Declaration of the Granting of Independence to Colonial Countries and Peoples (Decolonization Commission or Committee of 17, Committee of 24), 153, 194, 195, 201-05, 213; Visiting Mission, 75, 76, 153, 206, 208, 209
United States, Congress, 5, 7, 11, 18, 22, 24, 25, 26-27, 31, 39, 41, 52, 71, 77, 85, 92, 96, 108, 117, 120, 128; Constitution, 4, 5, 6, 7, 9, 19, 40-42, 91, 93, 95, 110; Department of Education, 42; federal law of (see, federal law); immigration, 10, 24, 57; Independence Act of 1934, 21, 22, 23-24, 25; Jones Act, 43-44, 94; Meritorious Claims Act, 115; Military Bases Agreement, 31; Navy, 19, 71, 90,

108; relationship with Associated States, general, 1, 2; relationship with Guam, 108 [Guam organic act, 116-17, 119, 125-26]; relationship with Philippines, 17-22; relationship with Puerto Rico, 39-47 [Foraker Act of 1900, 18, 39, 42, 59, 60]; relationship with Trust Territory, 71-76 [Compact, 83-89]; Supreme Court, 7, 18, 19, 22, 43, 51, 52, 58, 62, 126; Treasury, 11

Vieques, 35
Virgin Islands, 2, 4, 9, 85, 96, 105, 126-27

Webster, Roland, 188, 189
West Germany, 166
West Indies Associated States, 6, 174-92; constitution, 183-84; Federal Law, 184; Moyne Commission, 186; relationship with Great Britain, 180-83 [Grenada United Labor party, 192]; Supreme Court, 185; West Indies Act, 185
Whitlock, William, 188
Williams, Franklin, 78, 80, 81
Winship, Blanton, 45
Windward Islands, 177-80
Won Pat, A. B., 117, 119
World Health Organization, 58, 167

Yap, 69

ABOUT THE AUTHOR

ARNOLD H. LEIBOWITZ is an attorney in Washington, D.C., specializing in constitutional and federal problems. In addition, he is a Professor in the Graduate School of Public Administration at Howard University.

Mr. Leibowitz served as general counsel to the Status Commission of Puerto Rico (1964-66) and counsel to the Political Status Commission of the Twelfth Guam Legislature (1974). He has published several monographs on Puerto Rico and Guam.

He also served on the White House Task Force on the Virgin Islands and was a member of the U.S. Social and Economic Development Commission to Jamaica (1970-71). He served as counsel with the Development Loan Fund and was subsequently chief of the Financial Policy Division in the Agency for International Development. He now is president of the Institute for International Law and Economic Development which is studying the problems of developing nations.

Mr. Leibowitz received his A.B. degree from Columbia University and his LL.B from Yale Law School. He did postgraduate work at the University of Heidelberg in Germany.

RELATED TITLES
Published by
Praeger Special Studies

INTERNATIONAL POLITICS IN EAST ASIA SINCE WORLD WAR II*
        Donald F. Lach and
        Edmund S. Wehrle

MICRONESIA AND U.S. PACIFIC STRATEGY: A Blueprint for the 1980s
        James H. Webb, Jr.

PLANNING FOR TOURIST DEVELOPMENT: Quantitative Approaches
        Charles E. Gearing,
        William W. Swart, and
        Turgut Var

THE POLITICS OF THE WESTERN INDIAN OCEAN ISLANDS
        John M. Ostheimer

THE U.S. AND JAPAN IN EAST ASIA: Economic Relations and Stability*
        Peter A. Poole

*Also available in paperback as a PSS Student Edition.

LIBRARY OF DAVIDSON COLLEGE

Books on regular loan may be checked out for **two weeks**. Books must be presented at the Circulation Desk in order to be renewed.

A fine is charged after date due.

Special books are subject to special regulations at the discretion of library staff.